AS LONG AS GRASS GROWS

AS LONG AS GRASS GROWS

THE INDIGENOUS FIGHT FOR ENVIRONMENTAL JUSTICE, FROM COLONIZATION TO STANDING ROCK

DINA GILIO-WHITAKER

Beacon Press, Boston

Beacon Press
Boston, Massachusetts
www.beacon.org

Beacon Press books
are published under the auspices of
the Unitarian Universalist Association of Congregations.

22 21 20 19   8 7 6 5 4 3 2

This book is printed on acid-free paper that meets
the uncoated paper ANSI/NISO specifications for
permanence as revised in 1992.

Text design by Wilsted & Taylor Publishing Services

The names of some individuals in this book
have been changed to protect their privacy.

Library of Congress Cataloging-in-Publication Data

Names: Gilio-Whitaker, Dina, author.
Title: As long as grass grows : the indigenous fight for environmental
    justice, from colonization to Standing Rock / Dina Gilio-Whitaker.
Description: Boston : Beacon Press, [2019] | Includes bibliographical
    references and index.
Identifiers: LCCN 2018057540 (print) | LCCN 2019004334 (ebook) | ISBN
    9780807073797 (ebook) | ISBN 9780807073780 (hardcover : alk. paper)
Subjects: LCSH: Indians of North America—Social conditions. | Environmental
    justice—United States. | Indian activist—United States.
Classification: LCC E98.S67 (ebook) | LCC E98.S67 G55 2019 (print) | DDC
    970.004/97-dc23
LC record available at https://lccn.loc.gov/2018057540

For Water Protectors Everywhere

MNI WICONI!

Contents

Author's Note

Books are born for many reasons. This one emerged as a result of many years of research and activism, which for me has always focused on environmentalism, Native sovereignty, and their intersection. If what the preeminent Indian law scholar Felix Cohen said was true, that Indians are the United States' miner's canary that signals the poison gas of the political atmosphere, to extend the metaphor, then in the larger world dominated by the fossil fuel industry all humans have become the miner's canary. On a planet with a rapidly changing climate and undergoing what many scientists believe is the Earth's sixth mass extinction, the future of humanity is looking about as bright as it did for American Indians in 1953 when Cohen wrote those words railing against federal Indian policy (known as termination, which was every bit as menacing as it sounded). From an American Indian perspective, we're all on the reservation now.

In the past few decades it has become crystal clear that, as "the people," our common enemy is the entrenched corporate power of Big Oil and other toxic industries that buy political influence to protect their own corrupt interests in collusion with government, all in the name of democracy. This has come at the expense of countless marginalized people worldwide. In the US, that has always meant Indigenous people, other people of color, and those having low incomes. The overall goal of this book is to highlight the importance of building alliances across social and racial divides. To do this requires an honest interrogation of the history of the relationships between the environmental movement and Indian country.

In my years of research and writing on American Indian environmental justice (EJ), I have observed two locations where those conversations predominantly occur: in academia and in activist spaces. By "activist spaces," I am referring to points of contact between activist groups (such as spontaneous actions or movements, coalitions, and nonprofits),

governmental agencies in charge of implementing environmental policies, and business interests those policies may or may not regulate in
the process of development. Academics in environmental studies, Native studies, and other disciplines educate students on the histories and
principles of EJ in different EJ communities, but they face a dearth of
literature from which to teach on the topic relative to Indigenous peoples.
A similar lack of knowledge exists within governmental and nongovernmental institutions and businesses. People in these organizations might
have access to lawyers trained in federal Indian law, but law is only one
aspect of the EJ world, especially when it comes to Indian country, not to
mention the fact that federal Indian law is a creation of colonial forces and
not particularly designed to deliver justice to Indian people. Lawyers with
expertise in federal Indian law often are also neither versed in environmental justice history or principles nor are aware of other critical work by
historians and other academics that inform EJ praxis (that is, the way EJ
is imagined and implemented).

American Indian activists doing EJ work, however, tend to be quite
knowledgeable about the issues they are working for and the histories that
inform those issues. As a result, they inevitably end up having to educate,
with no additional financial compensation, the various groups they inter-
act with, people with whom they often have contentious relationships to
begin with. This points to an in-between space in Indigenous environmental justice organizing, where there is a need for education that helps
build the foundation for productive relationships. Thus, a primary goal of
this book is to help fill that gap by providing a broad overview about what
environmental injustice is for American Indians, describing what justice
looks like, and proposing avenues to get there. The only book of its kind to
date, my hope is that it will be used not only in classrooms but also by every
organization, institution, and individual that engages with Indigenous
peoples on the protection of the environment and their rights within it.

NOTE ON TERMINOLOGY

There are numerous terms used to describe and define American Indian
people. Some are more accurate or appropriate than others, depending on
context. Some are a matter of personal preference, while others are more
legal in nature. As a general rule of thumb, the most appropriate terms

are specific Native nation names, such as Lakota, Diné (aka Navajo), or Anishinaabe. But when referring to American Indians collectively, the older terms "American Indians," "Indians," and "tribes" are terms used in federal legal parlance, and tribal nations and individuals often still use these terms. "Native American" is more contemporary and also used in legal contexts, but many Native people prefer simply "Native" in addition to their specific tribal names. Native people often also prefer the term "nation" to "tribe," since "tribe" can imply cultural inferiority, while "nation" invokes Indians' historical, preinvasion self-determination and governing systems. The terms "Indigenous" and "fourth world" signal originality to place and also provide context for a more global category of people who share similar struggles against states. Accounting for these complexities, the terms are used interchangeably throughout the text. When discussing specific American states, except where naming specific states (such as Washington State), "state" (lowercase s) is used to distinguish the individual state from "State" (capital S) meaning the US nation-state.

The Standing Rock Saga

We are unapologetically Indigenous, we embody resistance,
everything we do from eating rubber bullets for breakfast to holding
our frontline has been done in a manner that is nothing but spiritual.

—RED WARRIOR CAMP COMMUNIQUE, DECEMBER 15, 2016[1]

As things often do in Indian country, it began with a story, this one a prophecy. Ancestors of today's Lakota, the people of Oceti Sakowin, had for generations warned about a black snake that would slither across the land, bringing destruction to the Earth and her people. The day representatives for Energy Transfer Partners entered the council chambers of the Standing Rock Sioux Tribe on September 30, 2014, to present plans for the Dakota Access Pipeline (DAPL), it perhaps came as no surprise to the tribal council that another pipeline was threatening Lakota lands. Other Lakota bands, Plains tribes, and white ranchers and farmers were, after all, already fighting the Keystone XL Pipeline. But nobody that day could have predicted the debacle the DAPL would turn into—the extremes to which Energy Transfer Partners (ETP) would go to put down tribal opposition to the project, beginning with CEO Kelsey Warren's lie that the tribe had not registered their dissent to the project early enough, and that if they had, the pipeline could have been rerouted. Or the human rights abuses by ETP's private security firms and militarized state police that would bring United Nations observers to the protest camps. Or the level of support the tribe would receive for a cause millions of people around the world found to be righteous. Then again, maybe they could have.

The startling truth is that there are 2.4 million miles of black snakes in the United States. These pipelines convey more crude oil, gasoline, home heating oil, and natural gas than any other country in the world.[2] Of the total miles, 72,000 are dedicated to crude. Pipelines are "an extremely safe way to transport energy across the country," says the oil industry's Pipeline101.com, claiming they are generally considered safer than truck or rail transport. Yet hundreds of pipeline leaks and ruptures occur each year, with consequences that range from relatively benign to catastrophic. And with the pipeline infrastructure aging, critics warn about increasing risk of accidents.

Pipelines are so ubiquitous and normalized in the American political (and actual) landscape that they aren't even heavily regulated. While numerous federal and state agencies oversee some aspects of the pipeline infrastructure, most government monitoring and enforcement is conducted through a small agency within the Department of Transportation called the Pipeline and Hazardous Materials Safety Administration, PHMSA ("fimsa") for short. The agency's mandate requires that only 7 percent of natural gas lines and 44 percent of all hazardous liquid lines be subject to rigorous and regular inspection criteria. The rest are inspected less often.[3]

So when Energy Transfer Partners initiated the permitting and construction process, it was business as usual. The pipeline—1,172 miles long and spanning four states—was designed to connect Bakken Oil Field crude to an oil field tank farm in Illinois, flowing 470,000 barrels per day. It's hard to say if ETP was caught off guard when they encountered a dramatic groundswell of protest in 2016. Not that there hadn't been indications of the possibility of a backlash; in 2015, farmers in Iowa registered their dissent against the project with letters to the Iowa Utilities Board. The following year a lawsuit was filed by thirty Iowans contesting the state's granting eminent domain to ETP. At the same time, opposition to the Keystone XL Pipeline had become so high profile, due to the cross-sectional organizing of many diverse groups, that President Barack Obama had rejected Keystone's permit, sealing its fate in 2015. Pipeline protests were nothing new, given that the history of pipeline opposition goes back to at least 1968 with the building of the Trans-Alaska Pipeline System, and the battle against the Trans-Alaska Pipeline is still considered the biggest pipeline battle in history.[4] What took ETP by surprise, however, was the Obama administration's order to halt the DAPL project in December 2016 as the result of a massive grassroots resistance movement that mobilized millions of people in the United States and beyond.

The resistance movement, organized around the hashtags #NoDAPL, #Mniwiconi, #Waterislife, and #Standwithstandingrock, officially began in April 2016 when a small group of women from the Standing Rock Sioux Tribe (SRST) set up camp and named it Camp of the Sacred Stones, or Sacred Stone Camp.[5] The idea was to monitor pipeline construction while registering tribal dissent in a tangible way and, they hoped, to stop the project. SRST had known about the DAPL project since at least 2014 when Energy Transfer Partners conducted their first meeting with the tribal council. As reported by the *Bismarck Tribune*, an audio recording from September 30 documents the first meeting between ETP and the tribal council in which the company outlines its planned route less than a mile from the reservation boundary and crossing under the Missouri River at Lake Oahe. The council argued that while the route was not within current reservation boundaries, it was well within the boundaries acknowledged in the 1851 Treaty of Fort Laramie, and the treaty of 1868. The council expressed its concern about the potential of desecrating sacred sites and the danger of contaminating the community's water supply in the event of a pipeline rupture. The tribal council informed company representatives at the meeting that in 2012 they had passed a resolution opposing all pipelines within the treaty boundaries.[6]

Even more significant, ETP did not mention that an earlier proposal had the pipeline crossing the Missouri River north of Bismarck (some seventy miles away), as documented by a map included with other documents provided to the North Dakota Public Service Commission (PSC) as part of the permitting process. The same document shows that a change to the route was made in September, the same month as the meeting with the tribal council. A permit for that route had been rejected by the Army Corps of Engineers (ACE) after an environmental assessment concluded that among other consequences, it posed too great a risk to wells that served Bismarck's municipal water supply.[7] This led to a charge of environmental racism by the Standing Rock tribal council, a claim the PSC dismissed. On July 27, 2016, SRST filed a lawsuit against the Army Corps, claiming multiple federal statutes were violated when it issued permits to ETP.[8] And a carefully orchestrated campaign to discredit the Standing Rock Sioux Tribe emerged, backed by fossil fuel interests in a state whose political machine is heavily influenced by industry money and where 90 percent of the population is white.

Meanwhile, back at Sacred Stone Camp, people kept coming. By late August there were thousands of people at what was being referred to generally as Standing Rock, and new camps were popping up. Sacred Stone, Oceti Sakowin, and Red Warrior were the three primary camps people came to. Hundreds of tribal nations in the United States sent their support, financial and otherwise, and messages of encouragement poured in from Indigenous and non-Indigenous communities all over the world. Oceti Sakowin came to be the central gathering place for new arrivals, who were visually greeted by the dozens of tribal nation flags that regally lined the road of the main entrance. People brought donations of firewood, tents, construction materials, clothing, sleeping bags, and anything and everything needed for life in the camps. Kitchens staffed with volunteers fed the masses with donated food. The demonstrators refused the term "protestors," referring to themselves instead as "water protectors," and their main organizing principle was peaceful prayer and ceremony. "*Mni Wiconi*" was their mantra, meaning "Water is life" in the Lakota language. Drugs, alcohol, and weapons were banned in the camps. Although violence was strictly eschewed, civil disobedience was embraced; people put their bodies in the way of the construction path, locked themselves to heavy equipment, and got arrested.

As remarkable as the gathering was, few outside Indian country or the environmental movement were initially aware of what was happening in North Dakota. The mainstream press had turned a blind eye—until the violence began. On September 3, 2016 (Labor Day), as people attempted to block the digging up of a sacred site, ETP brought in a private security firm armed with approximately eight attack dogs and mace. The security personnel sprayed people directly in the face and eyes and pushed the dogs to bite people. One dog was unleashed and ran into the crowd in attack mode.[9] At least five people and a horse were bitten, and around thirty people were injured by the chemical spray. Images and video of the dog attacks went viral on social media, thanks to the handful of journalists at the site, particularly Amy Goodman of the popular program *Democracy Now!*, for whom an arrest warrant was later issued by the Morton County Sheriff's Department. Footage of a German shepherd with its mouth covered in blood was viewed by millions of people. The mayhem and viciousness of attacks on American Indians was a chilling reminder of a history of brutality used against the Lakota Sioux by the US military in the staunch defense of their lands and freedom, and the dog attacks evoked the history of Christopher Columbus's savage rampage and genocide against the Arawaks on Hispaniola in which dogs were used. After that day the world started paying attention to the #NoDAPL movement at Standing Rock.

Instead of discouraging people from coming into what was increasingly turning into a risky situation, the Labor Day incident attracted even more people to the encampment as Standing Rock began currying widespread favor in the media. SRST tribal chairman Dave Archambault Jr. came to be the most recognizable face in what had grown into a global movement. Archambault (and other Lakota people like LaDonna Brave Bull Allard and Dallas Goldtooth) suddenly had a public platform to tell their stories, which described a long line of violent depredations against the seven nations of the Oceti Sakowin (literally "Seven Council Fires"), the Great Sioux Nation's traditional name for themselves. These accounts include centuries of genocidal policies, treaty violations, illegal land seizures, and environmental catastrophes perpetrated by the US settler government. The creation of Lake Oahe itself is one such environmental catastrophe against the Standing Rock people. Under the Pick-Sloan Missouri River Basin Program, the Lake Oahe Dam was one of five dams built in Oceti Sakowin treaty territory. Completed in 1962, the lake created by the dam destroyed more Native land than any other water project in the US, eliminating 90 percent of timberland on the Standing Rock and Cheyenne Sioux reservations and the loss of much grazing and agricultural land.[10] Altogether, the nations lost 309,584 acres of vital bottomlands and more than one thousand Native families were displaced without their consent. In the words of Kul Wicasa Lakota scholar Nick Estes, "Entire communities were removed to marginal reservation lands, and many more were forced to leave the reservation entirely."[11]

On one hand, the Dakota Access Pipeline was only the most recent intrusion into the Standing Rock Sioux's lands and sovereignty. On the other, it represented a breaking point, the final straw in which SRST sent the message that they would not tolerate the further desecration of their treaty lands and the potential contamination of their water—especially for the sake of profits of a fossil fuel conglomerate and for which the tribe would see no benefits whatsoever. Proponents of the DAPL argued that because the pipeline did not cross reservation boundaries, and because the company conducted a meeting with the tribal council, the Army Corps' permit was in compliance with the law. But SRST contended that the territory within the original treaty boundaries, which covers a far larger area than the current reservation boundaries, was legally subject to a more extensive environmental study than had been done.[12] The council also argued that the tribe should have been consulted much earlier and more thoroughly, especially given the presence of traditional burial grounds and Lake Oahe as the primary source of drinking water for the reservation.[13]

SRST consistently maintained that all they wanted was for an EIS, an environmental impact statement, to be performed and the pipeline rerouted away from the lake. Their legal team, the iconoclastic nonprofit Earthjustice, continually filed motions designed to halt construction, force the EIS, and push the Army Corps to deny the easement for the lake crossing. The court and even other departments of the federal government responded with a joint request for ETP to voluntarily halt construction, which the company declined to heed.[14] On September 16 a federal district court in Washington, DC, ordered the company to temporarily cease construction, but the company ignored the order and work continued.[15] On October 10 another joint statement was issued by the three federal departments—the Army Corps, the Department of Justice, and the Department of the Interior—repeating requests for a voluntary stoppage.[16] Still, the work continued. While the tribal council wrangled with lawyers, courts, and federal agencies, water protectors on the ground continued to put their bodies in the way of construction, and tensions mounted. Observers pointed out that instead of following their mandate to protect the public, the Morton County Sheriff's Department, becoming increasingly militarized, was in reality protecting Energy Transfer Partners pipeline project. And then the standoff at Standing Rock took a shocking turn for the worse.

Construction crews, whose drill pad was on a bluff adjacent to the Oceti Sakowin encampment, had drawn closer to the Lake Oahe crossing. A group of water protectors had set up a new camp—with tipis, tents, a small kitchen, and a sweat lodge—directly in the crew's path and blockaded the main road in and out of the area. They named it the 1851 Treaty Camp, in commemoration of the original Fort Laramie treaty. Media reports said the camp was on private land that the Dakota Access Pipeline had recently purchased, but water protectors asserted it was unceded treaty land, land that had been wrongfully taken to begin with.[17] A statement issued on October 24 by Mekasi Camp-Horinek, an Oceti Sakowin camp coordinator, read, "Today, the Oceti Sakowin has enacted eminent domain on DAPL lands, claiming 1851 treaty rights. This is unceded land. Highway 1806 as of this point is blockaded. We will be occupying this land and staying here until this pipeline is permanently stopped. We need bodies and we need people who are trained in nonviolent direct action. We are still staying nonviolent and we are still staying peaceful."[18] Three days later, on October 27, the militarized police conducted a violent sweep of the camp, with more than three hundred officers from five states in riot gear and aided by eight all-terrain vehicles, five armored vehicles, two helicopters, and numerous military grade Humvees.[19] Several live Facebook feeds captured police using high-tech sound weapons (known as Long Range Acoustic Device, or LRAD), tasers, beanbag guns, pepper spray, concussion grenades, and batons; and snipers were reportedly seen on the armored vehicles.[20] One horse was shot and later had to be put down. Police alleged that water protectors set fires to several vehicles and a bulldozer, that a Molotov cocktail was thrown at them, and that a woman fired three shots at police; claims that were unsubstantiated by any of the videos. The violence lasted several hours, and at the end of the day 141 people had been arrested and many people were injured, some severely.

Ironically, the same day Ammon and Ryan Bundy were acquitted of charges in the armed takeover of the Malheur Wildlife Refuge (formerly the Malheur Indian Reservation) in January 2016. Commentators noted the disproportionate use of police violence against the Standing Rock water protectors, compared to the way the Malheur situation was handled.[21] Indian people recalled the chilling parallel of militarized violence in 1973 during the seventy-one-day siege at Wounded Knee in South Dakota.

The numerous videos captured on October 27 went viral, further galvanizing the world's attention and support for Standing Rock's cause. The violence, however, didn't end there. On the evening of November 20, police again attacked peaceful water protectors with rubber bullets, tear gas, and mace after they attempted to remove a police blockade on Highway 1806. The violence became potentially lethal when police sprayed the crowd with a water cannon in the subfreezing temperatures. One young woman, Sophia Wilansky, was hit with an explosive device that nearly blew her arm off. Legal observers with the National Lawyers Guild said that numerous people lost consciousness after being shot. More than one hundred people were hurt and many were hospitalized, and there were speculations that the water cannon was mixed with mace. An elderly woman went into cardiac arrest and was revived on the scene.[22]

Throughout the months of the Standing Rock standoff, President Obama had remained mostly silent, aside from one interview with *NowThis News* on November 1, where he said, "We are monitoring this closely. I think as a general rule, my view is that there is a way for us to accommodate sacred lands of Native Americans. I think that right now the Army Corps is examining whether there are ways to reroute this pipeline."[23] Meanwhile, an extremely contentious presidential election was just a few days away, with polls favoring the Democrat, Hillary Clinton. Clinton had also been silent on the Standing Rock issue but finally issued a statement on October 27, the same day as the 1851 Treaty Camp incident and the Bundy decision. The only reason she said anything at all was because a contingent of Native youth stormed her campaign office in Brooklyn, New York, demanding some kind of acknowledgment. The statement was not what the #NoDAPL activists had hoped for. In a scant four sentences, Clinton said that "all voices should be heard" and that all parties involved needed to "find a path forward that serves the broadest public interest."[24] Indian country viewed Clinton's position as no less than a tacit endorsement for the DAPL project, or in the words of one commentator, "a crock."[25] As for the Republican candidate, Donald Trump, while he made no official statement, it was widely presumed what a Trump presidency—as outlandish as it seemed at the time—would mean for the DAPL: green lights all the way. It had been well publicized that Trump was an investor in Energy Transfer Partners, and that ETP had also donated a lot of money to the Trump campaign. It was, however, a matter of speculation about how a Clinton presidency would handle the DAPL. But then on Tuesday, November 9, the unthinkable happened, and Trump was elected president.

A few days after the election, with more than half the country in shock (especially Indian country and their allies in the environmental movement), Energy Transfer Partners CEO Kelsey Warren appeared on CBS News, breaking his own silence on the pipeline controversy. Noting that the pipeline was already 84 percent complete, Kelsey expressed that he was "100 percent confident" that the Trump administration would grant the contested easement and get the project completed. It was a bitter pill, yet no reasonable person could argue against it being probably true.[26]

But on December 4 the DAPL roller coaster took another surprising turn—the one that caught ETP off guard—when the Army Corps announced it would not grant the permit for the lake crossing. It clearly seemed to be a major victory for Standing Rock. The corps said that after discussions with the tribe and the company, more work was necessary, and that "the best way to complete that work responsibly and expeditiously is to explore alternate routes for the pipeline crossing." This could best be accomplished, the Army Corps said, through engaging full public input and analysis and an environmental impact statement "that could aid in future showdowns with President-elect Donald Trump's incoming administration."[27]

The #NoDAPL movement could bask for a moment in the glow from that victory. It was fragile, however, with the looming threat of what a Trump administration would bring, and everyone, especially water protectors, knew it wouldn't be good. Reality set in when Trump took office and within days started signing executive orders. One executive order after another, sometimes several a day, came for the first several weeks of his presidency, signaling his intention to make good on some of his more controversial campaign promises, like banning and deporting undocumented immigrants, building a border wall, and overturning the Affordable Care Act, among many others. Reviving the Dakota Access Pipeline was at the top of his list when on January 24, 2017, his second day in the White House, he signed a presidential memorandum "regarding construction of the Dakota Access Pipeline" and authorized both the Dakota Access Pipeline and the Keystone XL Pipeline.[28] The memorandum itself had no legal teeth to overturn the Army Corps' decision to order an EIS but did make clear the administration's pro-fossil-fuel agenda and intention to move the project forward. Two weeks later the environmental review had been canceled and the easement was granted by the Army Corps.

Attempts to evict the water protectors from the #NoDAPL encampments began in November. The evictions were supported by the Morton County Sheriff's Department, the Army Corps of Engineers, the Standing Rock tribal council, and, eventually, the Bureau of Indian Affairs. Deadlines were set and changed. Given that the winter had brought abundant snow and that the camps were in a known floodplain, officials were concerned about the impact of the snowmelt. Newly elected governor Doug Burgum ordered a final date, February 22. Under the supervision of hundreds of armed police, one hundred fifty or so of the people who remained at Oceti Sakowin ceremoniously marched out of camp, while fires burned wooden structures in the background and people drummed and sang prayer songs. A stalwart group of forty-six unarmed water protectors held their ground and the following day were arrested at gunpoint. The same day at a White House press conference, in response to a question about why the president hadn't yet intervened to try to negotiate a solution between Standing Rock and Energy Transfer Partners as promised, press secretary Sean Spicer stated that the president had "been in contact with all parties involved, . . . working and communicating back and forth."[29] Chairman Archambault responded that the claim was "absolutely false"; there had been no contact despite repeated requests for meetings with the Trump administration—just one in a myriad of "alternative facts" the new administration immediately became known for.

Although on the surface it appeared that the #NoDAPL movement was defeated in the wake of a hostile Trump administration, water protectors, Standing Rock Sioux Tribe, and Indian country more broadly claimed the nearly yearlong protest movement as a victory on many fronts. For one thing, it was the ground for a ceremonial reunification of the Seven Council Fires—including a revival of the term "Oceti Sakowin"—in a way that hadn't occurred since the Battle of the Little Big Horn. And it brought more than three hundred tribal nations together in solidarity for Standing Rock's cause and for environmental justice throughout Indian country. Beyond that, it was widely acknowledged by scholars and other commentators as the most significant Indigenous protest in recent US history. As part of the climate justice movement, it arose spontaneously and on the heels of the Idle No More movement and the less successful Occupy movement a few years earlier. By comparison, the last Native resistance movements of major consequence occurred in the 1960s and early '70s, beginning with the Fish Wars in the Pacific Northwest (approximately 1964–74) and the Alcatraz Island occupation of 1969–71. Then, the Trail of Broken Treaties and takeover of the Bureau of Indian Affairs building in 1972 and the seventy-one-day armed siege of Wounded Knee in 1973, while viewed as militant and violent, nonetheless contributed to a growing national consciousness about the United States' pattern of injustice toward American Indians. Collectively those actions led to sweeping changes in federal Indian policy, which included the Boldt Decision of 1974 (reaffirming tribal treaty rights) and Public Law 93-638, the Indian Self-Determination and Education Assistance Act of 1975. These and many more progressive legislative acts and court decisions constituted a reversal of previously oppressive federal policy and accorded new respect for government to government relationships between the United States and tribal nations, however imperfectly implemented.

Those previous victories happened amid a social revolution that resulted in new levels of enfranchisement for a number of historically marginalized people. Half a century later, the gains made during the civil rights era (approximately 1954–68) became threatened as a result of a growing conservative backlash during the Reagan years—and intensified despite eight years of an African American presidency—reaching startling proportions during the Trump campaign. Two decades of neoliberal policies under Democratic and Republican leadership led to the worst economic recession since the Great Depression. The subprime mortgage debacle and bank bailouts, ever-widening gaps in wealth and income, loss of the American manufacturing base and rampant offshoring of previously American-held jobs, and a health-care crisis became fertile ground for a blame game that pitted economically struggling people against each other. Renewed racial tensions evidenced in particular by disproportionate incarceration of people of color and rampant police brutality led to new movements like Black Lives Matter, while right-wing operatives like Donald Trump, the so-called alt-right, and a Republican-controlled Congress, were widely perceived as stoking the flames of xenophobia and racism. "Trumplicans" (Trump Republicans) seized power by promising extreme market fundamentalism reliant on fossil fuels, an authoritarianism that would have made Richard Nixon proud, and a toxic rejection of what they referred to as "political correctness," which was really just a dog-whistle invoking their hatred of Democratic values. Shored up by a disdain for the media and a loose relationship with the truth, the Trump administration was on a collision course with Standing Rock and served as little more than a thinly disguised sponsor for the Energy Transfer Partners' Dakota Access Pipeline.

It is no surprise that the #NoDAPL movement would spring up in Indian country. In the big picture, after all, it was just one more assault on the lands, resources, and self-determination of Native peoples since the beginning of American settler colonialism. As the Standing Rock story illustrates, the assaults have never ended. It also illustrates the trend in the past couple of decades of the uniting of the environmental movement with Indigenous peoples' movements all over the world, something that hasn't always been the case. Environmentalists recognize that the assaults on the environment committed by relentless corporate "extractivism" and development are assaults on the possibility for humans to sustain themselves in the future. They recognize that in some ways, what happened to the Indians is now happening to everybody not in the 1 percent.

This book is not about Standing Rock—but it takes Standing Rock as an excellent example of what environmental injustice in Indian country looks like. It starts from the assumption that colonization was not just a process of invasion and eventual domination of Indigenous populations by European settlers but also that the eliminatory impulse and structure it created in actuality began as environmental injustice. Seen in this light, settler colonialism itself is for Indigenous peoples a structure of environmental injustice. As this book will argue, however, the underlying assumptions of environmental injustice as it is commonly understood and deployed are grounded in racial and economic terms and defined by norms of distributive justice within a capitalist framework. Indigenous peoples' pursuit of environmental justice (EJ) requires the use of a different lens, one with a scope that can accommodate the full weight of the history of settler colonialism, on one hand, and embrace differences in the ways Indigenous peoples view land and nature, on the other. This includes an ability to acknowledge sacred sites as an issue of environmental justice—not merely religious freedom—and recognize and protect sites outside the boundaries of reservation lands or on aboriginal lands of nonfederally recognized tribes. Overall, a differentiated environmental justice framework—we could call this an "Indigenized" EJ—must acknowledge the political existence of Native nations and be capable of explicitly respecting principles of Indigenous nationhood and self-determination.

These principles of nationhood and self-determination are plainly evident in the ways Native peoples have always fought to defend and remain on their lands and the life those lands give them. From the intrusions of the earliest colonists into Native gardens, to the havoc wreaked by railroads and the imposition of reservation boundaries, to today's pipeline and fracking conflicts, Indigenous peoples have been forced into never-ending battles of resistance. As the #NoDAPL movement made clear through the slogan "Water is life," Native resistance is inextricably bound to worldviews that center not only the obvious life-sustaining forces of the natural world but also the respect accorded the natural world in relationships of reciprocity based on responsibility toward those life forms.[30] The implicit question this book asks is what does environmental justice look like when Indigenous peoples are at the center?

To that end, this book proceeds in eight chapters that identify Indigenous approaches to conceiving of environmental justice. Having laid the foundation with the Standing Rock story, it views environmental justice and injustice from a variety of angles, taking a view on the history of American Indians' relationship with the US as an environmental history. It uncompromisingly exposes the roots of white supremacy not only at the governmental level but even within the environmental movement itself, ultimately for the purpose of building effective alliances around issues of common concern. It recounts numerous examples of how Native and non-Native peoples are working together to build those partnerships, and the importance of women to these efforts, and takes you on a journey to Southern California to tell a story about how one coastal sacred site and iconic surf break were simultaneously saved as a result of successful coalition building and recognition of the sacred site's importance. Finally, the book looks for a way forward for environmental justice in Indian country by identifying positive trends and innovative ways communities are rallying together to build a more sane future in the face of relentless corporate power, an entrenched fossil fuel industry, and its collusion with the US State.

The most I hope to accomplish is to scratch the surface of what environmental justice means in Indian country, in terms of academic theory, activist praxis, and where the two meet in the formulation of government policies at all levels. It is a daunting (and humbling) task in which this is but one possible starting point; it is undoubtedly incomplete and imperfect, but one that I hope scholars more accomplished than I will expand and build upon in time.

Environmental Justice Theory and Its Limitations for Indigenous Peoples

You are now in a country where you can be happy; no white man shall ever again disturb you; the Arkansas [River] will protect your southern boundary when you get there. You will be protected on either side; the white shall never again encroach upon you, and you will have a great outlet to the West.

As long as water flows, or grass grows upon the earth, or the sun rises to show your pathway, or you kindle your camp fires, so long shall you be protected from your present habitations.

—PRESIDENT JAMES MONROE'S SPEECH
TO THE CHEROKEES, 1817

HISTORY, ORIGINS, AND DEFINITION OF ENVIRONMENTAL JUSTICE

"Environmental justice" did not enter common vernacular until the early 1980s. In 1982, when a landfill designed to accept PCBs (polychlorinated biphenyls, a highly toxic by-product of the chemical industry) was proposed to be placed in Warren County, North Carolina—a predominantly low-income African American community—it sparked a massive protest to try to stop the project. The protest failed to stop the dumping, but it stands nonetheless as a defining moment in the environmental movement and is generally hailed as the birth of the environmental justice movement. It was not the first incident of minority communities resisting exposure to hazardous environmental conditions. In the early 1960s, for example, Cesar Chavez organized Latino farmworkers to improve their working conditions, including protection from toxic insecticides. In 1968 black residents in West Harlem, New York, waged an unsuccessful campaign against siting a sewage plant in their community. Many more examples can be named, but it was the Warren County protests that galvanized national attention, leading to claims that the proliferation of toxic facilities in communities of color was environmental racism. Citizen groups from poor minority communities began forming beyond North Carolina; they believed they were being targeted by polluting industries, resulting in high rates of environmentally related illnesses.[1]

The Warren County incident led initially to several foundational studies designed to uncover the veracity of the claims being made by communities. In the first of the studies, commissioned by Congress, thanks to the influence of Democratic representative Walter Fauntroy, delegate to the House of Representatives from the District of Columbia, the US General Accountability Office confirmed that blacks made up the majority of the population in three of the four communities in a region where four off-site hazardous waste landfills were located (EPA Region Four, consisting of Alabama, Florida, Georgia, Kentucky, Mississippi, North and South Carolina, and Tennessee).[2]

In 1986 two cross-sectional studies were conducted to determine to what extent African Americans, Hispanic Americans, Asian Americans, Pacific Islanders, and Native Americans were exposed to uncontrolled toxic waste sites and commercial hazardous waste facilities in their communities. Those two studies—the first national studies of their kind— were brought together in another study in 1987, *Toxic Wastes and Race in the United States: A National Report on the Racial and Socio-Economic Characteristics of Communities with Hazardous Waste Sites*, which originated from the United Church of Christ's Commission for Racial Justice (CRJ), led by Ben Chavis. The findings revealed, among other things, the smoking gun: while socioeconomic status was implicated in siting hazardous waste facilities, race was the most significant variable, and three of every five black and Hispanic Americans and approximately half of all Asians, Pacific Islanders, and American Indians lived in communities with uncontrolled toxic waste sites.[3] Among the report's many recommendations, it urged the US president to issue an executive order mandating federal agencies to "consider the impact of current policies and regulations on racial and ethnic communities" and for the Environmental Protection Agency to establish an Office of Hazardous Waste and Racial and Ethnic Affairs.

It made sense that these early studies would emerge from the African

American community, given their leadership in the civil rights movement. It was a good and necessary start to articulating this new environmental justice movement, as the studies addressed long-standing, life-threatening problems in communities plagued by centuries of exploitation and marginalization. And they laid a solid foundation for other marginalized communities to build upon. What was true about the early research, however, was that as the *Toxic Wastes and Race* study exemplified, their predominant focus on the effects of siting of noxious facilities provided only a narrow window into how environmental racism played out in communities of color. But racial and ethnic minorities were being environmentally—and economically—exploited in ways that didn't involve incinerators or dumps. Between 1965 and 1971, for example, under the leadership of Cesar Chavez, Mexican farmworkers in California launched a historic resistance movement to organize a union not only in the interest of raising wages and improving working conditions but also to combat pesticide abuse, which was notorious for making workers sick. As leading environmental justice scholar Laura Pulido shows, the farmworkers' struggle brought together multiple issues that tied economic and political exploitation together with environmental abuse to show how hegemonic relationships disempower marginalized communities in many seemingly disparate but inevitably connected ways. As she writes, by fully appreciating the conditions structuring the lives of minorities and their precarious economic circumstances, it becomes apparent how new social movements and the environmental concerns of people of color differ dramatically, resulting in the need for a new understanding of environmentalism.[4]

The narrow focus of the early EJ research on the location of toxic and hazardous waste sites was only the beginning point for EJ research, and as it evolved, so would the nuances of the research. Important distinctions were yet to be made, such as how experiences varied across racial and ethnic minority groups (as the California farmworkers case demonstrates). It would become apparent that collapsing environmental discrimination against people of color into one monolithic group elided the experience of Indigenous peoples who had been undergoing environmental devastation of a particular, genocidal kind. For one thing, as the *Toxic Wastes and Race* study makes visible, it couldn't account for the ways Native Americans were being poisoned by uranium mine tailings in the hundreds of abandoned mines on and near reservations, the contaminated water the mines created, and how many had died as a result of uranium mining during the Manhattan Project era. Nor could collapsing all racial and ethnic minority groups' EJ experiences into one account for the ways forced displacement and assimilation over hundreds of years had disrupted traditional food systems to such an extent that chronic health problems and lower life expectancies in Native American and Native Hawaiian communities would be attributed to it. Or the ways foreign invasion and military occupation in Hawaii had rendered large swaths of land—including an entire island—not only off limits to Native Hawaiians but totally uninhabitable for generations to come.

Although the early studies initiated the important work of underscoring the ways in which environmental issues overlap with racial issues, the early studies also made visible wounds that had been festering for decades in communities of color and identified environmental justice as a civil rights issue. It wasn't until 1991, when the Commission for Racial Justice sponsored a landmark gathering, the first People of Color Environmental Leadership Summit in Washington, DC, that the first inklings of indigenized environmental justice could be seen. The summit produced a visionary document titled *Principles of Environmental Justice.* Its preamble reads:

> We, the people of color, gathered together at this multinational People of Color Environmental Leadership Summit, to begin to build a national and international movement of all peoples of color to fight the destruction and taking of our lands and communities, do hereby re-establish our spiritual interdependence to the sacredness of Mother Earth; to respect and celebrate each of our cultures, languages and beliefs about the natural world and our roles in healing ourselves; to ensure environmental justice; to promote economic alternatives which would contribute to the development of environmentally safe livelihoods; and to secure our political, economic and cultural liberation that has been denied for over 500 years of colonization and oppression, resulting in the poisoning of our communities and land and the genocide of our peoples, do affirm and adopt these Principles of Environmental Justice.[5]

As the language suggests, the seventeen-point proclamation represented a greater level of inclusion for Indigenous concerns than the preceding studies had, framing environmental justice in terms of colonial histories and oppressive political domination, even reflecting an Indigenous worldview by recognizing "our spiritual interdependence to the sacredness of Mother Earth." Specific to Indigenous peoples, principle eleven claims that "environmental justice must recognize a special legal and natural relationship of Native Peoples to the U.S. government through treaties, agreements, compacts, and covenants affirming sovereignty and self-determination," and principle fifteen, "Environmental justice opposes military occupation, repression and exploitation of lands, peoples and cultures, and other life forms." It was a big step forward in recognizing the distinctions between Indigenous populations and all others, necessary in framing legal approaches to environmental justice—a goal that has yet to be fully realized.

THE LEGAL LANDSCAPE OF EJ

The concept of environmental justice began finding its way into the federal regulatory terrain with the help of the Congressional Black Caucus. Since its inception in 1971 the CBC had been advocating for strong environmental policies, including the Clean Water Act (1972); the Marine Protection, Research, and Sanctuaries Act (1972); the Endangered Species Act (1973); the Safe Drinking Water Act (1974); the Toxic Substances Control Act (1976); the Comprehensive Environmental Response, Compensation, and Liability Act (1980); and the Nuclear Waste Policy Act (1982).[6] With the CBC's leadership, in 1990 the EPA established the Environmental Equity Work Group (EEWG) in response to findings by social scientists that "'racial minority and low-income populations bear a higher environmental risk burden than the general population' and that the EPA's inspections failed to adequately protect low-income communities of color."[7] Based on this knowledge, the EPA defines environmental justice as "the fair treatment and meaningful involvement of all people regardless of race, color, national origin, or income, with respect to the development, implementation, and enforcement of environmental laws, regulations, and policies."[8] The EEWG was tasked with two primary functions: first, to evaluate evidence that racial minority and low-income groups bear a disproportionate burden of environmental risks, and second, to identify factors that contribute to different risk burdens and suggest strategies for improvement.[9]

In 1992, one year after the People of Color Environmental Leadership Summit, the EPA formed the Office of Environmental Equity, and in 1993 it created the National Environmental Justice Advisory Council (NEJAC). By 1994 the office's name was changed to the Office of Environmental Justice. That same year President Bill Clinton issued Federal Actions to Address Environmental Justice in Minority Populations and Low-Income Populations, Executive Order 12898. The executive order created the Interagency Working Group on Environmental Justice, which was charged with conducting research, data collection, and analysis. To date, the executive order remains the cornerstone of environmental justice regulation in the US, with the EPA as its central arbiter. The EPA's primary EJ functions lie in standard setting, permitting of facilities, grant making, issuing licenses and regulations, and reviewing proposed actions of other federal agencies.[10]

Executive Order 12898 mandates federal agencies to ensure that recipients of federal funds comply with Title VI of the Civil Rights Act of 1964 "by conducting their programs in a non-discriminatory manner [based on race, color, or national origin]. Unlike Title VI, Executive Order 12898 does not create legally enforceable rights or obligations."[11] Some critics argue that Title VI is ineffective at addressing environmental injustice, in part because it is unlikely that section 602 (the clause prohibiting discrimination in federally funded projects) is privately enforceable.[12]

Legislative efforts to pass an EJ bill have been vexed for decades. The first attempt to pass an EJ bill—the Environmental Justice Act of 1992 (H.R. 2105)—died in committee in both the House and the Senate. Then, with a Republican takeover in 1994, Congress hamstrung further efforts to pass this progressive legislation. Subsequent attempts to pass environmental justice legislation went awry in 2007 and again in 2011 with a proposal by Representative Jesse Jackson Jr. (D-IL) to amend the Constitution, recognizing the "right to a clean, safe, and sustainable environment." Another congressional blow to EJ was delivered in 2009 when the Congressional Research Service stopped using the term "environmental justice" as a tool for citizens to track EJ-related legislation.[13]

In the court system, scholars generally recognize the limited results of EJ law. Legal scholars Clifford Rechtschaffen, Eileen Gauna, and Catherine O'Neill said in 2009 that legal challenges have met with "mixed success," where "claims alleging violations of the Equal Protection Clause of the U.S. Constitution have largely failed because of the difficulty of proving intentional discrimination. Other claims, some using traditional common law theories and environmental laws, have been somewhat more successful."[14] The authors contend that, overall, integrating EJ into environmental regulations in a meaningful way has proven to be extremely complex. More recently, another study found that courts have provided too few opportunities for environmental justice advocates to effect change when limited to Title VI of the Civil Rights Act of 1964, the Equal Protection Clause of the Fourteenth Amendment to the US Constitution, and the National Environmental Policy Act.[15]

EJ FRAMEWORKS IN THE CAPITALIST STATE

Changing the name of the Office of Environmental Equity to the Office of Environmental Justice in 1994 came on the heels of public criticism and reflects what remains a long-standing debate in activist, academic, and legal EJ circles.[16] As many have pointed out, the difference between environmental equity and environmental justice is in how risk is distributed. Equity says that the burden of environmental risk should be equally distributed among all populations, whereas justice guarantees protection from environmental degradation, prevention of adverse health impacts, mechanisms for accountability, and the availability of remedial action and resources. Justice guarantees three basic rights: the right to information, the right to a hearing, and the right to compensation;[17] or as EJ activist Mike Ewall succinctly states, "It represents the fundamental difference between the concepts of 'poison people equally' and 'stop poisoning people, period!' "[18]

While proving environmental racism is easier said than done when it comes to law, scholars also argue that simply defining terms like *environmental justice*, *environmental racism*, and even *environment* and *environmentalism* can be difficult and contentious. For instance, environmental racism is a narrow term that doesn't account for ways in which poor white communities are affected by polluting industries, or the ways it can ignore the historic and systemic nature of racism. From this perspective, the question is, is race or class responsible for discriminatory pollution? Similarly, how we understand *environment* raises questions about human presence in and use of the environment. In whatever ways we answer these questions, they are rooted in certain fundamental assumptions: first, they are based on a paradigm of social justice that presumes the authority of the State (nation-state), under which victims of social injustice are presumably subjected with their consent, even if as ethnic minorities they are "others." Scholars often call the ethnically diverse State the multicultural or multiethnic State. Second, the multicultural State is a form of democracy where justice is framed by principles embedded in a capitalist system. This leads to a third point: that justice is presumed to follow a distributive model. Let's briefly analyze each of these three points.

The multicultural nature of the State is capable of recognizing that ethnic and cultural groups have varied histories and interests, and sometimes those interests clash with each other. This is exemplified in the Southwest where hundreds of years of colonial interactions between Indigenous peoples, Hispano populations (Spanish descendants who were under Spanish and later Mexican rule prior to the Treaty of Guadalupe Hidalgo), and more recent white settlers have led to complicated and ongoing environmental battles based on conflicts over Spanish land grants and American treaties and laws and varied ideas about proper land use. For example, in northern New Mexico in the 1980s and '90s, environmentalists (predominantly white) came into conflict with the Hispano community of Ganados del Valle over the community's controlled use of elk-grazing habitat.[19] In another northern New Mexico example, battles over forest use demonstrated widely divergent beliefs among white environmentalists, state forest service officials, Chicano, Hispanic, and Latino activists, Indigenous peoples, and even nuclear scientists as a result of the Los Alamos Nuclear Laboratory.[20]

Bringing us to the second point, the logical question is how would an accurate EJ analysis account for these particularities, or differences, and can they coexist under the universalizing impulse of the State? Racism at its most basic level is the denial of the benefits of national citizenship (particularly equality), either covertly or overtly. In theory, equality in a democracy means that all people, regardless of ethnicity or race, have equal opportunity to enjoy the potential advantages available to them: a comfortable life with financial security, fair wages, a clean environment, education, and so on. These represent, in a capitalist democracy, the promise of material benefits for all.[21]

Third, if justice is a function of the capitalist State (which is imbued with the power to correct wrongs), when redress is sought for environmental injustices committed against ethnic minority groups, it is typically conceived of as distributive justice. That is, both the risks of environmental degradation and the benefits of a clean environment would be evenly distributed among citizens. However, some scholars contend that a distributive framework of justice is insufficient, because on a global scale, it doesn't account for the "social, cultural, symbolic, and institutional conditions *underlying* poor distribution in the first place."[22] This would also be true in the domestic sphere. In this line of reasoning, a focus on the distribution of goods and "bads" ignores group difference, perpetuating a lack of recognition and participation (for example, the right and institutional ability of activists and communities to speak for themselves). This relates directly to Indigenous peoples. One example is the United States' refusal to abide by the United Nations Declaration on the Rights of Indigenous Peoples (UNDRIP) in the Dakota Access Pipeline controversy, and its guarantee of the right of free, prior, and informed consent in projects that involve industrial development in traditional Indigenous lands.[23] Had the US Army Corps of Engineers taken seriously the United States' commitment to the UN declaration, in which the Standing Rock Sioux Tribe would have been given the opportunity to exercise their institutional ability to speak for themselves, one can imagine a different outcome to the Dakota Access Pipeline controversy.

THE POLITICAL DIFFERENCE OF INDIGENOUS PEOPLES

Emphasizing the ways that a solely distributive notion of environmental justice fails Indigenous peoples, EJ scholar David Schlosberg notes different conceptions of justice in the EJ movement, and that too often Indigenous conceptions of justice—and Indigenous ways of understanding land and human relations with it—are obstructed or not recognized at all. Even more problematic, as he points out, Indigenous nations in North America experience numerous barriers to their participation in the governance of environments. Broadening participation, he contends, would enhance recognition and validate diverse ways of valuing land.[24]

For a conception of environmental justice to be relevant to a group of people, it must fit within conceptual boundaries that are meaningful to them. Indigenous peoples fighting for political autonomy from the hegemony of the State are fighting the forces of colonialism while simultaneously fighting capitalism—all aimed at control of land and resources—with colonialism as the precondition for capitalism. The wealth generated in the Americas (much of it transferred to Europe) could only accumulate from centuries of violent Indigenous displacement, genocide, and land theft. Colonialism is inextricably bound up with slavery, having paved the way for the transatlantic slave trade initiated by Columbus in his first voyage to the "New World." Colonialism and slavery are also irrefutably linked to the unprecedented amassing of wealth in the United States. Karl Marx recognized colonialism as the genesis of what he called "primitive accumulation," connecting colonialism, slavery, and capitalism. He wrote, "The discovery of gold and silver in America, the extirpation, enslavement and entombment in mines of the aboriginal population, the beginning of the conquest and looting of the East Indies, the turning of Africa into a warren for the commercial hunting of blackskins, signalised the rosy dawn of the era of capitalist production. These idyllic proceedings are the chief momenta of primitive accumulation."[25] In the foundation of the US, slavery and capitalism are the two cornerstones made possible by colonial dispossession of Indigenous lands.

In settler colonialism, which is viewed not just as a historical event but also a structure designed to eliminate the Native via physical and political erasure, the purpose of political control and domination is to gain access to territory.[26] The political erasure of Indigenous peoples happens in many different ways, including the refusal of the State to fully recognize the nationhood of Native collective existence. In the US legal system, Native nationhood is expressed as federal recognition and the so-called government to government relationship.[27] In other words, the State has become the sole determiner of Native nationhood, despite the longevity of a people and a community that have been tied to a place since time immemorial and their collective ongoing Indigenous identity. Native peoples are thus in the position of fighting against the whims of the State not only to protect their lands but also for their continued existence as nations.

Central to Native nationhood is sovereignty. Federal law has long recognized the inherent sovereignty of Native nations based on treaty relationships, but it is a limited form dictated by legal doctrines as imagined by the US Supreme Court. The first three cases ever argued in front of the court involving Indians, referred to as the Marshall Trilogy, form the basis of today's canon of federal Indian law. The court created what legal scholars have widely called legal fictions that constructed Native peoples' relationships with the State that reached beyond the original intent of the treaties (the recognition of the independent existence of tribal nations), reining them in under federal control without their consent. In the first case, *Johnson v. M'Intosh* (1823), to settle a land dispute between two white men and out of a need to more clearly define land law in the fledgling country, the court articulated the so-called doctrine of discovery, the idea that European religious and cultural superiority gave the US the superior right of title to land by virtue of discovery, while Native nations merely possessed the right of occupation, or usufruct rights. In the 1831 case *Cherokee Nation v. Georgia*, the court denied the independent existence of the Cherokee Nation, claiming they were a "domestic dependent nation," likening the relationship as a ward to its guardian. The following year in the *Worcester* decision, the court asserted the primacy of the federal government to deal with Native nations, saying that the state of Georgia had no authority over Indian affairs and giving birth to the concept of inherent—but limited—sovereignty. More than one and a half centuries of legal decisions and legislation have chipped away at Native nations' control over their own lives and lands, resulting in a form of sovereignty they never agreed to, with many nations having been stripped of their sovereignty altogether. The legal framework that governs the tribal-federal nexus forms the core of what is thought of as a settler colonial structure in a relationship of domination.[28]

EJ for Indigenous peoples, therefore, must be capable of a political scale beyond the homogenizing, assimilationist, capitalist State. It must conform to a model that can frame issues in terms of their colonial condition and can affirm decolonization as a potential framework within which environmental justice can be made available to them. It must also recognize that racism is imbricated with colonialism in a logic that, as EJ geography scholars Anne Bonds and Joshua Inwood claim, "situates white supremacy not as an artifact of history or as an extreme position, but rather as the foundation for the continuous unfolding of practices of race and racism in settler states."[29]

We might think of this as a project to "Indigenize" environmental justice. Indigenizing EJ by centering Native issues means it should conform to principles outlined in decolonizing theories and Indigenous research methodologies, defined as "research by and for Indigenous peoples, using techniques and methods drawn from the traditions, and knowledges of those people."[30] While Indigenous peoples' lived experiences vary from place to place, there are common realities they all share in the experience of colonization that make it possible to generalize an Indigenous methodology while recognizing specific, localized conditions. Maori scholar Linda Tuhiwai Smith (who broke ground with her book on decolonizing methodologies), quoting Franke Wilmer, notes that "the Indigenous voice speaks critically to the narrative (some would say the myth) of the nation-state—the hierarchical, incorporative, coercive state that exists, in part, to facilitate the process of creating economic surplus on an international scale."[31] Creating economic surplus is possible from not only the exploitation of Indigenous lands but the commodification of them also—that is, the construction of land as property. Such an understanding necessitates the constant migration of people, which relies on Indigenous displacement and disappearance.[32]

From an Indigenous standpoint, justice must transcend the distributive, capitalist model. Indigenous modes of justice typically reflect a restorative orientation. A decolonized American justice system would also necessarily encompass both the colonized and the colonizer. In essence, justice for Indigenous peoples is about restoring balance in relationships that are out of balance.[33] In Western legal theory "laws hold insofar as those in economic and political power say they do," as legal scholars Wanda McCaslin and Denise Breton argue, but Indigenous peoples rarely experience Western law as either fair or equitable; for them, law is an enforcer of oppression.[34] For this reason, McCaslin and Breton argue three points: (1) that decolonization is good for both the colonizers and the colonized because it can restore right relationship to all involved; (2) rule by force cannot somehow become benevolent or even benign; it punishes the colonized for who they are; and (3) colonization has steered the colonizers away from their own ancestral wisdom. Decolonizing the colonizers is necessary so that they can once again learn how to respect themselves and others.

CULTURAL DIFFERENCE: CENTERING INDIGENOUS
WORLDVIEWS AND THE FAILURE OF THE EPA

The very thing that distinguishes Indigenous peoples from settler societies is their unbroken connection to ancestral homelands. Their cultures and identities are linked to their original places in ways that define them; they are reflected in language, place names, and cosmology (origin stories). In Indigenous worldviews, there is no separation between people and land, between people and other life forms, or between people and their ancient ancestors whose bones are infused in the land they inhabit and whose spirits permeate place. Potawatomi scholar Kyle Powys Whyte refers to these interconnections as systems of responsibility. Based on his study of various Indigenous philosophies and how Indigenous people relate to land and the environment, Whyte notes that environmental injustice occurs when systems of responsibility between humans and the land are disrupted through the processes of colonization:

> In these cases, environmental injustice cuts at the fabric of systems of responsibilities that connect [nonhuman] people to humans, nonhumans and ecosystems. Environmental injustice can be seen as an affront to peoples' capacities to experience themselves in the world as having responsibilities for the upkeep, or continuance, of their societies. . . . Environmental injustice can be seen as occurring when these systems of responsibilities are interfered with or erased by another society in ways that are too rapid for indigenous peoples to adapt to without facing significant harms that they would not ordinarily have faced.[35]

So, it is the interruption of the collective continuance of a people that disables their systems of responsibility, which are built upon place-based knowledge accumulated over eons. Throughout this book we will explore the nuances of these worldviews, particularly in chapter 7 on the topic of sacred sites and what constitutes them and their relationship to environmental justice. These are inevitably discussions about the spiritual foundations of Native peoples that inform all other aspects of life, including the political relationships that shape today's Native nations. This section of chapter 1, however, reveals how the philosophies undergirding cultural difference that Native peoples assert do, or conversely do not, find their way into State-based environmental justice frameworks.[36]

Although the Environmental Protection Agency was formed in 1970, American Indians were not substantively included in the EPA policy schema until 1984. That year, under the Reagan administration, the EPA issued its *Policy for the Administration of Environmental Programs on Indian Reservations*. Barely four pages long, the document's purpose was essentially to affirm the trust-based government to government relationship between tribal nations and federal agencies.[37] It acknowledged tribal governments as the primary parties for standard setting, decision making, and program management relative to environmental policy on reservations. It also promised to take affirmative steps to assist tribes in those duties, to remove legal and procedural impediments to working effectively with tribal governments. It assured that tribal concerns and interests were considered in EPA actions that may affect reservation environments, encouraged interagency cooperation with tribal governments, and pledged to incorporate all those principles into the agency's planning and management activities. Despite these promises, the federal government's efforts fell short and concerns were raised about the lack of effective consultation and collaboration between tribal governments and federal agencies. With the founding of the National Environmental Justice Advisory Council (NEJAC) in 1993, other policy statements were issued, such as the *Guide on Consultation and Collaboration with Indian Tribal Governments and the Public Participation of Indigenous Groups and Tribal Citizens* (November 2000), and *Meaningful Involvement and Fair Treatment by Tribal Environmental Regulatory Programs* (November 2004), both compiled by NEJAC's Indigenous Peoples Subcommittee.

Both reports built upon the 1984 document, elaborating on tribal sovereignty and fleshing out the finer details of things like federal Indian law, effective consultation practices, public participation, interagency cooperation, and other administrative functions of the State to better facilitate tribal-federal relationships in the realm of environmental policy and law. They reflect an expanding agenda that encompassed nonfederally recognized tribes, grassroots organizations, sacred sites, and international human rights and language that recognized tribal models of fair treatment and meaningful public participation.

In 2011 the EPA's Office of International and Tribal Affairs and Office of Environmental Justice commissioned another report "to provide advice and recommendations about how the Agency can most effectively

address the environmental justice issues in Indian country, including in Alaska and Hawaii and those facing indigenous peoples both on
and off reservations," asking Indigenous peoples for their input. Now
called the Indigenous Peoples Work Group (formed in 2011), in 2013 the
committee submitted its *Recommendations for Fostering Environmental
Justice for Tribes and Indigenous Peoples.* The IPWG was an ad hoc eleven-
member group of Indigenous advisors from diverse backgrounds, including representatives of tribal governments, Indigenous grassroots groups,
environmental organizations, academia, and elders and youth. The commissioned report was the first government effort to specifically and
comprehensively address environmental justice for Indigenous peoples.

The IPWG was certainly not the first committee to be composed of Indigenous advisors, as the prior two studies under the Indigenous Peoples
Subcommittee were also predominantly staffed by Native people. The
EPA recommendations from 2000 and 2004 are notable for their prosov-
ereignty and treaty-rights positions, empowering Native participation,
and incorporating Native values into the federal administrative appara-
tus relative to environmental programs. Ultimately, however, the focus
of the earlier recommendations was constrained by their deferral to federal law, problematically attempting to adapt Indigenous peoples' needs
to the existing domination-based legal structure. The historical context
of colonialism was almost completely absent. But what was significant
about the 2013 *Recommendations* document is its heightened attention to
history, explicitly naming the processes of dispossession that have led to
the environmental injustices faced by Indigenous peoples today. There is
no whitewashing or sugarcoating of history here:

> "Advanced" knowledge, innovation, technology and wealth have
> accelerated the insatiable need to feed, finance and advance
> growth and development, consuming natural resources at a rate
> that exceeds Mother Earth's ability to restore. At the same time,
> Indigenous peoples whose communities and nations pre-date
> the settler-state have maintained their unique relationships with
> the land, rivers, seas and sky. But in the 500 years since west-
> ern contact, indigenous peoples have experienced dispossession
> and disenfranchisement, rendering them one of the most vul-
> nerable subgroups on standard measures for quality of life and

sustainability such as: poor health, obesity, unemployment, teen pregnancies, high school drop-out rates, drug abuse, incarceration, etc. . . .

EPA must remain vigilant to the historical reality that federal policy recognizing tribes' separate political existence and sovereignty depends upon the cultural distinctiveness of tribes from the larger American society. Institutions of tribal governance include extended kinship networks that "do not exist to reproduce or replicate dominant canons appearing in state and federal courts." This "Dilemma of Difference" occurs even within tribes, such as the diversity of spiritual expression and the social contexts of tribal community members.[38]

The *Recommendations* document names some of the challenges facing Native peoples' ability to maintain traditional lifeways and ancestral places: sustainability of homelands, subsistence lifestyles, cultural and ancestral (sacred) sites, and environment-related health-care issues, including reproductive health and food insecurity. It recognizes the problems inherent in federal Indian law, which complicates EJ issues due to jurisdictional conflicts and whose sovereignty prevails. Further, it refers to President Obama's 2009 executive order on tribal consultation (Exec. Order No. 13175) and the UN Declaration on the Rights of Indigenous Peoples (UNDRIP) as established principles upon which to build a federal framework for Indigenous EJ. Several aspects of UNDRIP are invoked, including the right of free, prior, and informed consent. Numerous suggestions were made that would integrate various Native institutions, enabling the engagement of the best and brightest of Indigenous peoples' intelligentsia. One of its most important recommendations was for the EPA to establish a standing Indigenous Peoples Environmental Justice Committee or a standing NEJAC subcommittee. Overall, the document's twenty-four recommendations contained the most extensive Indigenous-centered solutions ever offered to build an EJ foundation for Indigenous peoples. It might also be said that the *Recommendations* document paralleled and reflected the trajectory of Indigenous studies scholarship, resisting the previous pattern of deferring to State-based law and statutory agendas.

In 2014, after receiving the recommendations from NEJAC's Indigenous Peoples Work Group, the EPA issued its *Policy on Environmental Justice for Working with Federally Recognized Tribes and Indigenous Peoples*, supplementing its *Plan EJ 2014*, a roadmap designed to help the EPA integrate EJ into the agency's programs, policies, and activities. It was written with the intent to create standards applicable to all Indigenous peoples on the US continent and in Hawaii, Puerto Rico, and the Mariana Islands.[39] In general, the seven-page document did not include any dramatically new policy statements, but for the most part simply reiterated many of the principles articulated in the previous guidelines, with updated language drawn from more recent executive orders and other policy implementation tools.

Noticeably absent from the new policy statement was any reference to the United States' colonial history or some of the more specific problems Indigenous communities face that the *Recommendations* document detailed (especially food insecurity and subsistence lifeways). What it does mention is the EPA's desire to integrate Indigenous traditional ecological knowledge into environmental science, policy, and decision-making processes "as appropriate and to the extent practicable and permitted by law," and it does affirm the "importance" of UNDRIP, but only to the extent that its principles are consistent with the mission and authority of the agency. It "seek[s] to be responsive to environmental justice concerns" and understand definitions of health and environment from Indigenous perspectives. No standing Indigenous people's committee was created as recommended. This policy statement, like the previous ones, emphasizes the language of "fair treatment and meaningful involvement" of Indigenous communities. The document closes with the following disclaimer:

> This document identifies internal Agency policies and procedures for EPA. This document is not a rule or regulation and it may not apply to a particular situation based upon the circumstances. This document does not change or substitute for any law, regulation, or any other legally-binding requirement and is not legally enforceable. As indicated by the use of non-mandatory language, this Policy does not create any judicially enforceable rights or obligations substantive or procedural in any person.[40]

The EPA's obvious weaknesses explain, at least in part, how things went so horribly wrong with Standing Rock. For one thing, the dis-claimer makes it clear that none of the Indigenous-affirming language used in the policy statement is legally binding, making the document aspirational only. A more cynical—or perhaps realistic—perspective would be that the EPA's entire Indigenous policy stance amounts to no more than a façade, a ruse to cover for the more standard project of the State to hamstring Indigenous peoples' rights to self-determination, as articulated in international rights agreements like UNDRIP and previ-ous covenants like the *International Covenant on Civil and Political Rights* (which was affirmed in NEJAC's 2004 policy report). And there's plenty of evidence for this argument. In the EPA's 2014 policy statement, the language emphasized tribal "consultation" and "involvement," as com-pared to language in UNDRIP, particularly the right to "free, prior, and informed consent." Consent implies the power to veto any action a tribal government or people disagrees with, whereas consultation means that even if a community objects to a proposed project (like a pipeline), it has no power to stop it, and the federal government will have theoretically met its legal obligation to "consult" with them, no matter how flimsy such a consultation may actually have been. This is in fact what happened in the Standing Rock case, leading to the three federal departments' (In-terior, Justice, and Army) announcement to halt the DAPL having recog-nized that the tribe had not been adequately consulted. Needless to say, it took months of high-profile demonstrations for the agencies to come to this conclusion. Further bolstering the argument that the federal govern-ment doesn't really believe in internationally based rights to Indigenous self-determination is that when the Obama administration endorsed UNDRIP in 2010, it issued a fifteen-page announcement littered with disclaimers.[41]

In the Obama announcement, the administration asserts the dubi-ous, unsupported claim that the "[UN] Declaration's call is to promote the development of a concept of self-determination for indigenous peoples that is different from the existing right of self-determination in interna-tional law."[42] It goes on to emphasize the disclaimer contained in UN-DRIP itself, that "the Declaration does not imply any right to take any action that would dismember or impair, totally or in part, the territorial integrity or political unity of sovereign and independent States"; in other words, moves toward independence. Put another way, the statement argues that the meaning of self-determination is limited to domestic law, which as we have seen, is a dictatorial and colonial approach to the recognition of Indigenous self-determination. The rest of the administration's announcement is spent in sanctimonious declarations about all the ways the US honors its relationship with Native Americans in its ongoing rehearsal of "benevolent supremacy."[43] Granted, Obama and his administration more than any other honored Native nations' political status, settled immense land claims, went out of the way to visit reservations, and signed important executive orders addressing some of the most pressing problems in Indian country. But never has the federal government officially acknowledged the term "colonialism" to describe the sociopolitical and legal structure that still governs the relationships between the US and Indigenous peoples. When the federal government does acknowledge its depredations, they are invariably sanitized as a simple "wrongdoing" or "mistreatment" consigned to a distant past.

To summarize, the extent to which the US government has incorporated Indigenous peoples into its environmental justice policy regime has, predictably, mirrored and replicated its hegemonic relationship to Native peoples in the language of benevolent supremacy. The political relationships are always evolving, always fragile, and subject to the unpredictable whims of the US political system. And it's been Indigenous peoples' initial assertions of sovereignty that have led to what advances have been made in distinguishing an Indigenized EJ from a more mainstream EJ, based on a differentiated cultural, legal, and political status. Next, we turn to specific histories and circumstances that constitute a broadly defined concept of environmental injustice, rooted in the history of the US settler State.

CHAPTER TWO

Genocide by Any Other Name

A History of Indigenous Environmental Injustice

> That those tribes cannot exist surrounded by our settlements and
> in continual contact with our citizens is certain. They have neither
> the intelligence, the industry, the moral habits, nor the desire of
> improvement which are essential to any favorable change in their
> condition. Established in the midst of another and a superior race,
> and without appreciating the causes of their inferiority or seeking to
> control them, they must necessarily yield to the force of circumstances
> and ere long disappear.
>
> —PRESIDENT ANDREW JACKSON,
>
> IN HIS FIFTH ANNUAL MESSAGE, DECEMBER 3, 1833[1]

Well before Andrew Jackson signed the Indian Removal Act in 1830, the writing was on the wall for the series of forced marches that would become known as the Trail of Tears. As early as 1822 the Chickasaw had begun moving west from their traditional lands in the Tennessee Valley, and thanks to the leadership and shrewd negotiating skills of their chief, Levi Colbert, their eventual relocation was better planned and financed compared to the other Southeastern tribes who were forced to move to the Indian territory in Oklahoma. Still, Colbert admonished the US government, saying,

> We never had a thought of exchanging our land for any other, as we think that we would not find a country that would suit us as well as this we now occupy, it being the land of our forefathers, if we should exchange our lands for any other, fearing the consequences may be similar to transplanting an old tree, which would wither and die away, and we're fearful we would come to

the same. . . . If we should consent [to come under the laws of the United States], we should be likened unto young corn growing and met with a drought that would kill it.[2]

Because of Colbert's foresight, the Chickasaw relocation would prove to be less horrific than that experienced by the Cherokee, Creek, and Choctaw. Contained in the chief's words is not only the anguish of forced removal; they also vividly capture a Native worldview that makes no distinction between people and land. The Chickasaw may have survived removal and adapted to their new environment west of the Mississippi, but in reality, there is no way to measure what was lost in the process of being deracinated from their homelands.[3] The same is true for all Native peoples who have been severed from their traditional territories and forced to adapt to a foreign society. As this chapter asserts, the origin of environmental injustice for Indigenous peoples is dispossession of land in all its forms; injustice is continually reproduced in what is inherently a culturally genocidal structure that systematically erases Indigenous peoples' relationships and responsibilities to their ancestral places.

As the previous chapter delineates, the language of environmental justice is still fairly new in the US. Scholars are working to more clearly articulate what environmental injustice is and what justice means in Indian country, beginning with understanding that the principles of EJ in Indigenous communities should be different from those of other populations. In this light, we might even question the EPA's definition of environmental justice for how well it does—or perhaps more important, does not—serve Native peoples. The statement "environmental justice is the fair treatment and meaningful involvement of all people regardless of race, color, national origin, or income, with respect to the development, implementation, and enforcement of environmental laws, regulations, and policies" clearly collapses "all people" into one conceptual category, without making distinctions based on varied histories, experience, or political status. This definition is a universalizing, unidimensional approach that fails to account for different histories. We have seen that Indigenous peoples are defined by vastly different cultural orientations and a political relationship to the State. As statistics consistently show, they also continue to suffer from a disproportionate excess of social ills and vulnerabilities as a result of their histories with the dominant settler society. These histories are critical to informing how environmental justice for Indigenous peoples is conceived.

Native American EJ research and the policies and programs that are informed by it must recognize these histories, but scholars note a lack of research that critically positions contemporary environmental inequalities within historical processes.[4] Take the example of a 1992 legal case with EJ repercussions. In *State v. Elliot* the court asserted that the Abenaki nation in New England no longer held aboriginal title to their ancestral homeland, negating their rights to fish outside the jurisdiction of the state of Vermont in keeping with federal Indian legal principles that protect treaty rights. At issue was whether the tribe could prove continual residence on their lands; the court rejected the tribe's argument despite an exceedingly complex historical record that proved an unbroken connection to the land.[5] The court's decision was a failure to acknowledge that the Abenaki had been systematically dispossessed of their lands, turning a blind eye on the history of violent settler incursions. In so doing the court contributed to a pattern of denial about the genocidal tendencies at the core of US history. Inquiries that ignore histories characterized by domination and oppression also ignore factors that shape perceptions of justice.[6] When courts disregard histories of dispossession, delivering legal precedents that future court decisions will build upon, the action constitutes a form of erasure and weakens the legal foundations upon which environmental justice might otherwise be constructed. Decontextualization, then—framing law absent documented history—is one way the State system fails Indigenous peoples' ability to experience environmental justice.

Justice is further compromised by an inherently racist legal system formulated on the ideologies of domination and white supremacy. Scholars have long noted the complexity and paternalism of federal Indian law. Even modern Supreme Court justices have critiqued the legal framework, stopping short, though, of providing commentary about its fundamental injustices.[7] As chapter 1 describes, the Marshall Trilogy forms the foundation of federal Indian law, beginning with the Christian doctrine of discovery, a framework that posits the innate cultural inferiority of Native people based on their non-Christian belief systems. The dictum of domestic dependent nationhood was built on the discovery theory, imposing a diminished conception of Indian self-determination, and created the trust doctrine in which the federal government assumes the role of trustee over Indian lands. But other legal doctrines at the core of federal Indian law place immense burdens of risk upon Native nations, most notably the plenary power doctrine. Plenary power is a legal invention affirmed by both the Supreme Court and the US legislature that vests Congress with plenary, or ultimate, authority over Indian affairs. There are times when Congress can be the friend of Indian country, even countering some of the court's worst decisions. But they have also been Indian country's worst nightmare, imposing laws and policies that erode tribal self-determination. And because of Congress's ever-changing nature, things can shift in unpredictable and disastrous ways depending on who is in power. Central to the discussion about the role of history in environmental justice is that these core legal premises themselves resulted from viewpoints of white men during periods of profound racism in American society. Their legal doctrines were paradoxically both ahistorical and founded in archaic religious doctrines of the Middle Ages Roman Catholic Church—and have never been repudiated.[8]

Evading history has other ramifications for Indigenous peoples when they are dislodged from their own social and political contexts. Kyle Powys Whyte poignantly argues this point when he claims that for Indigenous peoples,

> injustice also occurs when the social institutions of one society systematically erase certain sociological contexts, or horizons, that are vital for members of another society to experience themselves in the world as having responsibilities to other humans, nonhumans and the environment. Injustice, here, involves one society robbing another society of its capacities to experience the world as a place of collective life that its members feel responsible for maintaining. . . . Settler colonial societies seek to inscribe their own homelands over indigenous homelands, thereby erasing the history, lived experiences, social reality and possibilities of a future of indigenous peoples. . . . *Settler colonialism can be interpreted as a form environmental injustice* that wrongfully interferes with and erases the socioecological contexts required for indigenous populations to experience the world as a place infused with responsibilities to humans, nonhumans and ecosystems (emphasis added).[9]

Applying the lens of settler colonialism to the topic of environmental justice sheds a different light on the processes of history, providing irrefutable linkages between all eras and aspects of settler and Indigenous contact, environmental injustice, and genocide; they are inseparable. As a facet of settler colonialism, environmental injustice is linked with a larger ongoing process of Indigenous erasure that is built into the structure of the State. It began, and continues, as depriving Native peoples of the conditions necessary for life and the continuance of cultural existence, what can be called "environmental deprivation." "Environmental deprivation," as it is typically conveyed in academic literature and used by psychologists, refers to psychological and developmental health in children. Here, however, I seek to develop a different concept of environmental deprivation that relates to historical processes of land and resource dispossession calculated to bring about the destruction of Indigenous lives and cultures.[10] Environmental deprivation in this sense refers to actions by settlers and settler governments that are designed to block Native peoples' access to life-giving and culture-affirming resources. These actions are not new revelations of previously unknown US histories; they are familiar genocidal patterns, but viewed now through a lens focused on environmental factors. They are acts of ecological disruption that constitute the origin of injustices toward Native peoples in what might be called an Indigenous peoples' environmental history of the United States. What follows is a perspective on history viewed through a prism that centers the effects of environmental deprivation on Indigenous peoples in the US.

DISMANTLING AND REFRAMING HISTORICAL NARRATIVES

Conventional narratives of early US history have long been based on the virgin wilderness hypothesis, or what William Deneven (drawing upon a well-established American literary trope) in 1992 infamously called the "pristine myth." The virgin wilderness construct presupposes a landscape unadulterated by human intervention, which imagined the Indigenous inhabitants incapable of (or unwilling to) alter their environments. At the same time, paradoxically, it implied a landscape largely devoid of human presence.[11] Historians have long argued that diseases to which Indians had no immunity solely accounted for precipitous declines in Native populations over the first four centuries of European settlement.

In recent decades, however, researchers challenge the idea that disease is solely responsible for the rapid Indigenous population decline. The research identifies other aspects of European contact that had profoundly negative impacts on Native peoples' ability to survive foreign invasion: war, massacres, enslavement, overwork, deportation, the loss of will to live or reproduce, malnutrition and starvation from the breakdown of trade networks, and the loss of subsistence food production due to land loss.[12] These deliberate tactics of physical and cultural destruction were relentlessly repeated during the United States' expansionist march across the continent long after the initial European settlements. In one way or another these are all environmental factors that were rooted in settlers deliberately blocking Native peoples' access to resources necessary for maintaining an Indigenous way of life.

In her acclaimed 2014 book *An Indigenous Peoples' History of the United States,* Roxanne Dunbar-Ortiz renarrates the dominant story of American history, foregrounding the settler colonial practices that disrupted North American Indigenous ways of living, particularly their connection to land and water. *An Indigenous Peoples' History* presents the settler narrative as a genealogy of English colonialism and suggests that the settler colonial practices in the US have roots in England's colonization of Scotland and Ireland, when the early seventeenth-century conquest and forced removal of Indigenous Irish from their homelands resulted in the transfer of conquered Scottish populations to Ireland. It is this population of displaced Scots Irish, first the dominated, who then become the earliest settlers in North America, and eventually violent dominators, which became the model for English settlement in the New World.

Decentering the virgin wilderness myth, Dunbar-Ortiz "follows the corn" to reveal vital North American Indigenous civilizations, suggesting an environmental history. She retraces ancient trade routes between North and South America and reveals cultures built not on aimless nomadic wandering often narrated in conventional histories but on skillful cultivation of the land. Indigenous peoples up and down the Eastern Seaboard of North America and far inland maintained large farms where they grew corn, beans, squash, and other foods, while also practicing subsistence hunting and gathering. Successful game hunting was guaranteed by the deliberate maintenance of forest landscapes through management techniques like controlled burning. But the arrival of Europeans and their wars of domination led to massive disruption of Native life, setting off a cascade of catastrophic events. Dunbar-Ortiz notes, for example, that settler seizure and interruption of Indigenous trade routes led to food shortages, which weakened populations and forced Indigenous peoples' dependency on the colonizers.

Referencing the work of military historian John Grenier, Dunbar-Ortiz says that one tactic of war by seventeenth-century settlers was the deliberate targeting of crops: Indigenous agricultural resources were systematically destroyed with the intention of (successfully) starving people out of their ancestral areas. She contends that it was the onset of Bacon's Rebellion in 1674 that not only codified slavery of Africans in Virginia but also cemented genocidal policies against Indigenous peoples through the "creation of wealth based on landholding and the use of landless or land-poor settler-farmers as foot soldiers for moving the settler frontier deeper into Indigenous territories."[13]

Two particular aspects of history—slavery and forced removals—are worthy of closer inspection to understand how the US enacted the genocidal tool of environmental deprivation upon Native peoples. An analysis of slavery is relevant, considering recent scholarship that uncovers its extent in Indian country. Seldom is slavery discussed in connection with Indigenous peoples, and when it is, it is consigned to an ancient, pre-State past, not recent American history. But more recent studies reveal how various forms of Indigenous bondage contributed to genocidal environmental disruption in Native communities. Forced removal is often portrayed as limited to early American and pre-American history, with the Trail of Tears as the best-known example. But numerous other removal events and modes of Indigenous displacement occurred as a result of federal policy and deserve examination for the ways they constitute environmental and cultural disruption.

SLAVERY AND ENVIRONMENTAL DISRUPTION

One of the least known and studied aspects of US history involves the centuries-long trade in Indian slaves. Only in the last decade or two have scholars begun in earnest to piece together and analyze the trade in Indigenous bodies introduced by Christopher Columbus from his first voyage to the New World in 1492. Captivity and coerced labor was not a new phenomenon introduced by Europeans; numerous tribal groups across the continent practiced various forms of raiding and kidnapping, but such practices existed within cultural frameworks that ensured, among other things, a group's survival, not for profit as was the case for Europeans. Such was the case, for example, in the Mourning Wars of the Haudenosaunee where captives were taken to replace murdered family members, also functioning to balance a group's spiritual and political power. What was new to Indian country was the commodified practice of chattel slavery that defined the transatlantic economic system that swept them into the crosshairs of multiple colonizing powers. It's true that Indians at times benefitted from the slave-based economies that characterized the Southeast, Southwest, and parts of the Great Basin, as they became inextricably involved in an ever-changing economic landscape. As historian James Brooks showed, in the Southwest Indians were caught up in complex relationships of captivity and kinship through hundreds of years of interactions with Spanish, Mexican, and American settlers.[14] In the Great Lakes region, Native groups traded captives in diplomatic relations with the French.[15] But, overall, the research shows that far more often Native peoples were victimized by slavery, which became a bigger contributor to the disruption of Indigenous cultural existence than was previously understood.

In his 2016 book *The Other Slavery: The Uncovered Story of Indian Enslavement in America*, author Andrés Reséndez estimates that in a four-century span (1492 to the turn of the twentieth century) between 2.5 and 5 million Indigenous peoples succumbed to slavery, a range that roughly coincides with other research.[16] Studies on Native American slavery are generally concentrated regionally, owing to the wide variety of ways slavery manifested over four centuries in the US and pre-US. Reséndez contends that tracking this history is more difficult than African chattel slavery because, among other reasons, enslavement of American Indians was largely illegal and thus lacked a paper trail, while there is copious documentation and a clear set of laws governing African slavery and later, civil rights. The bondage of Native peoples proliferated after US Statehood, predominantly in the Southwest and California. "The American occupation of the West did not reduce the enslavement of Indians. In fact, the arrival of American settlers rekindled the traffic in humans," Reséndez writes, revealing Indigenous slavery as a key tactic of American settler colonialism.[17] Additionally, his research resonates with other important scholarship showing that the state of California had an explicit policy of genocide against the Indigenous population, with various forms of legalized bondage as part of its genocidal arsenal of weapons, well into the late nineteenth century.[18]

Bondage in any form meant catastrophic effects in the Native communities touched by it, inevitably involving the breakdown of communities, continued loss of land, lack of access to food, and starvation. In Southern California, for example, one way bondage shaped the lives of Native people during the 1850s was through slave markets in Los Angeles. California laws against Native peoples were so brutal that European Americans effectively "created the state in such a way as to make being a Native American in California basically illegal."[19] The law legalizing Indian bondage in California was euphemistically known as "An Act for the Government and Protection of Indians" (1850–65). It created a system of indentured servitude of children and adults, characterized as "apprenticeship." It also codified vagrancy, in which Indians were punished by being "hired" out to bidders in public auctions if they could not pay the bond or bail.[20]

With the constant illegal settler encroachments into Native lands after the Gold Rush, the legal system not only made it impossible for Indians to defend their lands but also falsely portrayed them as violent predators, thus justifying state and federally funded genocidal campaigns against them. In Los Angeles, the seizing of Native lands forced Indian people into a labor market designed to keep them in a revolving door of jail and unpaid labor, leading to extremely shortened life spans. The loss of lands and conscription into the labor market also meant the interruption of traditional food gathering and inability to tend to families. Calling it "an economy of slow starvation," historian Brendan Lindsay pointed out that Indigenous populations would normally have been gathering food throughout the year to store for lean times, but the new labor regime prevented it, making starvation an omnipresent possibility for California's Native population.[21] Native food sources were also routinely destroyed by ranchers' livestock roaming over crops and hunting into scarcity local game Native people depended on.[22]

In New Mexico, the military pursuit of the Diné (Navajos) from 1863 to 1865 to relocate them onto a reservation in the eastern part of the state resulted in the death and enslavement of thousands. Reséndez describes a scorched-earth policy undertaken by General James Carlton, whose forces "would ravage the land—burning crops, orchards, and food stores; setting fire to hogans and teepees; and tracking Navajos over long distances—all while denying them food and shelter until they became utterly exhausted. It would be a relentless chase through Navajo country."[23] The Diné had long been settled in the region they called Dinétah, enabling their population to grow to twelve thousand through the accumulation of large herds of sheep and development of fruit orchards and other crops that tied them to the land. Reséndez estimates that anywhere between one and three thousand Navajos fell victim to enslavement during this two-year period—upward of a quarter of the entire population—and that by the summer of 1865 "nearly all propertied New Mexicans, whether Hispanic or Anglo, held Indian slaves, primarily women and children of the Navajo nation."[24] This degree of disruption would have placed enormous strain on the Navajo's ability to maintain community life, and as was true for Chickasaw relocation, there is no way to know what was lost to the Diné people during this time.

The four-centuries-long history of Indigenous enslavement cannot be separated from the larger framework of US settler colonialism or dismissed as the irrelevant ghost of a bygone era. In the big picture, Indigenous people had been building their societies for at least twelve thousand years; four hundred years for them is recent history. Slavery's legacy must be recognized as an integral part of the systematic effort to eradicate Indigenous cultures by, as Whyte articulated, interrupting the sociological context for collective life characterized by human responsibilities not only to each other but also to other nonhuman relatives in their respective ecological niches. In an expanded understanding of environmental injustice that takes into account all forms of settler aggression, enslavement is but one weapon deployed to eradicate Indigenous existence by separating peoples from their lands and collective responsibilities to them.

RELOCATION AND DISPLACEMENT

The military campaign to contain the Diné is notoriously known as the Long Walk and is one of countless instances in US history of forced removal and other forms of displacement of Indigenous peoples from their homelands. Some, like the Long Walk and the Trail of Tears, were dramatic marches at gunpoint. The Long Walk relocated the Navajo to the Bosque Redondo prison camp at Fort Sumner, approximately three hundred miles from their homelands to the west. Three decades earlier the Trail of Tears, known as a particularly shameful era of American history, relocated the so-called Five Civilized Tribes—the Cherokee, Creek, Chickasaw, Seminole, and Choctaw—from their homes in various areas of the South to Indian Territory (today's Oklahoma) over a period of several years. Others, including the Chickasaw, voluntarily moved early on under pressure of relentless settler encroachment. But the Trail of Tears is more widely associated with the Indian Removal Act signed into law by President Andrew Jackson in 1830 and the nefarious Cherokee Treaty of New Echota (1835).[25] Aside from the loss of ancient connections to homelands and sacred sites, removal had immediately disastrous consequences, including the deaths of upward of 25 percent of those on the trail and the loss of life-sustaining livestock and crops. For most of those forcibly relocating from the southeastern United States, the new lands they came to in the central and eastern parts of Oklahoma resembled the lands they left behind, somewhat easing their transition, and they were able to resume most aspects of their previous farming and ranching lifeways. Choctaw and Chippewa historian Clara Sue Kidwell from the University of North Carolina at Chapel Hill tracked the environmental changes of the southeastern Indians who relocated to the new lands. She notes that while prior to removal they had already begun adapting to a cash-based, private-property economic system with their adoption of many European customs (including the practice of slave owning), after their move west they had become more deeply entrenched into the American economic system with the discovery of coal deposits and the western expansion of the railroads on and through their lands.[26] So while they adapted to their new environments, their relationship to land would change to fit the needs of an imposed capitalist system.

In the case of the Diné, the forced march to Bosque Redondo (called "Hwéeldi" in Navajo) on the banks of the Pecos River in 1864 had similarly devastating fallout. Several hundred of nine thousand died over eighteen days, and many more died after arriving to what was to be the first reservation in the west.[27] Initially intended for only five thousand people, the forty-square-mile section of land proved incapable of supporting a population almost double the planned size. The water was brackish and there was not enough firewood. Crops failed, as did the irrigation system when the river flooded. Conflicts with Apaches, who had been interned at Fort Sumner first, abounded, and mutual raiding between Comanches and the Fort Sumner prisoners added to the chaos. By 1868 the Bosque Redondo experiment had failed and the federal government entered into a treaty with the Navajos, sending them back to their traditional territory after four years marked by starvation and widespread suffering.

In a lesser-known incident, in coastal Northern California several Pomo groups were forcibly marched to what is today the Round Valley reservation in Mendocino County. In the mid-1850s Round Valley was known as Nome Cult (thought to mean "west place" in an unrelated Native language), the traditional dwelling place of the Yuki people. California was deeply engaged in its explicitly genocidal campaign against the Indigenous populations, and state and federally funded private militias identified Nome Cult as a convenient, out-of-the-way place to deposit Indian prisoners who had not otherwise been killed, even though much of it was now under white ownership. Around 1857 militia groups began clearing out entire villages as far south as Sonoma County, force-marching them under threat of violence in what has been passed down in Pomo oral histories as the "death march." The tales tell of the death of babies and elders, and great misery.[28] Once there, they faced hunger due to always-insufficient government food rations and the inability to gather enough wild foods on lands now claimed by whites. Rape was rampant, and children were always under threat of kidnapping to be sold into California's legalized slave trade.

Countless other displacements occurred before and after the Trail of Tears, the Long Walk, and the Pomo Death March, often accompanied by wars of annihilation or massacres. They fill volumes in a massive literature on American Indian history and need not all be recounted here to make the point that environmental disruption via forced displacement constitutes the foundation of what we think of today as Indigenous environmental injustice. Some removals were not as overtly deadly as others, but they nonetheless catastrophically interrupted an Indigenous community's ability to maintain itself and, as Whyte says, its "responsibilities to other humans, non-humans, and ecosystems."[29] Other notable displacements include the following examples. The Shawnee, originally an Eastern Woodlands people, were scattered into several bands due to relentless white encroachment beginning in 1793. As a result of numerous imposed treaties before and after the Civil War and further displacements, the Shawnee exist as three separate, federally recognized tribes in Oklahoma.

Like the Shawnee, the Kickapoo were split into several groups and removed from their territory in what became Illinois. A total of ten treaties between 1795 and 1854 divided them into the Kickapoo Tribe in Kansas, the Kickapoo Tribe in Oklahoma, the Texas Band of Kickapoo, and the Mexican Kickapoo.

The Ponca were driven out of their homelands by the Niobrara River in today's Nebraska in 1877 in what is remembered as the Ponca Trail of Tears. Over a period of eighteen months, about one-third of five hundred people died on their way to the swamplands of the Quapaw agency in northeastern Oklahoma. The Quapaw themselves had been relocated in 1834 from their original lands in Arkansas to the Indian Territory.

The Medicine Lodge Treaty in 1867 removed Comanches, Kiowas, and Kiowa Apaches (Plains Apache) from their territories in Texas, confining them to reservations in Oklahoma, where starvation and illness dramatically reduced their populations. The same treaty reduced the size of the reservation of the Southern Cheyenne and Arapaho in Oklahoma by more than half.[30]

Paiutes in southeastern Oregon were forced off their lands on the Malheur Indian Reservation after the cessation of the Bannock War in 1878 and moved to the Yakama Reservation in Washington, after which the federal government terminated the reservation and opened it to white settlement. In 1972 just 771 acres were restored to what is now the Burns Paiute Indian Reservation.[31]

The Modoc in northeastern California were forced into a treaty ceding their lands in exchange for their relocation to the Klamath reservation in 1864. With the land unable to provide sufficient food for all the Indians, a band of Modoc returned to their ceded lands at Tule Lake and engaged in an armed conflict with the US Army for several months before their defeat in 1873. Survivors were exiled to the Quapaw reservation, resulting in a Modoc diaspora between Oklahoma and Oregon.

Removal of Native communities from their ancestral lands was not confined to the earliest years of the republic, as the example of the Standing Rock and other Sioux nation reservations shows. As noted previously, the Pick Sloan Act of 1944 created a series of dams in the territory of the Great Sioux Nation that without consent displaced more than one thousand Native families. The building of dams has historically delivered some of the most devastating blows to Native communities. Flooding caused by dams dislocated entire towns and destroyed fishing sites, contributing to starvation and poverty inflicted by US policies. They were part of large-scale efforts to engineer landscapes to serve growing populations and accompanied a new belief in the need to "preserve" wilderness as the limits to continental expansion loomed. With the birth of the conservation and national parks movement in the mid-1800s, tribal peoples continued to be pushed out of their homes, fueled by the theory of Manifest Destiny and the view that Indians were an impediment to progress.

Finally, Native displacement continued under the federal government's mid-twentieth-century termination policy. Formulated as a "final solution" to the United States' "Indian problem," House Concurrent Resolution 108 (passed in 1953) and its companion Public Law 280 sought to end the government's treaty-based legal responsibility to Native people. Cloaked in the language of liberating Native peoples from US "supervision," termination envisioned the dissolution of reservations, the abdication of federal protections for tribal lands and cultures, and the end of federal services to Indians. Free from the yoke of federal paternalism, Indians would finally disappear into the social fabric of America, undifferentiated from all other American citizens. Termination included a plan to relocate reservation Indians to cities under the guise of a jobs program, where they were given one-way tickets to New York, Chicago, Los Angeles, San Francisco, Minneapolis, and other cities. Relocation amounted to a wholesale population transfer away from reservations to urban environments, and as a result, today most American Indians live away from their reservation communities. Under the termination policy 109 tribes lost their federal recognition (over one-third of them in California alone) and thus their political relationship to the US, affecting 1,369,000 acres of Indian lands and 12,000 Native people.[32]

While many urban Native people today maintain connection to their homelands, their lives and identities are mediated and shaped by these histories of dispossession and displacement. To be an urban Indian is to live under diasporic conditions, sometimes by choice, but more often by circumstances of birth. It is a state of disconnection from land and the culture and lifeways that emanate from land, such as language, ceremonial or religious practices, and traditional food and medicine knowledge. Even considering the remarkable resiliency Indigenous peoples have shown since European colonization, this legacy of loss has still come to be a defining characteristic of Indigenous identity. In both urban and reservation settings, Native identities are formed against a backdrop of historical tragedy and ongoing injustice, which often involves the continued struggle to defend what remains of ancestral lands, territories, resources, and cultures.

CONNECTING GENOCIDE AND ENVIRONMENTAL INJUSTICE

To be a person of direct Indigenous descent in the US today is to have survived a genocide of cataclysmic proportions. Some Native people have described the experience of living in today's world as postapocalyptic.[33] Based on sheer numbers, if we assume an estimate of eighteen million Indigenous people on the continent north of Mesoamerica in 1492 and compare that number to the Native American population count of roughly 228,000 in the 1890 census—the nadir of the Native American population—we see a population decline of approximately 99 percent.[34]

Well after the cessation of the Indian wars in the late nineteenth century, the legacy of loss continued with the imposition of a policy of assimilation and the systematic forced removal of children from their families during the boarding-school era (roughly 1887–1934)—what's been called the second of four removals.[35] This legacy cannot be overstated, and a growing awareness of intergenerational and historical trauma recognizes the social and psychological implications that histories of genocide and colonialism have had on American Indigenous populations.[36] Pervasive social problems such as substance abuse, mental illness, violence against women, and high suicide rates in Indigenous communities are broadly connected with oppressive government policies of the past and present, to which scholars often explicitly apply the terms "genocide" and "holocaust." And yet, while the US government has issued official apologies acknowledging its "mistreatment" of Native Americans (or its role in the illegal overthrow of the Native Hawaiian Kingdom government), it has never acknowledged genocide in any form.[37]

Genocide in the US context has been the topic of contentious debate among historians for decades—it is almost taboo—and only in the past decade or two has it become acceptable to even use the term, given the whitewashing that has characterized most US historical narratives. But a new generation of scholarship in genocide studies is articulating the subtler nuances of genocide, recognizing the ways it has manifested in modern history in varying contexts. Scholars have pointed out, for example, one problem in recognizing genocide is that the Jewish Holocaust (which gave rise to Raphaël Lemkin coining the term "genocide" in the mid-1940s) is too often the sole benchmark against which all other incidents of ethnic cleansing are measured, limiting the scope of what might rightly be seen as genocide. Some contend that too broad a definition can render the term meaningless. Others still have argued that genocide can be genocide only if there is evidence of a deliberate intent of a State or government to annihilate an entire population. Another strand in the research relative to the American Indian case is that assessing genocide might best be taken on a group-by-group or region-by-region basis, where intent is more obvious in certain places and cases. The best example is in California where, drawing again on the work of Brendan Lindsay and Benjamin Madley, the case for genocide against California Indians is far clearer.

The point of naming genocide as an aspect of United States history is not to create a legal case against the US based on international law, nor is it to assign hierarchies or degrees of victimhood. It is ultimately to establish a standard against which the inherent contradictions in US history and narratives of democracy and freedom might be understood —and how this history constructs the present, continuing to stifle Indigenous peoples' ability to experience justice. In his now-classic 2006 essay, "Settler Colonialism and the Elimination of the Native," the late Patrick Wolfe elaborates on the concept of genocide, linking it with settler colonialism. While not all genocidal events arise out of settler colonialism, he asserts, settler colonialism, with its mandate to eliminate the Native, is fundamentally genocidal. Arguing that settler colonialism is a "larger category than genocide," he suggests the term "structural genocide" to describe the logic of elimination at the foundation of a settler State like the US.[38] Structural genocide recognizes the myriad forms Native elimination takes and situates it as an ongoing process. Elimination as a process hinges on the expropriation of Indigenous lands and their transfer into settler possession via regimes of private property ownership, beginning with war, killing, and forced removal. All other techniques of elimination flow from there, including assimilation policies that remove children from families, imposition of citizenship, religious conversion, and blood quantum policies, among others.

Acknowledging environmental injustice as a process of settler colonialism means recognizing the larger historical arc of contact between Native and settler people and how the environmental disruptions imposed on Native people by that process linger today in myriad ways, as the many examples in this book reveal. It is beyond wrongdoing or mistreatment, a phenomenon consigned to the past. The United Nations 1948 Convention on Genocide and the Rome Statute of 2002 recognize genocide as a range of acts that aim to "destroy, in whole or in part, a national, ethnical, racial or religious group," including "deliberately inflicting on the group conditions of life calculated to bring about its physical destruction in whole or in part."[39] In a separate document, the United Nations incorporates into its analytical framework for determining genocide the assessment of "less obvious methods of destruction, such as the deliberate *deprivation of resources needed for the group's physical survival* and which are available to the rest of the population, such as clean water, food and medical services" (emphasis added).[40] While the analytic framework offered by the United Nations only briefly touches upon ways environmental deprivation is genocidal conduct, the history of the United States' relationship to Native peoples described in this chapter fits this description.

It is more than a little ironic that the historian Raphaël Lemkin, the one who defined genocide, was most influenced by his extensive study of European colonialism, including the United States, and not predominantly by the Jewish Holocaust, as is commonly asserted. The traits he identified in the genocidal behavior of Europeans were less outright physical killing and more the cultural effects of colonial invasion (which inevitably involved slavery). For Lemkin, cultural genocide precedes actual physical genocide. Genocide has two phases: first, the destruction of the national pattern of the oppressed and then the imposition of the national pattern of the oppressor. Fundamentally, "[Lemkin] regarded genocide as comprising an ensemble of policies and practices that attack the 'foundations of national life,'" write Michael McDonnell and A. Dirk Moses, scholars of Lemkin's work.[41] The environmental disruptions imposed upon American Indians as described in this chapter undeniably fit a pattern of destroying the foundations of national life. Had Lemkin understood the extent to which relationship to place and land formed national identity in the ways Native scholars articulate today, it's not difficult to imagine him factoring the imposed severing of these relationships into his conception of genocide.

The United Nations currently does not recognize colonialism as genocide, which is not surprising given that the most powerful members of the United Nations are colonial States. But a preponderance of the research in genocide studies in recent years recognizes Lemkin's foundation on cultural genocide and argues for expanded definitions of genocide. These new definitions include the concepts of social death and ecocide. Distinguished from mass killings, social death can be seen as the "central evil" of genocide: the loss of identity and social relationships as the context for community.[42] The minutia of social death is debated by scholars, but by and large social death describes cultural genocide.

Environmental injustice as environmental disruption and structurally based cultural genocide gives us another frame from which to conceive what environmental justice might look like, beyond the reductive and limited concept of environmental racism. To state it simply: if settler colonialism is environmental injustice and settler colonialism is a genocidal structure, then environmental justice as an analytic framework must be capable of acknowledging the extent to which historical environmental disruption structures Native lives today and should factor in to the formation of EJ laws and policies. Next, we turn to ways colonial impositions continue to complicate the rebuilding of Indigenous national life and interfere with Indigenous peoples' responsibilities to their nonhuman relatives.

CHAPTER THREE

The Complicated Legacy of Western Expansion and the Industrial Revolution

We knew that the White Man will search for the things that look good to him, that he will use many good ideas in order to obtain his heart's desire, and we knew that if he had strayed from the Great Spirit he would use any means to get what he wants. These things we were warned to watch, and we today know that those prophecies were true because we can see how many new and selfish ideas and plans were being put before us. We know that if we accept these things we will lose our land and give up our very lives.

—DAN KATCHONGVA, HOPI ELDER TO
CONGRESSIONAL COMMITTEE, 1955[1]

In an arresting painting by Yakama and Pawnee artist Bunky Echo-Hawk titled *Natural Resource Management*, two people are shown in the foreground wearing ominous-looking gas masks. One is dressed in suit and tie and is holding a briefcase, while the other is adorned in a feather headdress and dons a judge's robe, with what seems to be a gavel in hand, which is mysteriously connected to the gas mask. In the background is an oil-drilling rig and what appears to be an industrial facility, with purple snowcapped mountains rising skyward from behind. The painting is part of a series of gas mask paintings that Echo-Hawk describes in his original artist statement as signifying the ways the federal government has waged biological warfare on Indians, from the smallpox-infested blankets given to the Ottawas by Lord Jeffrey Amherst in 1763 to the nuclear waste leaked from the Hanford Nuclear Site in Washington State from 1944 to the 1970s, contaminating Yakama and Spokane reservation lands. The images also represent the dualities of traditional and contemporary Native life and the perseverance of culture and religion, "the stark reality that we have survived," Echo-Hawk says.[2] Another interpretation that might be drawn from this particular image, however, especially given the painting's title, hints at Native peoples' sometimes paradoxical relationship to the environment. In this paradox, the image suggests, Indigenous peoples' relationships with land is in potential conflict with their needs for economic development, leading to contentious battles and agonizing decisions in Native communities. The juxtaposition of undeveloped nature, on one hand, and industrial intervention on the environment, on the other, seems to insinuate difficult if not obvious questions: Can Native people respect the integrity of their nonhuman relations in accordance with their cultural imperatives to honor the land and simultaneously extract the Earth's resources to escape poverty? Are there ethical limits, and if so, how are they defined and implemented?

While Indigenous peoples' relationship to land is forged through thousands of years of experience, colonization has also imposed changes. In writing about Cherokee efforts to protect traditional medicinal plants, Cherokee ethnobotanist Clint Carroll points out how these changes have resulted in contrasting land management paradigms, rooted in the language of "resource-based" versus "relationship-based" approaches, a binary imposed on tribal governments by the Bureau of Indian Affairs through their historically paternalistic relationship.[3] Having consolidated its power over tribal lands during the height of the industrial revolution in the late 1800s, the federal government compelled Native peoples to use land productively (that is, profit generation via farming, ranching, and so on) in keeping with European standards of land use. This solidified into a deeply entrenched bureaucratic structure that still drives much of the federal-tribal relationship and determines how tribal governments use their lands, sometimes in ways that contribute to climate change and, in extreme cases, ways that lead to human rights abuses (as in the Three Affiliated Tribes of the Fort Berthold reservation's exploitation of the Bakken oil fields). Industrialism itself has played a central role in consolidating settler power over Native nations, contributing to their confinement to some of the most undesirable lands on the continent and cutting them off from some of the best. It was no small irony when some of those perceived "wastelands" were later found to contain valuable substances coveted by energy and new technology sectors, presenting what would be simultaneously a blessing and a curse for the nations. Bunky Echo-Hawk's haunting painting performs a visual critique of the confluence of political and economic greed imposed on North American Indigenous peoples in an ongoing struggle to balance economic development with environmental protection. While the entire history and structure of settler colonialism is riddled with environmentally disruptive events, this chapter examines ways the industrial revolution created for Indigenous peoples a complicated relationship between resource extraction and economic development that risks pitting Native peoples against their own values, and potentially even each other.

IMPERIAL DREAMS AND INDIGENOUS PERSPECTIVES

In the annals of US history, and as it is taught to American schoolchildren, westward expansion is a natural outgrowth of advances in technology that would revolutionize farming and other aspects of everyday life, facilitating the transition from an agriculturally based economy to an industrialized economy. With technology innovations imported to the New World from Britain in the 1700s, new inventions like steam-powered engines, for example, enabled the construction of large-scale mills and the invention of locomotives, which contributed to greater efficiency in farming. Advances in weaving technology and the invention of the cotton gin helped convert a mostly wool-based textile industry to cotton, reentrenching the slave trade in the South, which of course was a major cornerstone of the global economy until the US Civil War in the nineteenth century. With the explosive increase of immigration on the Eastern Seaboard and burgeoning urbanization, the insatiable demand for land placed pressure on the US settler government to continue invading Indigenous territories. Other factors, like the discovery of resource-rich land in Texas, California, and Alaska, also contributed to the US pursuit of westward expansion and territorial grabs.

Settler expropriation of Indigenous lands required a logic that could be woven into the legal fabric of the US. This logic was explicitly stated in 1823 in the first Supreme Court case involving Indians, *Johnson v. M'Intosh*, when Chief Justice John Marshall opined,

On the discovery of this immense continent, the great nations of Europe were eager to appropriate to themselves so much of it as they could respectively acquire. Its vast extent offered an ample field to the ambition and enterprise of all; and the character and religion of its inhabitants afforded an apology for considering them [the Indians] as a people over whom the superior genius of Europe might claim an ascendency.[4]

And just like that, with the stroke of a pen, Marshall invented the Christian doctrine of discovery, which would become the legal rationale for the continued violent appropriation of Indian lands and the engine powering federal Indian law still in place today. After the court's articulation of the discovery doctrine, President Jackson would sign the Indian Removal Act in 1830, expelling the Cherokee and the other four of the so-called Five Civilized Tribes from their homelands in Georgia and the broader south, setting the stage for removal as federal Indian policy. As Native peoples were being forced into new territories, the US continued its aggressive push westward under the mantra of Manifest Destiny, pressuring tribes for land-ceding treaties while Indigenous resistance in the Great Plains led to increased military violence and genocidal massacres.[5]

The religious underpinnings of both doctrines were not only obvious but shamelessly exploited as part of a white supremacist system bent on maintaining power over nonwhite, non-Christian people, as Justice John Marshall's language in *Johnson* makes clear. Marshall's views were backed by his colleague on the bench and close friend, Associate Justice Joseph Story, who elaborated on the concept of discovery, linking it to ancient Roman Catholic edicts contained in fifteenth-century papal bulls.[6] Story's opinion explicitly and extensively drew on the church's language about Indigenous ignorance, savagery, and heathenism to make the case that Christian European's "discovery" of the continent gave them superior rights to land title.[7] Unpacking the doctrine of discovery and how it constructs the United States' legal relationship with Native nations, Shawnee Lenape legal historian Steve Newcomb describes it as the "conqueror model." Simply put, the conqueror model is a cognitive construct created by the State to maintain a relationship of domination over Indigenous peoples based on the religious justifications provided by the

US Supreme Court. It implies that the State possesses a *divine right* to dominate and subdue Indigenous peoples.[8]

The religiously based conqueror model extended to an ideology of human superiority over the natural world; it is an anthropocentric worldview in which the world is there for human taking, manipulation, and exploitation without regard for the consequences to either human or nonhuman life. So it was that paradigms derived from ancient European religious and secular traditions provided the necessary justifications for violent land theft and control over Native peoples that made western expansion possible. The conceptual groundwork was laid for a capitalist future of hyperexploitation of the natural world, and with the intractable poverty the American system inflicted on Native nations, so too would they be subjugated to the new system, willingly or not.

RAILROADING THE NATIONS

With enough Indian lands surrendered across the continent, the US could continue expanding not only settlement but also its infrastructure, facilitated by the locomotive. This history is frequently told as a triumphal story of an era of explosive settler population growth and the consolidation of US control over the continent, which could occur only if the hundreds of tribal nations that existed across the vast expanse of land were sufficiently contained. The transcontinental railroads not only enabled this process but also accelerated it exponentially. The predominant narrative celebrates the railroads as the technological marvel necessary for the forward progress of a superior civilization with tragic consequences for Indian people. From an Indigenous perspective, however, it is the story of a misguided society's moral failing due to its desire for progress that foreclosed the ability of entire cultures to survive in their environments and maintain responsibilities to their nonhuman relations. Further, the expansion enabled by the railroads led to the construction of mythological narratives rooted in the vanishing Native trope that still prevents them from being perceived accurately (or fairly) by the dominant society.[9]

Consider that in 1840 there existed fewer than 3,000 miles of railroad track, which would increase tenfold over the next twenty years. By 1880 there were 115,000 miles of track traversing the US, facilitating the stunning national economic transformation that characterized the twentieth century.[10] This was made possible by the treaties aggressively pursued by US lawmakers, forcing massive land transfers with increasingly harsh terms as the nineteenth century progressed into the twentieth and the balance of military power shifted to favor the US (aided by the railroads themselves).[11]

The treaties also created reservations that would confine Native people to territories far smaller than they had for millennia been accustomed to, diminishing their ability to feed themselves. Efforts to push Indians out of the way to make room for the railroad, which included eliminating Native claims to the lands concerned, ramped up in the 1850s with the passage of the Kansas-Nebraska Act (1854) and persisted for a period of approximately twenty-five years. The period known as the Indian Wars, sparked by unrestricted and often illegal white settlement combined with Native resistance to confinement on reservations, roughly paralleled the building of the transcontinental railroad. With the completion of the railroads and the consolidation of US power over American Indians, the Indian Wars would come to an end. In 1883 General William Tecumseh Sherman connected these events, speculating that aside from "'occasional spasmodic and temporary alarms . . . the *railroad* . . . has become the *greater* cause.' The recent completion of the fourth transcontinental line, he [Sherman] added, 'has settled forever the Indian question.'"[12] In a very real way the railroads were the death knell to an independent Indigenous existence.

The railroads bisected huge tracts of Indian lands, cutting Native peoples off from their traditional homelands and even removing them altogether, as was the case with the Shawnee. Some were defrauded in other ways; the Delaware, Kickapoo, and Shoshone, for example, were deceitfully persuaded that their lands would be enhanced with a railroad running through them.[13] While the railroads wreaked havoc on Indian lives in numerous ways, one of the most destructive and tragic outcomes of the United States' industrial expansion was the near extermination of the Plains buffalo herds, with the railroads as the strategic prerequisite to carry out the plan. With numbers in the tens of millions in the early nineteenth century, buffalo had for centuries been an abundant resource that provided food and nearly everything else the hunting cultures of the Northern and Southern Plains peoples needed for a comfortable, sustainable lifestyle. Militant Indian resistance to reservation life vexed the United States' efforts to safely settle westbound migrating populations, so a more extreme strategy aimed at starving Indians into submission ensued. Historians identify General Sherman as its main architect, and the army principally responsible for the demise of the buffalo. Even Congress stepped in to try to curb the carnage; despite its attempt to pass legislation in 1874 to limit the buffalo slaughter, Sherman's malicious genius proved triumphant when army veteran and president Ulysses S. Grant vetoed the legislation. So extreme was the buffalo extermination that by the 1890s fewer than one thousand remained, scattered mostly on private ranches.[14] And without their ancient food source, the Indian nations were forced into confinement on remote reservations and succumbed to the next wave of oppressive federal Indian policy, assimilation.

The near disappearance of the buffalo directly paralleled the experience of Native nations when the 1890 census counted a scant 228,000 American Indians, the nadir of their population compared to precontact populations. A growing awareness of the apocalyptic collapse of the Native population, a national feeling of mourning for the closing of the American frontier, and anxieties about modernity combined to create a new American sensibility that waxed nostalgic about the tragedy of the American Indian. The country now made safe from marauding, savage Indians, Americans could afford to indulge their humanity and pity the "plight" of the Indian, who was perceived to be disappearing into the mists of time. In their rush to preserve the last remaining vestiges of the vanishing Indian, documentarians like Edward Curtis went to reservations to capture their images on film for posterity, even artificially staging many of the now famous photos. Hollywood filmmakers created the first moving pictures, which inevitably depicted Indians before their final disappearance. Anthropologists memorialized "extinct" Indian peoples, searching frantically for anything left to preserve of pure, "authentic" cultures and individuals, in what anthropologists today call salvage ethnography.

The persistence of the vanishing Indian narrative in American society represents a collective inability to perceive Native people as survivors—as peoples with viable, living cultures that although altered and adapted to modern circumstances are nonetheless authentic and vibrant. The narrative has spun off into dozens of stereotypes and misconceptions that dehumanize them and keep them frozen in racist legal and policy frameworks that continue to deny them full access to their own lands and control over their own lives and resources.

DAMMING RIVERS, DAMNING CULTURES

As the railroads were snaking their way across the continent, altering the landscape and disrupting Indigenous lives to build American economic and industrial infrastructure, engineering technology was also being put to service to harness the power of the continent's rivers and watersheds. In the words of one historian, Theodore Steinberg,

> As the [nineteenth] century progressed, a consensus emerged on the need to exploit and manipulate water for economic gain. A stunning cultural transformation was taking place, a shift in people's very perception of nature. By the latter part of the nineteenth century, it was commonly assumed, even expected, that water should be tapped, controlled, and dominated in the name of progress—a view clearly reflected in the law.[15]

Dams were central to accomplishing those goals. They were designed for a variety of purposes, including flood control, water storage and delivery, and electricity generation as an integral part of the US economy. But while dams were contributing to American prosperity, and at times provided benefits to Native communities (jobs, and eventually economic development and recreation opportunities), their net effect in Indian country has historically been disastrous, particularly throughout the twentieth century. Those impacts range from population displacement to environmental disruption so extreme that subsistence livelihoods were eliminated, which in turn has reflected in negative health outcomes for tribal communities and ongoing trauma. The environmental effects of dams are well known, including the inundation of entire ecosystems, impacts on temperatures and changes in nutrient and toxin concentration in rivers, and increasing erosion and sediment deposition.[16] Reservoirs created by dams encourage the proliferation of nonnative invasive species; and large dams contribute to the extinction of indigenous species of fish; disappearance of birds; loss of forests, wetlands, and farmlands; erosion of coastal deltas; and many other issues. Riverbed deepening ("incising") can even lower underground water tables.[17] Human communities are affected by the decline in traditional food sources when fish species (most notably salmon) and other riparian and wildlife food sources disappear.

Decreased reliance on traditional foods is directly related to increases in food-related diseases, such as diabetes.

Studies show that population displacement has especially damaging consequences on children and the elderly, due to a lack of basic necessities for good health, such as shelter, food, water, health care, and loss of social networks.[18] Such was the case in the story of the Standing Rock Sioux, who experienced dramatic displacement as a result of the dam system created by the Pick-Sloan Act, which as the Dakota Access Pipeline controversy demonstrates, still has ramifications to this day. In some cases, displacement was irreparably calamitous, such as the O'Shaughnessy Dam, which created the Hetch Hetchy Reservoir in Yosemite Valley in 1923. Already severely disrupted by the formation of the national park and the California genocide, the Ahwaneechee Miwok along with other regional tribal groups lost villages, food sources, sacred sites, and the center of their spiritual world.[19] In the 1930s, as a result of the Bonneville, and later the John Day, and the Dalles dams, dozens of Nez Perce, Umatilla, Yakama, and Warm Springs families were relocated from at least three villages on the Columbia River with promises of new housing to replace those lost in the flooding—promises that as late as 2013 were not kept for some families.[20] In New York, six hundred residents of the Seneca Nation were forcibly relocated to make room for the building of the Kinzua Dam in 1965.

Displacement was not the only way that dams disrupted Indigenous communities environmentally. Waters were diverted, interrupting farming practices; ancient food sources were eliminated; tribal self-determination was compromised with dams built on treaty lands; entire ecosystems were altered, interrupting cultural practices and dividing families; trauma inflicted by the disruptions contributed to failing health conditions in tribal communities. Some of the largest and most damaging dams were built during the Public Works Administration, a New Deal program to combat poverty during the Great Depression, but at the expense of traditional Native lifeways and economies. In general, most of the dams that affect American Indians were built in the first half of the twentieth century, while the second half ushered in a movement to remove some of them. All told, the dam-building era represents one seldom-mentioned aspect of the US cultural genocide against Indigenous peoples.

Examples of tribal communities who were hardest hit still linger. Perhaps nowhere were dams more destructive to Native lives and the ecosystems that supported them than in the Columbia River basin. More than sixty dams shape a profoundly remade landscape designed to serve human "progress" within the 1,214-mile-long Columbia River watershed, in what has been called an "organic machine."[21] From British Columbia in the north to northern Nevada in the south, Idaho and parts of Wyoming in the east, and Coast Salish territory to the west, the Columbia and her numerous tributaries have been put to work to advance postindustrial American capitalism, simultaneously drowning fisheries tens of thousands of years old and interrupting migrating salmon populations to the point of near extinction. In this massive region there is no tribal nation that has not suffered devastating cultural impacts from the extensive damming, contributing to ongoing intergenerational trauma of the Columbia's river people.[22] On the Columbia Plateau ancient cultures connected to each other through a vast system of canoe- and later horse-based transportation. They were the last Indigenous people to be contacted by Europeans within the continental US. This meant that as long as they had their fisheries their cultures remained largely intact, even after colonization and the ceding of large swaths of land through the imposition of treaties, like the Yakama Treaty of 1855. The sudden loss of salmon-based economies and spiritual traditions was a seismic shock to the cultures and psyches of people who collectively call themselves Salmon People. But because the history of the Columbia Plateau is one of the least-studied regions of the US, narratives of the "genius" of human innovation and technology in the region still dominate, and ancient Indigenous regional history continues as a footnote in mainstream historic narratives.

Also noteworthy, the Coolidge Dam in Arizona contributed to water diversion problems that for a century impinged the farming abilities of the Maricopa Pima people, leading to starvation and, generations later, contributing to a dramatic diabetes epidemic. A series of dams on the Klamath River in Northern California has resulted in the near extinction of salmon runs, severely interrupting the fishing-based traditions of the Yurok, Karuk, Winnemum Wintu, Shasta, and other nations. And two early twentieth-century dams, the Elwha and Glines Canyon, permanently altered the watershed and blocked salmon and steelhead runs of the Klallam people, who since time immemorial lived along the Elwha River in Washington State, and flooded the nation's spiritual center.[23]

ENERGY, EXTRACTIVISM, AND ECOCIDE

The various eras of US land acquisition through treaty making (and other Indian land grabs) produced a noticeable pattern long recognized in Indian country: that the best lands were often those ceded (or taken), and the reserved lands were the least desired by settlers. The most desirable lands were those perceived to be most productive and suitable for farming or grazing. Prior to the early twentieth century, land acquisition occurred before particular resources had been found or recognized to be valuable. With the twentieth century came new technologies, increased need for energy, and discoveries of substances on Indian lands that would be coveted by extractive industries. The most notable of these are oil, coal, and uranium. Found in some of the most desolate regions in the country on lands that belong to some of the most desperately poor people in the United States, these substances brought promises of poverty relief and a better future for upcoming generations. And they did, in sometimes dramatic ways, but far less often they did not. Also unknown were the devastating environmental consequences that mining or drilling for these substances would bring to the nations, or the ways they would be swindled in shady business deals, or even murdered for their wealth. This latter point became obvious in the early twentieth century in an episode of history that was little-known but notoriously referred to as the Osage Reign of Terror.

After being pushed out of their homelands in what is today Missouri, Arkansas, and Oklahoma in the early nineteenth century to what became Kansas, the Osage people were forced to move again in 1871 to a remote corner of northeast Oklahoma, where oil was discovered on their new reservation. Beginning around 1895, the Osage oil boom had produced so much black gold and gas that by the roaring 1920s, the two-thousand-member Osage nation had become the wealthiest people per capita in the world, drawing millions of dollars in oil royalties. Their new wealth brought all the opulence one would expect—mansions, brand-new cars, servants. They sent their children to the best schools and traveled to Europe, and across the country their fortune was a news sensation. Dusty cow towns like Pawhuska were transformed into thriving cities, and businesses flourished as the proverbial American dream appeared to come true for the Osages and those around them. But where such fantastic wealth is found, so is corruption and treachery of the most heinous kind, and by 1925 the Osage dream had become one of the worst nightmares in American history. What followed was a string of gruesome murders between 1921 and 1925 that left dozens of people dead, mostly Osage—and in one case an entire family—in a vast conspiracy carried out by multiple white men in order to gain access to Indian lands and inherit Osage oil wealth through calculated intermarriage.

Contributing to the formation of the Federal Bureau of Investigation in the early twentieth century, the Osage Reign of Terror to this day has lingered as a sordid tale of unsolved murders and unanswered questions. And though it's a relatively unknown chapter of American history, it's been the topic of Hollywood films and numerous books, including the 2017 *New York Times* bestseller *Killers of the Flower Moon: The Osage Murders and the Birth of the FBI*, by Daniel Grann. Examining new evidence, Grann concluded that there were at least sixty deaths, many of which went uninvestigated, and that the entire town of Pawhuska was complicit in one way or another in the deaths and corruption that resulted in the skimming and scamming of Osage money.[24]

But sadly, the Osage murders represent only the beginning of the deadly avarice that would accompany resource extraction in Indian country. In the following decade, scientists in Berkeley, California, were hard at work learning how to split the atom. By 1945 the Manhattan Project had given birth to the world's first atomic bomb, and with it the nuclear weapons industry. The uranium it took to create those first-generation weapons came predominantly from the lands of the Navajo Nation, at a cost that Navajo and other Native peoples are still paying in human and nonhuman life today.

The story of the Navajo experience with uranium mining is notorious. Feminist scholar Tracy Voyles refers to "wastelanding" (in a book by the same name), a process where particular lands and particular bodies—in this case desert "wastelands" and Indigenous Navajo bodies—are deemed pollutable.[25] In the settler colonial context where the irreducible objective is attaining Native territory and resources, these bodies and lands are sacrificial and inevitably expendable because they are viewed and treated as worthless. And nowhere is this more apparent than the Four Corners region of the American Southwest. The Colorado Plateau, where most of the United States' uranium deposits lie, is the home of the Navajo Nation and Pueblo peoples. Uranium mining was predated by the mining of vanadium for the new car-manufacturing industry at the turn of the century; uranium was a by-product of vanadium extraction, and while uranium had limited industrial uses, with the discovery of its radioactive properties in 1917 the stage was set for the United States' soon-to-be born nuclear weapons program.

With roughly half the United States' recoverable uranium in New Mexico and half of that within the borders of the Navajo Nation, the Kerr-McGee Company in 1948 set up mining operations with a readymade workforce of under- or unemployed Southwest Indigenous peoples, predominantly Navajo.[26] The business-friendly environment was ideal for the company, with no taxes, cheap labor, and no health, safety, or pollution regulations. Within minutes of blasting, miners were sent into shallow tunnels without equipment of any kind to protect them from breathing radioactive dust where they loaded radioactive ore into wheelbarrows as though it were coal. After approximately a half century of uranium mining on the Navajo reservation, all the expended mines were abandoned, and radioactive mine tailings were left exposed to the elements, becoming airborne and contaminating above and underground water sources and ecosystems. Within a few decades lung-cancer death rates skyrocketed on the reservation, and children suffered radiation burns from playing around the mines or in the water exposed to the waste. Making matters worse, four months after the Three Mile Island nuclear plant meltdown in July 1979, on the Navajo reservation near Church Rock, New Mexico, an earthen dam disposal pool containing uranium mine waste burst, releasing a toxic stew of ninety-three million gallons of acidic, radioactive tailings and solid radioactive waste into the Rio Puerco River, poisoning the drinking and irrigation water of thousands of Navajo people as far as eighty miles downstream. The Rio Puerco catastrophe is generally thought of as the worst radiation spill in American history, even though it received nowhere near the attention of Three Mile Island.

The same year, the US Senate held hearings on the history of uranium mining in New Mexico, probing the Navajo cancer epidemic. It condemned Kerr-McGee's lack of safety protocols as deliberate negligence, in light of the knowledge that by 1930 radioactivity in uranium mines was linked to lung cancer. Further, although scientific evidence connecting radon gas to radiation-related illness existed after 1949, the company still did nothing to properly ventilate the mines as they stepped up their mining operations. Even worse, the Public Health Service monitored the health of more than four thousand miners between 1954 and 1960 without ever informing them of the threat to their health.[27] In 1990 Congress passed the Radiation Exposure Compensation Act (RECA), targeting a compassionate payment program to former miners, their widows, and other "downwinders" for their pain and suffering, but a tangle of bureaucratic roadblocks made compensation functionally unattainable to most of the victims of radiogenic disease, and RECA was expanded in 2000. As of 2015, awards to Native Americans totaled approximately $264 million among seventeen tribes. Members of the Navajo Nation alone received at least $212 million based on 2,800 claims.[28]

In 2005 the Navajo Nation took a stand against uranium mining by passing the Diné Natural Resources Protection Act, prohibiting its mining and processing on the reservation. But the vestiges of uranium mining on the Navajo Nation is ongoing with upward of two thousand abandoned mines that remain, which are still contaminating Navajo lands and waters, and with widespread health problems related to uranium contamination.[29] A lawsuit against Kerr-McGee and its parent company, Anadarko Petroleum, for its legacy of industrial pollution across the US was settled in 2014 for $5.15 billion, with $1 billion earmarked for cleanup on the Navajo Nation. That amount, however, will clean up only forty-nine mines, leaving the rest untouched.

The cases of the Osage murders and Navajo uranium mining are only two of the most obvious examples of how twentieth-century postindustrial expansion has delivered an excruciatingly mixed bag of economic benefits and fatal consequences to Indian country, especially when accompanied by a lack of disclosure of the impacts of industrial mineral extraction or equal partnership with Native governments. Many more can be named, like the decades-long Peabody Coal battle at Big Mountain–Black Mesa, which not only had devastating ecological impacts but also pitted Navajo and Hopi people against each other after centuries of peaceful coexistence. The manufactured conflict between the Hopi and Navajo peoples resulted in the forced removal of thousands of Navajos, a court-acknowledged violation of their human and environmental rights (aided by Interior Department corruption and congressional collusion), desecrated sacred sites, and the substantial depletion of an underground desert aquifer. The environmental threats of coal mining are also felt on the Northern Cheyenne reservation in Montana, which is surrounded by massive coal deposits and where the largest coal strip mine in the United States—aptly named Colstrip—and four coal-fired power plants are situated adjacent to the reservation border. Electricity generation from the plants produces such bad air quality that it causes respiratory diseases and low birthrates.[30] The Northern Cheyenne have battled the coal industry for decades to protect their otherwise pristine environment. In April 2017 the latest insult came when the Trump administration moved to lift a coal mining moratorium on public lands without consulting the tribe, which violated federal regulations and triggered one lawsuit by the tribe and another by a coalition of conservation and citizen groups.[31]

On the Spokane Indian Reservation in Washington State, high cancer rates still haunt the community, with the remains of two Cold War–era open-pit uranium mines, the Sherwood and Midnight Mines, scarring the landscape and continuing to poison the people. Peripherally related, the Hanford Nuclear Reservation in Washington, which processed uranium for the nuclear weapons industry from 1943 until its decommissioning in 1987, contaminated the Columbia River with routine dumping of radioactive materials directly into the river or onto the ground. Elevated rates of cancer and rare birth defects still plague the Yakama reservation and surrounding communities.[32] Efforts to conduct serious studies on the effects of Hanford's contamination have consistently been thwarted, especially by government entities. Uranium mining also took its toll in the Great Plains on the Pine Ridge Reservation in South Dakota. A uranium mine spill in 1962 in Edgemont, South Dakota, dumped radioactive waste into the Cheyenne River, contaminating the reservation's underground water source at Red Shirt Table, but had gone undetected for years. Not until 1980 did the Indian Health Service test the water after 38 percent of the pregnant women at Pine Ridge miscarried in the fifth month. In addition, of the children who were born, 60 to 70 percent exhibited birth defects ranging from undeveloped lungs to cleft palate and club foot.[33] More than one thousand open-pit mines dot the four-state region of North and South Dakota, Wyoming, and Montana, including the Lakota sacred lands of the Black Hills. On the Wind River reservation in Wyoming, home to the Eastern Shoshone and Northern Arapaho, uranium mining and processing at the Susquehanna-Western uranium mill tailings site left a legacy of increased incidents of cancer.[34]

In 2014, *Indian Country Today* reported that of the United States' 1,322 Superfund sites, 532 of them were located on Indian lands—an astoundingly disproportionate figure considering how little of the US land base is Indian trust land. Superfund sites are designated under the Comprehensive Environmental Response, Compensation, and Liability Act (CERCLA) of 1980. These sites are not just uranium or coal mines either. Some Superfund sites, like the General Motors and the Alcoa aluminum facilities, both in Massena, New York, adjacent to the Saint Regis Mohawk Reservation, were polluted due to manufacturing processes that leached PCBs and other hazardous substances into local water sources and ecosystems. Of the toxic sites the *Indian Country Today* story listed, however, the majority were the result of extractive industries. Some were well known, like the Midnight Mine in Washington. Others less so, like Salt Chuck Mine in southeast Alaska on the traditional lands of the Organized Village of Kasaan, which operated as a copper, palladium, gold, and silver mine from 1916 to 1941. Or the Sulfur Bank Mercury Mine, which is now the home of the Elem Band of Pomo Indians in Northern California, where mercury poisons people's bodies and contaminated nearby Clearlake—a traditional source of fish for the tribe—making it the most mercury-polluted lake in the world. Or the abandoned Rio Tinto Copper Mine site in Nevada near the lands of the Shoshone Paiute Tribes of Duck Valley, where the mine operated from 1932 to 1976 and whose mill tailings made Mill Creek uninhabitable for redband trout, an important cultural food source.[35]

The extensive environmental devastation as described above is often referred to as "ecocide." "Ecocide" was first named in international legal circles in the early 1970s to describe the destruction of ecosystems, implicating the behavior of governments and corporations all over the world—particularly in Indigenous and other marginalized communities—and has been applied in the American Indian context.[36] A decades-long effort to include ecocide alongside the four crimes against peace of the ICC's Rome Statute (the four being genocide, war crimes, crimes against humanity, and crimes of aggression) succeeded, but the revised statute limits ecocide to a crime only during wartime. Ecocide is part of the burgeoning field of "green criminology," a branch of criminology studies that links ecosystem destruction with corporate crime and environmental justice, seeing the environment as an independent entity invested with rights. But another strand of green criminology research sheds light on the underexamined connections between ecocide and genocide, recognizing the human rights implications when ecocide interferes with a culture's ability to perpetuate itself. By understanding the nexus of ecocide and cultural genocide, these researchers aim to ultimately produce new international laws that prevent the ongoing destruction of cultures due to extreme energy development technology such as fracking, or what British genocide scholar Damien Short calls "bottom of the barrel" development.[37]

FOSSIL FUEL EXTRACTION: INDIAN COUNTRY'S FAUSTIAN BARGAIN?

It's one thing when Indigenous communities are placed in harm's way or their lands are destroyed by extractive industries without being fully informed about the risks or having given their informed consent to extractive projects that will affect them. The robbing of Indigenous agency by State governments is, after all, the hallmark of hegemonic colonial relationships. But things get ethically complicated when Native nation governments willingly choose to engage in resource extraction—especially fossil fuels—given the environmental harm they cause, both in the extracting and in the production of climate-changing greenhouse gases. The need to escape poverty and assert sovereignty, weighed against cultural obligations to protect land, forces tribes into what can seem like an impossible double bind. It is a realm of difficult choices that exists beyond binaries of black and white and right and wrong, necessitated by the unforgiving and unrelenting demands of capitalism.

Most of the cases discussed above occurred during periods of oppressive federal Indian policy, before any meaningful articulations of tribal sovereignty had been built into federal regulatory regimes. But by the late 1950s things had begun to change, with tribes able to establish their rights of resource ownership and consent authority, enabling them to negotiate with multinational corporations for leases and royalties.[38] A turning point occurred in 1975 with the passage of the Indian Self-Determination and Education Assistance Act, ushering in a new framework that would stress the government to government relationship, the United States' trust responsibility, and tribal sovereignty. This new era signaled a loosening of the federal reins on Indian country, largely to promote economic self-sufficiency, which could be accomplished in a number of ways including by greater resource extraction. Armed with their enhanced powers of self-government and the need to combat the intractable poverty that gripped their communities, some tribal governments in resource-rich regions have chosen this route.

Some have fared quite well, like the Southern Utes in Colorado, who have built a financial empire based on natural gas production, which in 2005 was worth $650 million.[39] Similarly, the Three Affiliated Tribes of the Fort Berthold Indian Reservation was already doing well for itself by leasing its lands for oil and gas development in the North Dakota Bakken oil fields. In 2015 the tribe formed its own oil drilling company to gain greater control over production, increasing its profits and improving living conditions on the reservation. But in addition to the issue of the greenhouse gases produced by fossil fuels, both the Southern Utes and Three Affiliated use fracking technology to access shale-embedded gas and oil. Fracking is highly controversial for its environmental impacts, including the polluting and depletion of ground and surface water, inducing seismic activity, and radon and methane gas emissions. And paradoxically, in the case of Three Affiliated, their Bakken field–produced oil flows through the Dakota Access Pipeline that the Standing Rock Sioux Tribe fought so hard to stop and gave birth to workers' "man camps," which has resulted in increasing rates of violent crimes against Native women.

Whatever shade of gray Native energy development falls into and the ethical challenges it may pose, tribal nations have the undisputed right to develop their lands in whatever ways they like (always under the supervision of federal law, that is). Still, the relationship between nation building and extractive land use is a conundrum that exposes profound contradictions, considering the very real cultural values that view the Earth as a living relative to be honored, not harmed—especially now with the looming specter of irreversible climate change. This worldview is consistent across all Native nations and is encoded in the cultural fabric of Indigenous societies through their origin stories, often referred to as "original instructions." As author and Native studies scholar Melissa K. Nelson writes, "They are natural laws that, when ignored, have natural consequences."[40] The original instructions are roadmaps for right relationship between humans and between humans and their nonhuman relatives.

This is the message of a growing number of Indigenous activists working to raise awareness so that tribes can transcend the seduction of fossil fuel extraction. Clayton Thomas-Muller, a member of Mathias Colomb Cree Nation (Canada) and an activist with Indigenous Environmental Network, wrote in 2008 of his work to educate tribal nations about the dangers of extractive industries, especially oil.[41] Calling it energy colonization, Thomas-Muller likens energy companies to proselytizing Jesuit missionaries who targeted Indigenous communities knowing that their poverty made them vulnerable to tempting promises of a better way of life. Yet, worldwide Indigenous communities are disproportionately affected by the "river of destruction," as Thomas-Muller puts it, from the extraction process to refining to the burning of oil in cars and airplanes. Every aspect of oil production from beginning to end is toxic and has long-ranging impacts to the environment and human health. Yaqui legal scholar Rebecca Tsosie points out that Indigenous nations need to measure short-term benefits against long-term harms with their energy projects, especially considering that in the big picture, it is the global south that will suffer the worst consequences of climate change. Because of the political power of the US and its global position, she argues, some tribal nations will be "climate change winners."[42] The Navajo Nation, for example, would benefit from the proposed Desert Rock coal-fired power plant in jobs and revenue generation from leases and taxes, but shouldn't they care about others who will be the climate change losers, Tsosie asks, like Arctic peoples and other Indigenous peoples who will be disproportionately affected?[43] For the Navajo, the answers can be found in the Fundamental Law, a set of guiding principles based on the instructions of the Holy People at the time of creation and woven into the Navajo Nation governing system. It offers an ethical framework that stresses the interrelatedness of all living things and the maintenance of right relationship.[44]

Tsosie's point is that sovereignty functions on two levels: governmental and cultural. The activism of grassroots people can function as a check and balance on tribal governments who might otherwise make choices based purely on economic self-interest, not long-term environmental health and spiritual balance, as was the case in the defeat of the Desert Rock power plant.[45] At the same time, Native people must be vigilant not to see themselves through the reductive lens of stereotypes that are imposed on them by outsiders, and not fall victim to beliefs that tribal economic development and cultural preservation and responsibility are mutually exclusive. By adhering to their original instructions, Native nations "may be the only governmental entities that can bring these multiple aspects of development into the ethical calculation of what is appropriate energy policy for the twenty-first century." [46]

As this chapter has shown, the relationship between industrialism, resource extraction, and infrastructure development exposes the collusion between corporate interests and government that has been a core process of the US settler State. It was propelled by western expansion and imperialism, based on ideologies of racial, cultural, and religious superiority of European American settlers. The technological innovations and Indian land cessions that made westward movement possible have always benefitted settler populations at the expense of Indigenous populations. When viewed through the lens of the Dakota Access Pipeline conflict, we can see that the hasty granting of permits to Energy Transfer Partners without a full environmental impact statement or proper tribal consultation was business as usual in the grand scheme of history. At the same time, that the pipeline conveys Bakken oil derived at least in part from Indian lands on the Fort Berthold reservation reveals the tension between the tribal exploitation of resources, on one hand, and Indigenous imperatives to care for other-than-human life, on the other. And as the artwork of Bunky Echo-Hawk so poignantly reminds us, modernity's challenge to Native governments is to balance the material needs of the nation with the original instructions of the Creator within a governing structure that forces choices between resource-based and relationship-based management.

The effect of this system is not only continual political tightrope walking and environmental compromise. Environmental disruption from land dispossession and imposed infrastructure development has also netted very real harm to the physical health of Native people, as we turn to in the next chapter.

CHAPTER FOUR

Food Is Medicine, Water Is Life

American Indian Health and the Environment

Our traditional foods are a pillar of our culture, and they
feed much more than our physical bodies; they feed our spirits.

—VALERIE SEGREST,
MUCKLESHOOT TRIBAL MEMBER, 2013

The mixed terrain of verdant mountain forests and dry, open steppe plains of the Upper Columbia River basin near what is today the Colville Indian Reservation was a land rich in food sources that produced some of the healthiest people on the North American continent prior to European invasion. Plants such as bitterroot, hazelnuts, soap berries, chokecherries, and numerous varieties of camas bulbs combined with protein sources like deer, elk, and other smaller game to form a balanced and highly nutritious diet. The imposition of the reservation system disrupted our ancestors' access to these original foods, which were gradually replaced with the high-starch, high-fat foods characteristic of the European diet. At the center of Colville food traditions was salmon. For millennia, my Sinixt ancestors thrived, as had all the nations of the Columbia River, on a food source as sacred to the people of the mighty Columbia as buffalo was to the people of the Plains. Salmon fishing in this region of the plateau revolved around a place known in English as Kettle Falls—Swah-netk-qhu to the Indians[1]—a massive fishery that had sustained plateau people until the Grand Coulee Dam submerged the falls in the early 1940s, simultaneously ripping out the heart of Colville culture. The dam obliterated the abundant salmon runs, delivering a final blow to our traditional diets and collective health. Today, Colvilles suffer disproportionately high rates of diabetes, cancer, tuberculosis, heart disease, and a host of other health conditions related to poor diet and lack of good medical care. On average, American Indians still die younger than non-Natives, and a startling 2008 Department of Health report found that American Indian babies died at a rate 44 percent greater than a decade previously.[2] The reasons for our health disparities stem from the history of colonialization and are exacerbated by federal neglect.[3]

The harsh reality of Colville people's health issues is that they are typical of Indian country more broadly and a direct result of disruptions to Native peoples' traditional food systems. According to the Indian Health Service (IHS), between 2008 and 2010, American Indians died at a rate roughly 30 percent higher than non-Indians, from a range of causes.[4] Among those causes (which include accidents, suicide, violence, and other illnesses) what stands out relative to nutritionally related diseases is the rate of death from diabetes, which is three times the national average. It is ironic but perhaps not surprising that IHS attributes American Indian health disparities to "inadequate education, disproportionate poverty, discrimination in the delivery of health services, and cultural differences. These are broad quality of life issues rooted in economic adversity and poor social conditions."[5] While IHS does acknowledge the problem of inadequate funding and makes vague references to structural inequality, nowhere is the United States' history of violence and land dispossession implicated as the source of these health problems. According to one 2014 IHS report that claims the diabetes epidemic is slowing, 15.9 percent of Alaska Natives and American Indians have diabetes, compared to an overall national rate of 11.7 percent.[6] The problem, however, is worse in some groups than others. For example, a 2014 study by the Navajo Nation's Diné Policy Institute found a rise in diabetes in the Navajo population that went from 22 percent in 1990 to 33 percent in 2014. It elaborated:

Indian Health Service now estimates that 1 in 3 Navajos are either diagnosed with type-2 diabetes or are pre-diabetic. This equates to nearly 100,000 Navajos or approximately 33% of the Navajo population. As the incidence of diabetes is more heavily concentrated within the boundaries of Navajo Nation, the rate of diabetes may be closer to 50% for the population of the Navajo Nation; IHS workers have anecdotally stated that they are diagnosing diabetes for 1 in 2 patients in some regions.[7]

Diabetes is a clear and present danger and at the forefront of discussions about health problems in Indian country, but it provides only one window into a multiplicity of health problems related to Indigenous environmental disruption and modern uses of land. We have seen how the legacy of uranium mining and nuclear waste still affects Native communities on the Colorado Plateau and in other places. And another study in 2017 revealed that continual exposure to low-level inorganic arsenic in well water is linked to impaired neuropsychological functioning in American Indian elders throughout the western United States.[8] Clint Carroll, one of the authors of the study, contends that it is also a direct threat to culture, since it is elders who carry so much of the cultural knowledge of a nation; neuropsychological functioning raises concerns, he says, about the transmission of that knowledge to future generations.[9]

If we understand settler colonialism as a genocidal structure, the health disparities (and virtually all the negative sociopolitical indicators that characterize the American Indian demographic[10]) can clearly be linked as elements of environmental injustice. All over the world food is a defining characteristic of cultures, and for Native people whose roots have been established in particular geographical regions for thousands of years, physical bodies became adapted to those places from where their food derives. Food is the conduit between people and place that ensures cultural longevity and personal physical vitality. When those food sources are disrupted, health and culture are disrupted, triggering a cascade of sociological repercussions. Turning once again to the work of Michigan State University's Kyle Powys Whyte, it's a pattern, he says, that is reflected in Indigenous peoples' relationships with settler-industrial States worldwide. Adding another layer of specificity to an analysis of settler colonialism, settler *industrialism* refers to the ways settler societies inscribe themselves on top of Indigenous homelands by means of industrial processes, "from military technologies to large-scale mineral and fossil fuel extraction operations to sweeping landscape-transforming regimes of commodity agriculture."[11] He describes the disruption of Indigenous food systems as interference in Indigenous peoples' collective capacity to self-determine how they adapt to "metascale forces" like climate change and economic transitions, forces not of their making and beyond their control but which they were swept into. According to Whyte, colonization is one such force that affected every aspect of Native life including their food systems, which he contends are really ecological systems. Given the place-based nature of their existence, Indigenous cultures are often described as holistic, and a disruption to one aspect of community life has reverberations into all other aspects of it; thus, the disruptions to Indigenous food systems are part of the environmental disruption that defines settler colonization. This also includes medicinal plants and other resources, a topic this chapter will also discuss. But first, let us consider these topics within a historical context.

PRECONTACT LIFEWAYS AND COLONIAL IMPACTS ON DIET AND HEALTH

Studies about the food patterns of Indigenous peoples confirm the robustness of pre-Columbian peoples' health. At the time of first contact, Native peoples in North America were using around two thousand types of plant-based foods, and it was this nutritional diversity that ensured physical vitality. Native North Americans were among the healthiest in the world (notwithstanding the imported diseases brought by the Europeans responsible for massive depopulation in the first centuries of contact[12]) well into the modern era, before the advent of the modern American diet.[13] Such was not the case in Europe, where nutrition- and vitamin- deficiency-related diseases were commonplace. Dental health studies of Indigenous peoples worldwide, for example, confirm that the extreme change in diets is responsible for the chronic health issues and degenerative diseases that plague Native American communities (and other Indigenous peoples) today.[14]

Evidence suggests that food cultivation in the Southwest dates as far back as eight to ten thousand years ago, in what has been called the Lakeshore Ecology Phase, when Pueblo peoples began the transition from hunter-gatherer societies to agriculturists.[15] After the end of the last ice age as big game became more and more scarce, Native people evolved agricultural practices that rivaled those of the Fertile Crescent in the Middle East, the so-called birthplace of civilization. It was not just the type of food that sustained Native health, but also their relationship to those foods, which existed on a spiritual continuum of reciprocity that nourished their spirits as well. Food traditions evolved to become inseparable from religious traditions, and sacred foods were perhaps unsurprisingly also their most nutritious foods, especially corn.[16] Corn is so important to the Pueblo people that their origin stories are constructed around it. Corn, beans, and squash were known affectionately by the Haudenosaunee people (also known as the Iroquois Confederacy) as the Three Sisters. As was true in Pueblo societies, the Haudenosaunee viewed their world as a network of intertwined relationships of which they were only a part, not the center. In this relationship, respect for their plant relatives and their environments ensured their health as well as the health of the people. Not only was the nutritional value of these sacred foods known to them but their farming techniques also ensured the future viability of the ground where they grew. The same was true with the Pueblo dryland farming techniques, which produced abundant harvests in one of the most arid regions of the continent. In a place where drought was common, the success of Pueblo farmers' gardens "was accomplished through the use of multiple, strategically placed garden plots and the construction of many check dams and terraced plots."[17] They worked ingeniously within the constraints of their environmental limitations in ways that sustained them for millennia. In other words, it was the symbiotic relationship with place and their sense of responsibility to those places that guaranteed the health of the people.

In the Pacific Northwest on the Enumclaw Plateau in Washington State, where large-scale farming similar to the Pueblo and Haudenosaunee was unnecessary, Lushootseed people (today's Muckleshoot and their relatives the Puyallup and Duwamish and others on the coast) survived on the abundance provided by the ocean, rivers, and forest and mountain plains. Prior to colonization, their high-protein diet was derived from fish, shellfish, small and large wild game, and, most important, salmon. Twenty to thirty percent of their caloric intake was plant based, derived from camas, chocolate lily, mustard, nettles, balsamroot, wild onion, and dozens of other plants, edible roots, nuts, and berries. But they also practiced a form of food cultivation that nurtured the growth of their wild root crops in estuaries, supplementing their diets when salmon runs and other food sources were less bountiful.[18] Camas bulbs are high in protein, fiber, calcium, iron, and inulin, while balsamroot contains antifungal and antibacterial properties, and both can be eaten in many different ways. Like the Pueblo and Haudenosaunee peoples' relationship to corn, Northwest people consider their traditional foods to be sacred, and they are deeply intertwined in religious traditions in ceremonies widely known as the potlatch. Potlatch ceremonies, held in longhouses that served as the hub for communities, were gatherings that celebrated the sharing of wealth by the more affluent in society with the less affluent. Central to the potlatch celebrations was feasting, which brought people together in extensive food gathering and preparation activities. For Pacific Northwest peoples, as for peoples all over the world, food is central to culture.

With American domination and the influx of foreigners to Lushootseed territory came the loss of access to traditional foods and the poisoning of the environment where those foods historically grew. Even in areas where traditional foods still grow, the ecological systems are often so polluted and toxic that those foods are rendered inedible. Invasive plant species also choke out indigenous species. The Muckleshoot situation is not unique; all over North America this story plays out in Indigenous communities in one form or another. North America is known to be one of the most biodiverse land masses on the planet. According to the Cultural Conservancy's Melissa Nelson (Turtle Mountain Band of Chippewa Indians), as many as four thousand food varieties and species are unique to the continent, but one-third of them are ecologically or culturally at risk of extinction or abandonment. As she notes, "Biological diversity and cultural diversity go hand in hand. When one becomes endangered the other becomes endangered,"[19] and this is reflected in the declining health of American Indian people.

OTHER THREATS TO TRADITIONAL FOODS AND MEDICINES

There is no Indigenous group in the US whose relationships to ancestral foods has not been severely impacted, if not completely disrupted. Some of these are well known, having been extensively documented, and no one has written more powerfully or prolifically on the issue than Winona LaDuke. LaDuke is the quintessential Indigenous eco-warrior, making her mark in larger Indigenous environmental justice conversation not only as a researcher but also as an activist who has worked tirelessly for decades in her own White Earth reservation community to protect Ojibwe access to wild rice, known to them as *manoomin*. For as long as the Ojibwe (also known as Anishinaabeg) have resided in the woodlands of the Great Lakes region in today's Minnesota, they have relied on manoomin as a primary food source. Not surprising, their ancient origin stories reference it. Long ago it was prophesied that when the people found the "food that grows on the water" it would end their westward migration, from the land of their Wampanoag, Lenape, and Abenaki relatives, and it was the Ojibwe cultural hero Nanaboozhoo who would find it and bring it to them.[20] With colonization came a declining dependence on manoomin, but at the same time, in the modern era, ricing became an important economic resource. Recognizing its potential as a unique cash crop, the state of Minnesota domesticated wild rice, opening it up to commercial production under the misleading term "Indian wild rice" as far away as California (where no rice grows wild). Unleashing the triple evils of cultural appropriation, genetic modification, and patent ownership propagated by conglomerates like DuPont, Monsanto, Syngenta, and a host of others has not only resulted in truth-in-advertising legal battles but also exposed manoomin to the possibility of transgenic contamination.[21] The mixing of genetically engineered rice organisms—which are bred to not produce seeds—with manoomin could render the true wild varieties sterile, irreversibly upsetting the balance of the Ojibwe's relationship to wild rice and its ecosystem—a possibility the Ojibwe are unwilling to accept.[22] Further, the Ojibwe consider granting gene patents to corporations an act of "biopiracy" based on the belief that no one should possess rights of ownership to what was given by the Creator as a gift to the people.[23] Patents constitute the interference of the Ojibwe's reciprocal relationship with manoomin, but some argue that it also potentially violates the Ojibwe's treaty rights.[24]

Another high-profile issue LaDuke has written about is the disruption of the Klamath nation's relationship with salmon and sucker fish. The Klamath people have been sustained by their relationship with the Klamath River for thousands of years, but as is true for many river-dwelling peoples, changes to the physical environment combined with political intrusions have severely interrupted access to their most sacred food sources. In Indian country the Klamath are most well known for the termination of their tribal status by the Bureau of Indian Affairs in 1954 and the devastating loss of their reservation in Oregon with its rich timber resources that supported the tribe economically. The termination of their tribal status translated into a decline in every socioeconomic indicator possible, including health.[25] While their federal recognition was restored in 1986, only a small fraction of their land was returned. But decades of dam building and agriculture left the Klamath River an ecological disaster, leading not only to massive salmon and sucker fish depopulation but also to an intense culture war between Klamath tribal members and the settler population over water allocation. At issue was how to draw enough water for farm irrigation and still maintain healthy river flows for fish populations. Finally, after years of community bridge building and negotiations, a series of agreements were signed between multiple stakeholders, including the Klamath tribe, to simultaneously restore the river's health and allocate water for irrigation.[26]

Countless other stories can be told about the disruption to rivers and other ecosystems and the foods they produce, and their relationships with Native peoples. In Maine, despite a legal victory in 2016 to protect the Penobscot people's sustenance fishing rights, consuming fish from the Penobscot River is a health hazard due to toxic contamination of the river and the state's unwillingness to set adequate water quality standards.[27] In California, Indians carefully managed landscapes with controlled burning and other cultivation techniques to ensure abundant access to hazelnuts, acorns, and numerous other plant and animal species endemic to traditional diets and cultural practices.[28] But a history of mission enslavement, land theft, federal and state government corruption (and a policy of extermination), and relentless development has proven to be the most intractable of obstacles to these resources. In Washington State, decades of radioactive leaks into the Columbia River from the Hanford Nuclear Site have caused disproportionately high rates of cancer and fatal birth defects like anencephaly (a malformation of the brain in which the forebrain and cerebrum fail to form) on the Yakama Reservation, just downriver from the site. And even though Chinook salmon are experiencing a comeback, tribal members don't trust the health of the fish enough to eat it. Back home on the Colville Reservation, on a one-hundred-fifty-mile stretch of the Columbia River above the Grand Coulee Dam, the Canadian lead-smelting company Teck Resources dumped dozens of toxic chemicals into the river, including mercury, for nearly a century, toxifying what few salmon and other fish were left and finally triggering a lawsuit in 2004 that the tribe would win in 2012.

When food systems are interrupted, the costs to life and culture are incalculable, but we do know that the lingering result of losing legacy foods is the presence of diseases Indian people never used to have. The imposition of the reservation system marks a time of dramatic shift in food patterns, especially in the west when Indians were forced to adopt more sedentary lives and were confined to the artificial boundaries created by treaties. With dramatically reduced territories for hunting and fishing, and after buffalo eradication on the Plains, Indians were forced to rely on government rations consisting of beef, flour, lard, salt, beans, and sometimes sugar and coffee. These food rations were often inadequate or nonexistent when pilfered by corrupt Indian agents, as was all too common in many places. My great-uncle Vern used to tell stories about how on the Colville reservation the distribution of rations pitted families and bands against each when there was not enough to go around, resulting in long-standing resentments generations later.[29]

These new foods were high in calories and fat and low in fiber and nutritional value, compared to the nutritious and diverse foods Native people had been used to, and led to a state of food insecurity. In the mid-twentieth century, the US Food and Drug Administration (USFDA) implemented new food programs to combat hunger in American society. With chronic poverty and food insecurity in reservation communities a way of life and recognition that malnutrition was a serious problem as late as 1967, the government also instituted the commodity food program, in addition to the food stamp program, school lunch program, and others. Typical commodity food included canned meats, soups, and juices; pasta; cereal; rice; cheese; peanut butter; corn syrup; flour; dry, evaporated milk; and vegetable oil. In other words, like the rations of earlier days, they were foods high in calories and low in nutritional content. Astoundingly, within one generation the problem of malnutrition turned into a problem of obesity, what Indian people often refer to as the "commod bod."[30]

One theory about the dramatic rise in obesity in American Indian communities suggests that the rapid shift away from hunting-gathering lifeways led to a change in metabolism that Indian bodies couldn't adjust to—the so-called thrifty gene hypothesis. While the thrifty gene hypothesis has never been conclusively proven, lifestyle is nonetheless implicated when more active lives spent hunting and food gathering gave way to more sedentary habits. Combined with systemic barriers to good quality food in reservation communities—what are often referred to as "food deserts"—that is enough, researchers tend to argue, to account for the epidemics in obesity, diabetes, and heart disease. Consequently, programs designed to combat obesity and diabetes focus on prevention through lifestyle change, meaning increased physical activity and improved diets, including a return to traditional foods as much as possible.

PLANT MEDICINES

With the loss of access to traditional foods has come the loss of access to traditional medicinal plants. Where Indigenous peoples once controlled the entire continent, now only 56.2 million acres remain in the jurisdiction of Indigenous governments on reservations and other types of American Indian communities, such as Rancherias in California and villages in Alaska, constituting only about 1 to 2 percent of the entire US land mass.[31] The imposed political and social frameworks that limit access to those spaces (land theft via treaty abrogation, federal policies of removal and assimilation, federal Indian law that assumes white European superiority, and so on) thus means that original nations' ability to reclaim their foods and medicines is limited to a minute fraction of land.

The history of oppressive federal policies that dictated how Indian lands should be used still informs the jurisdictional frameworks tribal governments have adopted. Reservations were established during an era that imposed a policy of assimilation based on a philosophy of "appropriate" (white European) land use. As we saw in the previous chapter, Clint Carroll's work has shown that resource versus relationship-based land management ultimately has meant using the land for cash-crop farming and other income-generating activities like cattle grazing and timber harvesting, which has been all overseen by the Bureau of Indian Affairs. Even as policy shifted and changed throughout the twentieth century, affording greater freedom of choice for tribal governments, for the most part those land practices have remained intact (as has their accountability to the BIA), becoming cemented as depended-upon revenue streams. The problem, however, is that cattle grazing and forestry can be highly destructive to other plant and cultural resources, and that includes medicinal plants.

The loss of medicinal plant use also came as a result of the assimilation process itself, as Native people became increasingly acculturated to dominant American society and adopted Western medicine. Not all traditional knowledge, however, was completely devalued and abandoned; even when Native religious traditions (which invariably involved plants) were banned by the federal government, much of the knowledge went underground.[32] The knowledge was often held within the purview of specific clans or families, and this included the knowledge of plant medicine. That carefully guarded information is still passed down in families today. American Indian cultural revitalization includes a return to traditional medicine practices, but with current land use practices that result in the loss of medicinal plants, tribes must balance their land management practices to simultaneously meet economic and cultural needs. This can be a source of conflict between heavily bureaucratic tribal governments accountable to the BIA and grassroots community members, given the diametrically opposed mandates to maintain tribal incomes on one hand and maintain sensitive ecosystems for cultural resources on the other.[33]

The extent of tribal land loss means a loss of jurisdiction over territories that contain important cultural resources like medicinal plants. But it's especially true in areas of extreme land loss, such as California, where very little land was retained, and reservations that are heavily checkerboarded.[34] In these contexts, maintaining access to cultural resources is ultimately a matter of environmental justice because of the need to engage with non-Native governments and communities.

WATER

As the example of the Standing Rock Sioux Tribe's battle against the Dakota Access Pipeline dramatically revealed, there are few issues more sensitive than water: its availability, quality, accessibility, and even its power to destroy human life and permanently alter the existence of communities. The creation of Lake Oahe itself embodies all these complicated realities, having delivered devastating blows to the lives of the Standing Rock people, with the dams imposed by the Pick-Sloane Act.[35] Now, paradoxically, in the twenty-first century, with extractive industries' ongoing incursions into Indian country and a changing climate, Lake Oahe represents a lifeline to Standing Rock's future existence as a community. Water is indeed life, the activists at Sacred Stone and Oceti Sakowin reminded us, and the threat of a pipeline leak underneath that source was too great a risk to idly accept.

The Dakota Access Pipeline was not, however, the first recent threat to water in Great Plains Indian country. Barely five months before the #NoDAPL movement began in early 2016, coalitions of Native and non-Native people alike successfully prevented the permitting of the Keystone XL Pipeline, a 1,179-mile section that would convey Alberta tar sands oil through Montana, South Dakota, and Nebraska, connecting it to the southern leg of the pipeline already running from the Southern Plains to the Gulf of Mexico. After a four-year-long campaign that galvanized Canadian First Nations, several US tribal governments, environmentalists, and white ranchers—organized as the Cowboy Indian Alliance—activists convinced the Obama administration that the risks of the pipeline outweighed the benefits. While President Obama emphasized climate change as the biggest reason for denying the permit, among the unacceptable risks for the coalitions was the pipeline's potential to contaminate the Ogallala Aquifer, a massive but shallow and vulnerable underground water table that spans eight states from South Dakota in the north to the Texas Panhandle in the south and yields approximately 30 percent of the nation's groundwater used for irrigation.[36]

US water law is complex and its history is deeply intertwined with Indian treaty rights, regulated through the Winter's Doctrine of 1908. Predating other water-use law due to the creation of the reservations, the Winter's Doctrine affirms the reserved rights of Indian access to water, especially in the arid western states where most reservations are, placing legal power in federal courts. The law does not quantify the amount of water that prioritizes Indian allocation, and these rights are often challenged and litigated, and made more complicated by the 1952 McCarran Amendment in which Congress extended jurisdiction to state courts to hear disputes on reserved Indian rights.[37] Despite the "first in time, first in right" foundation of the law, securing actual access to water often means decades-long legal battles and, beginning in the 1980s, led to negotiated settlements. As of 2015, there were at least twenty-seven confirmed congressional water settlements, thirty-two tribes with federal settlement teams to negotiate in litigated cases, and roughly two hundred fifty tribes with unquantified water rights.[38] Prior to the era of water settlements and despite the reserved rights doctrine, throughout most of the twentieth century tribes were on the losing side of water conflicts, and the long-term effect of these negotiated settlements remains unclear.

What is clear is that "losing" means tribal loss of access to water, which is common is some communities.[39] According to one study, for example, 13 percent of Alaska Natives and 25–40 percent of people on the Navajo Nation still rely on hauling water. Hauling water is more than a matter of inconvenience; it is a health issue, given that it makes them more susceptible to water-borne diseases and that exposure to climate change leads to increased vulnerability.[40]

The issue of water quality is equally complicated. For one thing, under the Clean Water Act federal law treats the authority of tribes the same as states and allows jurisdiction over non-Indians within and even beyond reservation boundaries, which adds to the legal complexities.[41] In one well-known example, the Pueblo of Isleta in New Mexico won a Supreme Court case in 1998, which upheld the tribe's ability to enforce water quality standards for the city of Albuquerque. But having the right to enforce those standards doesn't guarantee pollution won't happen anyway. According to one story in 2015, violations of the Clean Water Act by the upstream entities of Albuquerque, Santa Fe, Rio Rancho, and Kirtland Air Force Base are so consistent and egregious that Isleta sometimes has to stop using river water for religious ceremonies, which the tribe perceives as a threat to its very existence. With toxic contaminants such as undertreated sewage water, arsenic, aluminum, PCBs, and lead, it also raises questions about the health of people who eat crops irrigated by that same water.[42]

Also in 2015, the San Juan River, which runs through the Navajo Nation in northern New Mexico, was poisoned when an abandoned gold mine, known as the Gold King Mine, near Silverton, Colorado, spilled three million gallons of acidic wastewater containing iron, aluminum, manganese, lead, copper, and other heavy metals into the Animas River, a tributary of the San Juan. The spill turned the rivers a sickening yellow-orange, and underground wells used for drinking water were also contaminated. The rivers are used by the Navajos and other communities for ranching and irrigation; around two thousand Navajos were affected, and crop damage to Navajo farms was widespread. The Gold King Mine was managed by the EPA, which admitted responsibility and promised to pay $4.5 million in emergency costs to state, local, and tribal governments. But they rebuffed accountability to the victims of the disaster when in January 2017 they announced that they would refuse to pay seventy-three claims filed against them—to the tune of $20.4 million—based on sovereign immunity, which bars most lawsuits against the federal government.[43] The EPA reported the same month that there were no long-term effects to the water quality of the rivers. The Navajo Nation is, understandably, not so easily convinced, given their history with uranium mining on the reservation, and is conducting its own studies in conjunction with Northern Arizona University, University of Arizona, Fort Lewis College, and Diné College to understand the long-term ramifications to the Navajo community.[44]

Climate change poses an entirely new set of problems relative to water's ability to sustain life in tribal communities. Hydrologists and other climate change scientists identify various impacts climate change is having on tribal water resources, including (1) supply and management, (2) aquatic species important for culture and subsistence, (3) ranching and agriculture due to weather extremes like droughts and floods, (4) sovereignty and rights, and (5) soil quality, as it is affected by coastal and riverine erosion (causing the need to relocate) or from drought-related land degradation.[45] In Alaska—home to 227 federally recognized Native villages—subsistence hunting of land- and ocean-based animals like caribou and walrus and salmon fishing are still a way of life. Global warming results in thinning and other changes to sea ice, in turn altering hunting patterns. Permafrost thawing makes the traditional practice of food storage in underground cellars less reliable, contributes to riverine erosion, and because the ground can absorb more water it can decrease lake water levels, causing water supply problems and increased risk for water-borne diseases.[46] In the lower forty-eight states, climate change poses numerous problems that compromise traditional practices, especially related to food systems. Warming air and water temperatures and decreased water levels disrupt river flows necessary for healthy salmon populations. In coastal areas, encroaching seas inundate freshwater habitats, threatening shellfish resources and traditional foods like roots and berries. Increasing aridity and drought in the west result in loss of grazing lands and native plant species, in addition to diminished water supplies. In the Great Plains and Midwest, drought interferes with water supplies and the ability to feed livestock. Low water levels result in warmer waters, algal blooms, and fish die-offs. Earlier snowmelts compromise late season irrigation. Unreliable temperatures cause wild and cultivated crop losses. Extreme fluctuations between drought and flood, for example, interrupted manoomin harvesting in 2007 for the Bad River Band of the Lake Superior Tribe of Chippewa in Wisconsin and in 2013 for the Fond du Lac Reservation. In the east and south, increased flooding, early snowmelt, warmer water temperatures, sea level rise, and coastal erosion deplete fish and shellfish resources in tribal communities that still rely on these traditional food sources.[47] The first climate refugees in the US are the Biloxi Chitimacha people of Isle de Jean Charles, whose island home in southern Louisiana is being inundated due to rising sea levels. The relocation of the Biloxi Chitimacha people is also particularly complex, because it involves the relocation of an entire community, not just individuals.

In short, settler colonialism and the industrial revolution set into motion a torrent of environmental effects that have been detrimental to the health of Native peoples for centuries and are exacerbated in the present by climate change. But despite the odds, Native people have survived because of their ability to creatively resist, adapt, and meet the challenges modernity has thrown at them. And now in the twenty-first century, the creative resistance and adaptability of Native nations is reflected in the ways they are reclaiming their food traditions and taking control of their food systems.

FOOD SYSTEMS AND SOVEREIGNTY MOVEMENT

"When I first heard the term 'food sovereignty,' I thought, Hmmm, does that mean that plants and animals will have treaty rights and reservations?" says Valerie Segrest, community nutritionist, Native foods educator, and coordinator of the food sovereignty project of the Muckleshoot Indian Tribe. "Because in tribal communities that term 'sovereignty' carries significant meaning. It upholds our right to practice our culture," she tells the audience in her TEDxRainer talk in 2013.[48] She goes on to tell the story of how her ancestor, one of the original negotiators of the treaty of Point Elliott in 1855, expressed that his number one priority was for the ability of the Muckleshoot people to maintain access to traditional foods. "At the core of tribal sovereignty is food sovereignty. This is significant because we know that our traditional foods are a pillar of our culture, and that they feed much more than our physical bodies; they feed our spirits. . . . They are living links with our land and our legacy, helping us to remember who we are and where we come from," Segrest declares with a confident but demure smile.

In Indian country, the Muckleshoot Food Sovereignty Project (MFSP) is often a model for other tribal food sovereignty projects, and Segrest is a leader in the movement. Food systems studies and food sovereignty projects are often initiated with funding from academic, government, or philanthropic institutions. The University of Arkansas School of Law's Indigenous Food and Agriculture Initiative, for example, produced the *Feeding Ourselves Report* in 2015, in partnership with the American Heart Association, the Robert Wood Johnson Foundation, and two private Native organizations, Echo Hawk Consulting and Pipestem Law. The eighty-four-page report clarified the relationship between the United States' history of colonization and current health disparities with a focus on food and made recommendations for funders, policy makers, and stakeholders about how to engage more deeply with the issues and work toward real solutions.[49] Covering every conceivable aspect of tribal food systems, the report connected the dots between the historical impacts of federal Indian policy and the changes it brought to Indian people's health, current food access problems, Native agriculture, federal food programs, community development, funding, training, and education, and it offered tribally centered and specific approaches to healthy food production in Indian country.

Some corporate funding for food system projects, such as that provided by the W. K. Kellogg Foundation, filters down to Native-run granting organizations like the First Nations Development Institute. Between 2011 and 2017, the foundation awarded nearly $4 million to First Nations, which in turn made grants to dozens of Native nations all over the United States, including Alaska and Hawaii. The movement has gained tremendous momentum over the past few years, and First Nations holds an annual food sovereignty conference, bringing together Native nations from all over the US who are interested in gaining greater control over their food systems.[50] The food sovereignty movement sweeping through Indian country is sophisticated and broad, and it's transformational on numerous levels, representing one of the most powerful ways Native nations can exercise their political sovereignty while simultaneously reclaiming their cultural sovereignty. While the federal government is bound by a treaty-based relationship of trust to tribal nations on one hand, on the other, self-determination is a process of transcending a relationship of dependency that has kept Native people trapped in cycles of poverty and failing health. The assertion of cultural and political sovereignty enables Native communities to take greater control over their lives and lands while holding the federal government accountable to its legal responsibilities.

The Muckleshoot Food Sovereignty Project is a larger framework encompassing distinct projects that all contribute to the goal of increasing expertise regarding tribal food systems and improving the quality of the food Muckleshoot people eat, all with a focus on revitalizing culture through traditional foods. It is holistic in that it also contains an economic component that identifies the MFSP as a vehicle for economic sustainability by reforming the Muckleshoot food distribution system while it also improves community food quality. In the most recent phase of the MFSP, for example, an extensive community-wide food sovereignty assessment conducted in 2016–17 revealed not only that community members overwhelmingly desired to restore traditional foods to their diets but also that the reliance upon grocery stores outside the Muckleshoot community resulted in a net loss to the Muckleshoot economy of between $1.04 and $3.14 million each year.[51] This has opened up new discussions about how the tribe can attain greater economic control as part of its efforts to generate greater control of its food system. As the examples of other tribal communities show, this might include a tribally run grocery store, farmer's market, and other kinds of food production capacity building.

The Oneida Nation of Wisconsin, for instance, have a five-pronged integrated food system designed to combat diabetes, which includes food production (and a farm-to-school program), building local economies, food outlets, a community elder center, and sustainable practices. The Oneida Market in Green Bay features products created by tribal businesses, including black angus beef and bison, handmade herbal teas, herbal remedies and essential oils, and other food items. Holistic approaches to food system transformation are inventive in other ways, not the least of which for the ways they include youth development. The Suquamish community in Washington State has a program where elders teach youth about wild plant harvesting as part of a youth internship. The extensive ten-week program spans food systems, traditional plant knowledge, and tribal culture. In other examples, the Muscogee Creeks' Food Sovereignty Initiative includes the establishment of a Food and

Fitness Policy Council as a first step toward encouraging more healthy food choices in the community. And the Lummi Nation adopted a "Stop the Pop" campaign to encourage healthier choices in school vending machines and at tribal events.

The history of American Indians in the twentieth century is the story of a comeback from the brink of almost total annihilation at the hands of a settler population that benefitted from the demise of the Indigenous. Indian "survivance" has always been a matter of Native ingenuity aided by allies and accomplices working against the genocidal impulse of the State—sometimes within the State governmental structure itself but often outside it—in support of tribal self-determination.[52] In the twenty-first century, the food sovereignty movement may be the epitome of these partnerships, with organizations borne from, or at least influenced by, the environmental movement. As this book attempts to show, environmental justice and injustice are threads woven throughout all aspects of Native life, and linkages between the health of Indigenous bodies, the agency of tribal nations, the altruism of allies, and the environmental movement have taken a long time to build, and are in fact still developing. But friends have always been hard to find in Indian country, and things have not always been smooth between Native peoples and the environmental movement, as we will see in the following pages.

CHAPTER FIVE

(Not So) Strange Bedfellows

*Indian Country's Ambivalent Relationship
with the Environmental Movement*

> *In the old days there used to be lots more game—deer, quail, gray
> squirrels, rabbits. They burned to keep down the brush. The fires
> wouldn't get away from you. It wouldn't take all the timber like it
> would now. In those times the creeks ran all year round. You could fish
> all season. Now you can't because there's no water. Timber and brush
> now take all the water. . . . I remember Yosemite when I was a kid;
> You could see from one end of the Valley to the other. Now you can't
> even see off the road. There were big oaks and big pines and no brush.
> There were nice meadows in there.*
>
> —JAMES RUST, SOUTHERN SIERRA MIWOK[1]

There is a long-standing debate within the environmental movement
about its historical origins. Some point to the 1962 publication of Rachel
Carson's seminal book *Silent Spring* and accounts of the first Earth Day in
1970. Depending on the author, either of these two events is hailed as the
beginning of the modern environmental movement. With her ground-
breaking book, Rachel Carson alerted postwar America about the unin-
tended consequences of the chemical industry on the natural world—and
inevitably humans—leading to the banning of DDT in the US. Then, in
1969 a massive oil spill off the coast of Santa Barbara—the worst spill in
US history until the Exxon *Valdez* disaster in 1989—led to the creation
of the National Environmental Protection Act later that year and the Environmental Protection Agency in 1970. Growing awareness of environmental pollution, driven in large part by a burgeoning counterculture

movement, inspired international Earth Day proclamations in 1970, signaling the awakening of a global environmental consciousness.

But a deeper history, one that depicts a continuum of environmental thought in the US, dates back more than a century before the teach-ins of tie-dyed liberal college students who are sometimes associated with birthing today's environmentalism. Many historians trace the genealogy of the modern environmental movement to the ideals of mid-nineteenth-century naturalists and the creation of the national park system, and the preservation movement that started it. Born from the Manifest Destiny ideologies of western expansion, the preservation movement was deeply influenced by a national fixation on the imagined pre-Columbian pristine American wilderness and the social Darwinist values of white superiority. As this chapter reveals, those legacies carried forth into twentieth-century environmental organizing. The result was a contentious—and sometimes openly antagonistic—relationship between modern environmentalists and American Indians, making the attainment of environmental justice for Native people more difficult. It outlines patterns of divergence—where the goals of environmentalists worked in opposition to Native peoples—and more recently where they meet in a convergence of shared objectives that characterize the changing nature of the relationship, resulting in more productive partnerships and greater justice for both the environment and Native peoples.

THE PRESERVATION MOVEMENT AND NATIONAL PARKS

Historians of the environmental movement often locate the movement's genesis in mid-nineteenth-century literature, most commonly invoking writers such as Ralph Waldo Emerson, Henry David Thoreau, and John Muir. After Emerson composed a book titled *Nature* in 1836, a new, mystical religious and philosophical movement called transcendentalism began to emerge in Boston, Emerson its founder, with the help of Thoreau and others. Believing that a direct experience with the divine could be attained through intimate interaction with nature, both became known as naturalists in what was a new, highly romanticized, and particularly American version of naturalism.[2] While Emerson and Thoreau were paving fresh intellectual ground in the East, the artist George Catlin (who was unconnected to the Transcendentalist movement) was traveling out west documenting the last of the "wild" Indian tribes, becoming famous for the hundreds of paintings that are now his legacy and for beginning a national dialogue on the need for national parks. He published several books, among them the classic *Letters and Notes on the Manners, Customs, and Condition of the North American Indians* in 1841. In the book, Catlin lamented what he believed was the beginning of the extinction of the buffalo and the tribes who depended on them. He proposed that the US should create a "Nations' park containing man and beast, in all the wild and freshness of their nature's beauty!" Catlin's work was influential and widely acclaimed, and while the idea for a national park was not yet taken seriously, a growing national angst about modernity made conditions ripe for it by the early 1870s.

The national park system has long been lauded as "America's greatest idea," but only relatively recently has it begun to be more deeply questioned. In his 1999 book *Dispossessing the Wilderness: Indian Removal and the Making of the National Parks*, Mark David Spence delivered a long-overdue critique that linked the creation of the first national parks with the federal policy of Indian removal. Spence points out that the first so-called wilderness areas that had been deemed in need of preserving were not only and in actuality Indigenous-occupied landscapes when the first national parks were established, but also that an uninhabited wilderness *had to first be created*. He examines the creation of Yellowstone, Glacier, and Yosemite National Parks in particular to illustrate the way the myth of uninhabited virgin wilderness has for more than a century obscured a history of Native land dispossession in the name of preservation and conservation and serves as the foundation of the environmental movement.[3] The creation of Yellowstone as the first national park is instructive for understanding how the language of preservation evolved over time. What is today Yellowstone National Park (which lies predominantly within the northwest corner of Wyoming and slightly within Montana and Idaho) was originally the territory of numerous tribal nations, including Shoshone, Bannock, Crow, Nez Perce, and other smaller tribes and bands. The treaties of Fort Bridger and Fort Laramie in 1868 ceded large tracts of land to the US and created separate reservations for the tribes but retained the right of the continued use of the ceded lands for hunting and other subsistence activities. Although early settlers had claimed the Indians avoided the Yellowstone area due to superstitions about the geysers, they in fact had long used the lands, a rich source of game and medicinal and edible plants, for spiritual ceremonies and other purposes.

After the park's establishment in 1872 the Indians continued to frequent the area, especially since limited reservation land and government food rations were insufficient to feed the people, and the threat of starvation constantly loomed. According to Spence, Yellowstone, with its mesmerizing geysers and otherworldly geologic formations, was set aside initially not in the interest of preserving wilderness but as a "wonderland" for its unique natural features—an ideal tourist attraction. But the threat of private development such as mining interests, timber exploitation, and railroads combined with fears about the depletion of game, fish, and timber, changed the government's rationale for the park. By 1886 the Department of Interior's stated purpose for the park's existence was the preservation of the wilderness (animals, fish, and trees), to be enforced by the military, which was already aggressively pursuing resistant Indians throughout the Plains. Anxiety about hunting in the park over the next few years led to the passage of the Lacey Act in 1894, a law prohibiting all hunting within park boundaries, including Indian hunting—in direct violation of treaty protections. A legal challenge to the law resulted in the US Supreme Court case *Ward v. Race Horse* in 1896 in which, as Spence contends, the court ruled that the creation of Yellowstone National Park and the Lacey Act effectively signaled Congress's plenary authority to nullify Indian hunting rights at will, at a time when both judicial and congressional decisions persistently eroded Indian rights. *Race Horse* was overruled by the Supreme Court in a 1999 case brought by Minnesota's Mille Lacs Band of Chippewa Indians, but in a separate 2016 case a Wyoming state court rejected the Crow's treaty right to hunt on federal lands within the state. That case is still pending in a state appellate court. These cases demonstrate the contradictions in law when state and federal law conflict relative to Indian treaty rights.

The lingering result of the Yellowstone story is that coded within the language of preservation, "wilderness" landscapes—always already in need of protection—are, or should be, free from human presence. But this logic completely evades the fact of ancient Indigenous habitation and cultural use of such places. In Spence's words, "the context and motives that led to the idealization of uninhabited wilderness not only helps to explain what national parks actually preserve but also reveals the degree to which older cultural values continue to shape current environmentalist and preservationist thinking."[4] In other words, the paradigm of human-free wilderness articulated by early preservationists laid a foundation for the twentieth-century environmental movement in extremely problematic ways. When environmentalists laud "America's best idea" and reiterate narratives about pristine national park environments, they are participating in the erasure of Indigenous peoples, thus replicating colonial patterns of white supremacy and settler privilege.

THE MYTH OF THE WILDERNESS AND
THE REALITY OF INDIAN LAND MANAGEMENT

If anyone were to be called the patron saint of the environmental movement it would surely be Thoreau. Although he was not widely read in his time, the real impact of his work would manifest later, particularly as a result of his (and Emerson's) influence on John Muir. Both Thoreau's and Muir's views on nature and what humans' relationship to it ought to be were shaped by their experience with Indians, about whom both wrote in published and unpublished manuscripts.[5] Biographers of Thoreau and Muir tend to admire Thoreau and Muir's views on American Indians, praising them as progressive "Indianists" at a time of intensifying violent colonization of the continent, but also tend to downplay the extent to which both men were influenced by popular anthropological narratives of Indian inferiority—what we today call the savage and noble savage tropes. In the process, these commentators often reinforce the patronizing, romanticized views that prevented Americans from seeing Native peoples as fully human in the first place. The overly romantic and fetishized view of Indian closeness with nature (conceived, for example, as "mystical," "primeval," and "primal") inevitably invokes Indians as child-like and intellectually unevolved. Worse, it evades US accountability for its genocidal expropriation of the continent—based on the very justification of Indian inferiority—and the violation of its own constitutional law about treaties being the supreme law of the land.[6]

Thoreau, especially, wrote extensively about American Indians. Fascinated by the Indians' closeness to nature, he studied their history and cultures and later in his life befriended Penobscots Joe Aitteon and Joe Polis, whom he had hired as guides, documenting his adventures with them in his classic work *The Maine Woods*. He clearly had a great admiration for the way Indians lived, and he perceived in their spirituality a mysticism that appealed to his own Transcendentalist orientation. Yet inescapably woven throughout Thoreau's writings about Indians is also a romantic draw to the "wildness" of Indian life—the noble savagery of the Indian, who by virtue of his primitiveness is worthy of respect, because, at least in part, he resists the corruption of the white man's civilization. Thoreau may have appreciated Indians more than most European Americans, but he was still a man of his times and reflected popular social Darwinist views when he wrote in 1858,

> Who can doubt this essential and innate difference between man and man, when he considers a whole race, like the Indian, inevitably and resignedly passing away in spite of our efforts to Christianize and educate them? Individuals accept their fate and live according to it, as the Indian does. Everybody notices that the Indian retains his habits wonderfully, is still the same man that the discoverers found. The fact is, the history of the white man is a history of improvement, that of the red man a history of fixed habits of stagnation.[7]

Thoreau read Samuel George Morton's *Crania Americana* (1839), and embraced Morton's theories of Indian cultural and intellectual lowliness.[8] Even as he occupied himself with absorbing all he could about Indian life, fixating on everything from the Indian physique to funeral customs, Thoreau seemed never to have grasped that the New England wilderness, already so altered by European settlement in his time, had in the precolonial period been a cultural landscape shaped by centuries of Indian intervention on the land, not the untouched pristine environment he and many of his contemporaries imagined.[9]

The history of national parks, shaped by ideologies of preservation and conservation that Thoreau and similar naturalists inspired, has a long track record of severing Indians from living on, or traditional uses of, their ancestral lands. Similar versions of the Yellowstone story played out in the early days of numerous national parks, including Glacier, Mount Rainier, Mount McKinley (now Denali), Death Valley, Grand Canyon, Mesa Verde, and many others. National park historians Robert

Keller and Michael Turek identify four phases the national park system exhibited as it gradually improved its relationship with tribes, particularly in the latter half of the twentieth century, but by then the stubborn narratives about Indian savagery and inferiority that justified their removal from parklands had cemented themselves into the national imagination and infiltrated the consciousness of early environmentalists.[10] The racist tropes are found throughout the historical literature of the late nineteenth and early twentieth centuries and are all too familiar: Indians were lazy, stupid, and childlike, conniving beggars and treacherous liars. But ironically, they were also sometimes characterized as ignorant of their own environments, wasteful users of the land. In 1923, for instance, one ranger in Glacier National Park, enforcing no-hunting laws (which violated the treaty rights of the Blackfeet) inside the park, commented that "unless the Indians are curbed in their desire to kill everything in sight Glacier Park will soon have no game."[11]

The view that Native peoples were incapable of managing their own lands in intelligent and innovative ways was evident in the early years of government management of Yosemite, but it also reflects the very different cultural values that shaped their own use of the land. When the first white settlers observed the magnificent "cathedral" of Yosemite Valley, they described vast open meadows covered in "luxuriant native grasses and flowering plants,"[12] a place that "presented the appearance of a well-kept park,"[13] "an appearance of a prairie planted with fruit trees."[14] These observers were there early enough to witness how the valley had been managed for centuries by Native peoples. With techniques like controlled burns and even hand removal of young willows and cottonwoods, the growth of a thick and highly combustible understory was averted, helping to prevent uncontrollable fires. Ethnobotanist M. Kat Anderson, whose voluminous analysis of California Indian land management broke intellectual ground in Native studies, noted that "much of the landscape in California that so impressed early writers, photographers, and landscape painters was in fact a cultural landscape, not the wilderness they imagined. While they extolled the 'natural' qualities of the California landscape, they were really responding to its human influence."[15] But, as the epigraph to this chapter indicates, within a few short decades of bureaucratic management Yosemite Valley would become almost unrecognizable to its Indigenous inhabitants.

Before it became a national park in 1890, Yosemite was a state park under a grant from President Abraham Lincoln in 1864, but its history with Indians differs from that of Yellowstone and Glacier. The Yosemite Indians were violently expelled from the valley with the Mariposa Indian War of 1850–51, but unlike the Rocky Mountain Indians, the Yosemites were gradually allowed to return within a few years and resume much of their previous customary land-based practices, including hunting, fishing, and food gathering.[16] Limited numbers of them lived in the park for another century, contributing to the Yosemite tourist economy through the exploitation of their labor and culture. Yosemite was established as a tourist destination from its earliest days, and the presence of Indians still living largely in their traditional manner lent an aura of authenticity and mystique to park visitors' "wilderness experience," rationalizing their continued existence in the park to the bureaucrats who maintained it. But with the tight controls of government bureaucracies came the loss of traditional environmental management Yosemite's Indigenous peoples had maintained for centuries.

As the federal government evolved its wilderness management practices, so did its philosophical slant toward it. From the national parks' inception in 1916 until well into the 1930s, the "wonderland"[17] approach to land management prevailed, and as early as 1872 the national parks were conceived of as national "pleasuring grounds."[18] Ironically, the Park Service's guiding philosophy was more about catering to tourists than it was about actually preserving wilderness—however problematic the concept of wilderness was. Even the national parks' Organic Act (its founding document) directed park managers to manipulate the landscape as necessary to improve views, which could be achieved by "dispos[ing] of timber" or killing predatory animals that reduced populations of popular game animals like deer and mountain sheep, which tourists expected to see.[19] In Yosemite, Indians were prohibited in the late 1800s from hunting and their controlled burning practices. So, by the turn of the century the valley had become transformed from an Indigenous cared-for cultural landscape to a cultural landscape based on the projection of an imagined, commodified, European American wilderness.[20]

Unpacking the philosophical foundations of the early conservation and preservation movements is crucial to understanding how the formal, organized environmental movement would unfold throughout the twentieth century, informed as it was by its not-so-hidden prejudices and stereotypes about American Indian people and the overarching master narrative of white supremacy, and also by wilderness as a historically contingent, socially constructed idea. John Muir and the founding of the Sierra Club was at the temporal intersection of these eras, bridging the nineteenth-century era's savagist narratives and the twentieth-century federal move toward (re)recognizing Native sovereignty and self-determination. But they were far from the only ones.

WHITE SUPREMACY AND THE SEEDS OF THE ENVIRONMENTAL MOVEMENT

Few terms in American vernacular English can elicit the kind of emotionally charged response that "white supremacy" can. Americans like to think that since the civil rights era, we have achieved the postracial, meritocratic, multicultural state where color blindness and equal opportunity prevails. Both liberals and conservatives like to think that racism is defined only by hostile behavior from which individuals can excuse themselves because they have friends, employees, perhaps an old lover or two who are people of color. In this way of thinking, white supremacy is an ideology restricted only to rogue alt-right neo-Nazis or white-nationalist fringe groups, and certainly not well-meaning everyday people, whether conservative or liberal. While white supremacy is most definitely at the root of those regressive social movements, as a foundational worldview constructed by centuries of white European settlement of the United States, it is far broader than that. It is the thread from which the American social fabric is woven. A few decades of laws promoting racial justice have failed to unravel the systemic forms that white supremacy has taken, reflected by a range of social indicators from chronic wealth inequality to negative educational outcomes to disproportionate rates of violence (police, sexual, and domestic) and incarceration in communities of color. Centuries of dehumanization of American Indians, African Americans, and ethnic minority "others" has left its mark on the American mind and in its institutions, refusing to die.

In Indian country, white supremacy was never limited to just racial inferiority, since ideologies of religious and cultural inadequacy predated it, as the previous discussion on the foundations of federal Indian law, particularly the doctrine of Christian discovery, revealed. That Native

Native

people were inferior to white Europeans was a given and widely accepted by the general public well before and after the nineteenth century. It was as true for John Muir as it was for his predecessor Henry Thoreau. Some writers claim that Muir's racist views on Indians stemmed from his postimmigration childhood in Wisconsin's Winnebago territory and became intensified after coming to California. When Muir arrived in San Francisco in 1868, California was engaged in an open campaign of extermination of California Indians, which he didn't seem to ever have actively opposed. Instrumental in the creation of Yosemite National Park, he supported the expulsion of the Yosemite Indians from their ancient home in the valley and journaled his experiences with and thoughts about California "digger" Indians (a derogatory term even then), whom he found dirty, lazy, ugly, and altogether disappointing. Muir's apologists like to point out that his views about Indians evolved over time, especially after his travels to Alaska where he spent time among Tlingits and other Alaska and Pacific Northwest Natives, gradually growing more favorable ideas about Indigenous peoples. It's true that his opinions improved over time, but Muir never fully shed his views of Indigenous inferiority that were shaped by his religious upbringing. In Alaska Natives he may have been more able to see a noble culture that lived in harmony with its environment, but even in this case he never transcended a deeply ingrained pattern of Christian paternalism that presupposed Natives as culturally deficient and in need of Christian improvement.[21] At a time of profound oppression of Native people, Muir's "evolution" can be said to have risen to no more than old-fashioned European American benevolent supremacy.

The idea of wilderness as conceived by preservationists and conservationists was a white-settler social construct. It imagined an unpeopled, wild landscape as pristine, pure, and unspoiled, and as the environmental historian Carolyn Merchant asserts, reflected values that equated wilderness with whiteness and, after postbellum black urban migration, cities with darkness and depravity. These tropes, rooted in policies of removal and segregation, she argues, led to the ideal of an American "colonized Eden," a "controlled, managed garden" from which colonized Indigenous peoples, immigrants, and people of color were systematically excluded and which led to patterns of toxic waste dumping in communities of color.[22]

It is against this backdrop that the Sierra Club, the United States' first nongovernmental, environmentally focused organization, was founded in 1892, with John Muir at the helm as one of its founding members and first elected president. Established initially as a mountaineering enthusiast club, its mission was "'to explore, enjoy, and render accessible the mountain regions of the Pacific Coast; to publish authentic information concerning them,' and 'to enlist the support and cooperation of the people and government in preserving the forests and other natural features of the Sierra Nevada.'"[23] From its inception the Sierra Club's agenda was to protect Northern California's wilderness areas, which by then had been largely cleared of California's Indigenous population, with the survivors of the state's genocidal policies confined to small rancherias and reservations. It also dovetailed with the federal policy of forced assimilation legislated by the 1887 Dawes Act in the immediate post-Indian-war period. Nationwide, with the Indian population at record low numbers, safely contained within reservation boundaries and guarded by strictly enforced laws against hunting outside those bounds, the stage was set for a burgeoning new phase aimed at protecting what remained of the United States' "wild" places and animals. On the heels of the industrial revolution and western expansion, and with a still-growing national infrastructure, protecting the environment—framed as preservation and conservation—would be a matter of balancing the needs of development with wise use of land and natural resources.

The first few decades of the twentieth century saw the establishment of numerous nongovernmental organizations and governmental agencies and laws oriented toward preservation and conservation. Among them are the National Audubon Society (1905), Antiquities Act (1906), National Park Service (1916), National Parks Conservation Association (1919), Izaak Walton League (1922), Wilderness Society (1922), Civilian Conservation Corps (1933), National Wildlife Federation (1936), Defenders of Wildlife (1947), and Nature Conservancy (1951). While naturalists worked to protect lands acquired through centuries of aggressively imposed treaties and a variety of other legally sanctioned land grabs, tribes struggled to hold on to what remained of their land bases and cultures. By 1934, with the passage of the Wheeler Howard Act, a new policy direction was ushered in, influenced by a new generation of Western-educated

Indians. Also called the Indian Reorganization Act, or the "Indian New Deal," the law allowed tribes to organize their own tribal governments patterned after the US Constitution. It reversed the assimilation policy and empowered newly reconstituted tribal governments to have greater management of their own land and mineral rights (still, however, under the close supervision of the Bureau of Indian Affairs), building capacity for economic development as the answer to the intractable poverty that choked tribal communities.

By 1949, under the Truman administration, assimilation was back on the table, and in 1953 Congress passed House Concurrent Resolution 108, also known as the termination bill. Conceived as a final solution to the "Indian problem," termination was framed as the liberation of tribes from the yoke of federal supervision. In reality, it was no less than another push for the federal government to abrogate its treaty obligations and end its administrative responsibilities to Indians, and another land grab. Under termination, tribal governments were dissolved, their lands transferred into white settler ownership, and more than twelve thousand individual Indians absorbed into the American mainstream, no longer legally recognized as Indians. The termination policy's relocation program transferred thousands of Indians from their reservation homes to large cities, causing a population shift away from the reservations. More than one hundred tribes were terminated throughout the 1950s and '60s—at least forty-six in California alone—with particularly disastrous effects on the Menominee in Wisconsin and Klamath in southern Oregon. But the winds of change were blowing in the US with a growing civil rights movement and once again Indians were organizing, this time on college campuses and in urban areas like Minneapolis, San Francisco, Los Angeles, Seattle, and beyond. The new Red Power movement activated Indian people on and off reservations who argued for resistance to termination and for honoring the treaty relationship. A policy shift to self-determination solidified a government to government relationship, which by the 1980s would come to be articulated in the legal language of tribal sovereignty. New laws enabled tribal governments to pursue economic development projects, from resource development to gaming, by reacquiring federal recognition and traditional homelands and revitalizing cultural practices—sending them at times on a collision course with the new environmental movement.

THE MODERN ENVIRONMENTAL MOVEMENT
AND CLASHES WITH INDIAN COUNTRY

The Red Power movement was just one aspect of the social revolution that swept across the American social landscape in the 1960s and '70s, paralleling other ethnic nationalisms, women's liberation, the antiwar movement, and the emergence of a new, rebellious, and predominantly white middle-class counterculture. Disenchanted with the conservative values of their parents' generation and witnessing the increasing degradation of the environment, countercultural youth looked to other cultures for answers to existential questions they perceived as unavailable in mainstream American society. In American Indians they, like Thoreau and Muir before them, saw a relationship to nature that should be emulated, inspiring a back-to-the-land movement and an aesthetic that unequivocally evoked the Indian—long hair, headbands, moccasins, beads and feathers, leather and fringe, turquoise and silver.

In 1971, just a few months after the first Earth Day signaled the beginning of a modern environmental movement, Indians unwittingly became the symbol of the new movement with the famous "Crying Indian" antilittering commercial released by Keep America Beautiful, Inc. The image of a buckskin-clad Indian, with a single tear rolling down his face as a factory spews toxic smoke in the background and trash thrown from a car lands on his beaded moccasins, seared itself into America's collective consciousness. Never mind that the Indian, Iron Eyes Cody, was no Indian at all, but a 100 percent Sicilian American actor named Espera Oscar de Corti who had built an entire career—and personal life—on Indian impersonation. The Crying Indian represented what anthropologist Shepard Krech III called the "ecological Indian," a revamped version of the noble savage who became the stand-in for an environmental ethic the US should aspire to.[24] In a strangely visceral way, the deception of Iron Eyes Cody mirrored the falseness of the ecological Indian stereotype, because like de Corti's fake, hyper-Indian image,[25] the new stereotype set an impossibly high standard to which white environmentalists would hold Native people for the next several decades. It came at a time when tribal governments had finally regained enough power to exercise self-determination in nation-building projects that often involved exploiting the only things they had—natural resources—setting the stage for future conflict and discord.

The relationship between the counterculture and Indian country was complicated from the beginning. Desiring a deeper connection with the Earth and a more meaningful form of spirituality, hippies made pilgrimages to reservations searching for the mystical Indian wisdom they had read about in books like John Neihardt's *Black Elk Speaks* and Carlos Castaneda's wildly successful but fraudulent series about the Yaqui shaman Don Juan Matus.[26] Other ethnic frauds infested the literary counterculture over the next few decades, exploiting the gullibility of the spiritually starved and building a lucrative New Age industry in the process.[27] The problem was not so much that hippies looked to Indian country for answers. It was that as settlers they unconsciously brought with them worldviews and behavior patterns that were inconsistent with Indigenous paradigms and tried to fit Indigenous worldviews and practices into their own cognitive frameworks. Predominant among their settler culture frameworks are the pursuit of universal truth and personal edification, both particularly Christian ideas in the context of the US. If truth is universal, the logic goes, then the truths perceived in Native cultures must be applicable to all people everywhere, and in the United States everyone has the right to practice whatever religion they choose. Non-Natives couldn't comprehend that Native spiritual principles evolved over eons based on ancient relationships to place and was reflected in language and specific histories, and that the function of Indigenous ceremonies was primarily for the perpetuation of particular communities, not personal enlightenment. An orientation based on rugged individualism combined with a deeply ingrained sense of entitlement (Manifest Destiny in its modern form) translated into the toxic mimicry that today we call cultural appropriation, which takes a multitude of forms. At its core, cultural appropriation is always an invocation of "authentic" Indians and Indian culture as constructed by settlers, however falsely. The fetishized authentic Indian is the representational production of the culturally and biologically "pure" Indian, and the ecological Indian trope was just the counterculture and environmental movement's version of it.

The Indian-inspired back-to-the-land sensibility cultivated by the counterculture emerged as another iteration of the environmental movement, but it was expressed in distinctly spiritual terms drawn from Native peoples, as the literary examples of Carlos Castaneda and many others demonstrate, however problematically. Sometimes referred to as "second-wave environmentalism," countercultural hippies, despite their blatant appropriations, did at times work constructively with Indian country. As historian Sherry L. Smith documents, the Pacific Northwest Fish Wars, the cultural revolution in California, the Wounded Knee occupation, and other places and events saw productive partnerships between hippies and Native people who were working for Indian rights alongside calls for other social justice reforms. Indians sometimes even exploited non-Natives' misplaced beliefs about Native cultural authenticity, but overall "most leftists did not understand that their adulation and reverence carried this darker undercurrent [of colonialism and racism]."[28] Historian Paul Rosier contends that the mainstream environmental movement developed in tandem with an American Indian environmentalism during the 1960s and '70s, sometimes intersecting in interesting ways (the Fish Wars is a good example, and literary examples include Ken Kesey's blockbuster *One Flew Over the Cuckoo's Nest* and Edward Abbey's 1975 cult classic *The Monkey Wrench Gang*). "An important element of this story," Rosier writes, "is thus the conversation and collaboration among Indians and non-Indians on environmental problems in their efforts to find common ground; the process was an exchange of ideas and political support rather than a one-way act of appropriation or cultural imperialism."[29] But as the years progressed, the cultural appropriation and imperialism intensified with the rise of the New Age movement, and the conversations and collaborations weren't always smooth, or even present at all, when they should have been.

With the 1975 shift in federal policy to tribal self-determination and as tribal governments sought economic development, land use projects, land return, and cultural revitalization, clashes between tribes and white environmental groups were on the rise by the early 1980s, exposing the groups' historic roots in (white) settler privilege and racism. In 1983, for instance, the Nature Conservancy purchased four hundred acres of land on the White Earth Reservation and donated it back to the state of Minnesota, not the tribe.[30] In 1985 the Sierra Club sued to prevent Tlingit and Haida in Alaska from logging on Admiralty Island, after the US had returned twenty-three thousand acres as part of a land claims settlement. In 1992 the Sierra Club refused to support the White Earth Land Recovery Project's effort to have returned the northern half of the Tamarac Wildlife Refuge to the White Earth Band on the grounds that the club would not have a say in refuge management.[31] In 1999, after years of legal, cultural, and spiritual groundwork, the Makah tribe in Washington State successfully hunted and killed their first gray whale in more than seventy years from a traditional cedar canoe. The reprisals were swift and furious, coming from a variety of antiwhaling and animal rights groups, the most vocal from the Sea Shepherd Conservation Society's Paul Watson, a founding member of Greenpeace.[32] The Makah received death threats, hate mail, public harassment, and the inevitable challenges to the authenticity of the tribe's culture.

Conservationist mythologies of Native people living in untouched pristine nature have dogged them even into recent years. The Timbisha Shoshone in California's Death Valley were dispossessed of their lands with the creation of Death Valley National Monument in 1933, ending the tribe's ancient land management when their homeland came under the management of the National Park Service. In 1983 the tribe gained federal recognition, but because federal recognition did not come with the return of land, it would take many more years of legal battles to finally reacquire 7,754 acres within the park, under the Timbisha Homeland Act. Decades of landscape neglect resulted in the deterioration of the honey mesquite and single-leaf piñon groves—both important food sources—and in 2000 the Timbisha requested comanagement with the Park Service to resume their traditional management practices, but they faced bitter opposition from numerous environmental groups and individuals, including the local Sierra Club chapter. In the public commenting process of a legislative environmental impact assessment, a dominant theme running through the comments was objection to tribal management. Public opposition was based on the tired, old belief of a pristine wilderness, as though the valley had been uninhabited and unmanaged for millennia. Eventually the conflict was resolved, and today the Timbisha Shoshone are engaged with the Park Service in experimental projects to rehabilitate the natural habitat with traditional techniques.[33]

Opposition to gaming has also been a platform upon which environmentalists have battled with tribes. I began my career as a journalist with one particularly ugly episode in 2003 in the Northern California community of Sonoma County. I chronicled an explosive controversy over plans of the Federated Indians of the Graton Rancheria (FIGR) to build a casino and hotel resort within its traditional territory of Rohnert Park, a town that was part of the county's growing urban sprawl and where I

happened to live. Sonoma County and neighboring Napa Valley are better known as California's wine country, and tribal gaming had long been
perceived as a corrupting influence in an otherwise politically liberal and
expanding economic climate. Prior tribal gaming ventures had faced bitter opposition and vitriolic fights. Initial promises not to pursue a gaming
operation were made by tribal leaders under pressure from congressional members as a condition of the tribe's federal recognition bill, which
had passed only three years earlier. But when the recognition bill passed
without an antigaming clause, the tribal council changed its mind; well-
funded gaming industry backers had courted them based on what was
sure to be a lucrative location. Terminated in the 1950s and with widespread poverty in its community, the tribe had regained its recognition
but had no land base. The project would first require the acquisition of
land that would then be taken into federal trust, making it a reservation.
Once the site was chosen and the purchase initiated, the organized casino opposition kicked into high gear, becoming a spectacle of modern
bipartisan anti-Indianism and invoking the ghosts of California's not-so-
distant genocidal past. Like the Makah, the tribe faced death threats and
public hate speech, inaccurate and unfair media representation, and vi-
cious racist attacks. And it went on for years.

Lawsuits failed to stop the project. The conflict raised issues of the
tribe's sovereignty, its right to economic development, and the historical
injustices it had faced on one hand, and on the other, an ideologically
driven disapproval of gaming by a surprisingly large and diverse segment
of the local population. The result was a toxic brew of highly public and
far-reaching anti-Indian rhetoric. After a 360-acre parcel of farmland
had been purchased and the land taken into trust in 2010, the opposition group Stop the Casino 101 Coalition tried numerous tactics to block
construction, including appeals to environmental harm. The Center for
Biological Diversity was brought in and determined that the habitat of
the endangered tiger salamander would be affected. Adding fuel to an
already raging political conflagration, public debates then centered on the
need to balance economic development (not tribal sovereignty) with environmental protection. Efforts to stop the project based on the endangered
salamander ultimately failed, however, and the casino opened in 2013.
The highly divisive public battle led all the way to the US Supreme Court,
with the court declining to hear the case in 2015. In the end, challenges
based on salamander habitat resulted in the US Fish and Wildlife Service's

designation of a 47,383-acre salamander protection zone, an exemption of 252 acres of FIGR's property from the zone,[34] and the tribe setting aside 180 acres and $24 million for environmental mitigation projects.

Legal strategies aimed at protecting the salamander may have failed to stop the project, but it raised troubling and provocative questions about what it means for non-Indians to use environmental issues as a political wedge against tribes' right to exercise sovereignty, especially if seen through a lens that recognizes settler colonialism as an ongoing process of environmental injustice. If settler colonialism is a structure that disrupts Indigenous peoples' relationships to their environments (as clearly happened to FIGR) and the exercise of sovereignty is at least a partial effort to reverse that structure, then opposition to it would be read as favoring a system that continues to commit environmental injustice against Indigenous peoples. It also highlights why environmental injustice is an issue that for Indigenous peoples goes beyond environmental racism. To what degree is environmentalism deployed as just another weapon of colonial domination in unpopular tribal economic development projects? Connecting the issue more broadly to ethical land use in energy projects, how can environmental awareness and protection be balanced with histories of injustice and respect for tribal sovereignty? If environmentalists (and the broader public) were more knowledgeable about tribal histories, sovereignty, and colonialism, could they transcend narratives that reduce debates about tribal economic development projects to environment versus development or in the case of gaming, communities versus tribal gaming? Finally, how can education about settler privilege, white supremacy, and systemic racism improve relations between Indian and non-Indian activist communities and the broader American population overall?

WORKING TOWARD PRODUCTIVE PARTNERSHIPS

A milestone in the environmental movement occurred in 1992 with the convening of the United Nations Conference on Environment and Development, also known as the Rio de Janeiro Earth Summit. The Rio Summit was, among other things, the world's governments formal acknowledgment of climate change and resulted in several binding agreements, including the Framework Convention on Climate Change. By then, Indigenous peoples had been organizing around environmental issues at the international level since at least 1972, when a delegation of

Hopi and Navajo activists attended the United Nations Conference on the Human Environment in Stockholm, the United Nation's first major international conference on the environment.[35] Climate change agreements like the Kyoto Protocol and the Paris Accords eventually followed, and by 2000 a robust climate justice movement was mobilized. On a large scale, climate change activism married the environmental movement— which had morphed into one wing of an international nonprofit industrial complex—with grassroots activism. It signaled that environmental justice was a global but distinct aspect of the environmental movement, since the detrimental effects of climate change were unevenly distributed between the so-called developed and undeveloped worlds. Whereas the environmental movement writ large was concerned with the myriad ways humans were causing environmental degradation, climate change, caused by greenhouse gases produced primarily by burning fossil fuels, pinpointed the blame on Big Oil and its far too cozy relationship with governments. But Indigenous and fourth world people were on the frontlines of climate change, as people living in closer relationships to the Earth felt its impacts first: loss of land due to sea level rise, desertification, drought, disruptions to subsistence-based food systems, intensifying storms, loss of sea ice, and a host of related ecosystem changes. Yet they had been largely excluded from United Nations climate change talks, and worse, the Kyoto Protocol's creation of a market-based system of carbon trading exposed Indigenous peoples to new abuses by States. It was thus natural that Indigenous peoples would rise as global leaders of the climate justice movement.

During the 1990s new kinds of stories began to appear in American environmental literature and media, conceding the ways the environmental movement had marginalized and alienated Native peoples. New alliances between tribal nations and people with whom they had historical enmities (not just environmental groups) increasingly formed to oppose environmentally destructive development. Indigenous environmental groups sprang up, like the Indigenous Environmental Network (1990), Honor the Earth (1993), and other locally based tribal and non-Native coalitions, such as the Shundahai Network (a Shoshone effort to resist the Nevada Nuclear Test Site), the Environmentally Concerned Citizens of Lakeland Areas (Lac du Flambeau Ojibwe citizens' opposition to a sulfide mine in Wisconsin), Sweetgrass Hills Protective Association (multiple tribes aligned with non-Natives to fight a gold mining operation in northern Montana), to name just a few. In the second decade of the twenty-first century, with the oil industry posting record profits, proliferating fracking operations,[36] and massive new pipelines planned— exacerbating tensions created by the 2008 recession and skyrocketing wealth inequality—public fury grew. By 2015, high-profile demonstrations succeeded in convincing the Obama administration to reject the Keystone XL Pipeline, uniting Native and non-Native people in mounting demands to transition away from a fossil fuel economy. By April 2016, when a handful of Lakota women and youth were quietly setting up the Sacred Stone Camp to protest the Dakota Access Pipeline, a critical mass had been reached and the ground laid for what would become the biggest tribally led act of civil disobedience in US history.

The #NoDAPL protest at Standing Rock was precedent setting on numerous fronts, not the least of which for the degree of collaboration between Native and non-Native people it inspired. For the better part of a year, non–Native Americans poured out their support in social and news media, with financial and other donations of everything from food and clothing to building materials, and side by side risked their lives with Indian people, braving brutal police attacks, harassment, and jail. Thousands of non-Native veterans put their bodies on the line in life-threatening weather conditions, and led by Wesley Clark Jr., son of the retired army general and Democratic presidential candidate Wesley Clark Sr., they publicly asked forgiveness for centuries of military aggression against Indian people. More than a few stars showed up, lending their celebrity to draw attention to the Standing Rock tribe's cause. After hundreds of years of hostility between Native and non-Native people, the cooperation between them at Oceti Sakowin seemed to suggest a new level of conciliation for at least some segment of the population. Yet even in light of this heightened spirit of cooperation and goodwill, underlying tensions bubbled to the surface in old, familiar ways, as we explore in the following chapter. It found a particular expression among the women, which might not be surprising, given it was women who established the camps and were largely in charge to begin with. This gendered cultural clash opens a space to examine in detail how things can so easily go wrong between Native and non-Native activists when entrenched patterns of white supremacy and racism are unconsciously repeated, maintaining obstacles to true partnership and respect.

CHAPTER SIX

Hearts Not on the Ground

Indigenous Women's Leadership and More Cultural Clashes

> A nation is not defeated until the
> hearts of its women are on the ground.

—OLD INDIAN PROVERB

Ladonna Brave Bull Allard, a Standing Rock Sioux tribal historian and founder of the Sacred Stone Camp, stands on a grassy green knoll looking out over Lake Oahe, wistfully reflecting on the past. The North Dakota prairie wind blows her thick salt-and-pepper hair away from her face, accentuating her elegant Indian grandma features. She tells the story of how her great-great grandmother Nape Hote Win (Mary Big Moccasin) survived the Whitestone Massacre in 1863, and about a time before the dam when the Missouri River was called Wakangapi Wakpa, River that Makes the Sacred Stones, for a large whirlpool that created large, spherical sandstone formations. The lake claimed those sacred stones, and it was for them that Allard named her place the Camp of the Sacred Stones. "I was a girl when the floods came and desecrated our burial sites and Sun Dance grounds. Our people are in that water. This river holds the story of my life," hinting at the bittersweetness of the lake, at once a giver and taker of life.[1] This is the way it has always been done throughout Indian country, elders telling stories that keep the memories of their people alive—the ancestors and their enemies, life and death, good and bad. Women have always been valued storytellers in their communities, keepers of culture and defenders of their lands, alongside and equal to but different from men, often sharing political power and leadership roles. It is the same today, but not without alteration, loss, and reclamation.

Examining the history of Native women's political activism provides context for understanding how the Standing Rock resistance camps came to be and lays the groundwork for a discussion on how activists and scholars talk about Indigenous feminist theory, demonstrating the important roles women have always played in American Indian communities and the United States more broadly. This then opens a space to discuss the ways in which conflict entered the camps in some of the ways discussed in the previous chapter, but also in particularly gendered ways among women, revealing the cultural differences and unspoken assumptions that often still interfere with non-Native activists' ability to be respectful, effective allies and accomplices. These are critical ruptures that shouldn't be overlooked so that we can "all just get along." An unflinching assessment can help well-meaning non-Native allies break down the systemic barriers of colonially based racism that still construct relationships between Indians and non-Indians, build more constructive partnerships, and eviscerate the destructive patterns of white supremacy and saviorism.

THE INDIGENOUS ROOTS OF MODERN FEMINISM

Long before there was ever a concept called "feminism" in the US settler State, there was the knowledge of women's power in Indigenous communities. The imposition of foreign cultures, and Christianity in particular, was corrosive to societies that were typically matrilineal or matrifocal, were foundationally equitable in the distribution of power between the genders, and often respected the existence of a third gender and non-hetero relationships. As Christianity swept over the continent, it instilled Indigenous societies with patriarchal values that sought not only to diminish women's inherent cultural power but also to pathologize alternative gender identities, relationships, and marriage practices outside the bounds of monogamy, establishing a general pattern of gender and relationship suppression that constructs modern American society and reordered Native societies.

Feminism as we know it today is a concept that emerged primarily from the experience of white settler women in the mid-nineteenth century. Historically, European women were little more than the property of men and did not have the same political rights as men did, such as the right to vote or own property. Once they were married they had no rights to their own bodies or even to their children, amounting to no legal existence, as feminist historian Sally Roesch Wagner recounts. So it was logical that their struggles focused on the ability to achieve equality, which would mean, among other things, legal standing and rights. Less well recognized today is the way early women's rights activists were shaped by American Indians. Studying the writings of some of the earliest recognized founders of the feminist movement, such as Lucretia Mott, Elizabeth Cady Stanton, and Matilda Joselyn Gage, Wagner noted the ways they were influenced by Haudenosaunee (Iroquois) cultures with whom they were neighbors in the Northeast. These settler women observed that Haudenosaunee women were free from constrictive, torturous clothing, were farmers, played sports, owned property, and were free from rape and other violence. They were not the property of men. Haudenosaunee women were highly respected in their societies, and a Clan Mother society guided much of the governance of the Haudenosaunee Six Nations Confederacy (Mohawk, Oneida, Onondaga, Cayuga, Seneca, and Tuscarora) by choosing and overseeing the male chiefs. In Haudenosaunee society, children's identity was inherited through the mother's clan (compared to Western societies, which trace identity patrilineally), making the concept of illegitimate children completely foreign. This meant that women had far more control over their bodies than did their white counterparts. While there were norms that governed Haudenosaunee life, women's sexuality was not policed and condemned the way white women's was.[2]

White women, in other words, were fighting for the social equity that most Native women traditionally enjoyed in their societies. The work of white women activists in the nineteenth century, often referred to as "first-wave feminism," gradually bore fruit, and by 1920 white women had won the right to vote. But paradoxically, while white women were gaining rights, Native women's rights were still being eroded through centuries of forced assimilation into the US political landscape. The bestowal of citizenship upon American Indians in 1924, for example, was (and still is to an extent) controversial in Indian country. For the federal government, citizenship was a strategy of assimilation, but it was also advocated by the Society of American Indians, the first Indian-run rights organization, which was in existence from 1911 to 1923. Citizenship was one of SAI's primary agenda issues and was viewed as a mechanism to advance Indians' status beyond "wards of the government" and a "fight for a place as full, modern, and dynamic participants in American life."[3] But as Wagner also points out, many Haudenosaunee women opposed citizenship because it would subject Native women to the same legal system that continued to oppress white women even after suffrage.[4]

NATIVE WOMEN'S ACTIVISM IS BORN

The mid-twentieth century brought with it intense social unrest as traditionally marginalized communities fought to end oppressive policies like segregation and combat poverty borne of their marginalization. The women's liberation movement, firmly rooted in the white middle class and now referred to as "second-wave feminism," pressed forward with demands for equality, which would ideally be solidified into an Equal Rights Amendment to the constitution and was first unsuccessfully proposed in 1923. A renewed movement to pass the ERA in the 1970s failed in large part due to obstacles imposed by conservative women. In the meantime, as the feminist and ethnic nationalist movements advanced through the 1970s and beyond, women of color activists and scholars articulated differences between their struggles and those of middle-class white women. Their struggles, they said, were inseparable from their particular histories of racial and colonial oppression. Not all American Indian women, however, agreed that feminism was an appropriate framework, claiming that it opposed traditional practices and forms of social organization. Many of today's Native feminists counter the claims that feminism was inappropriate, however, and argue for an Indigenous conception of feminism, which recognizes their cultural diversity and that what they do share is their histories of colonial domination. In the words of Native feminist scholars Shari Huhndorf and Cheryl Suzack, an Indigenous feminism "centers on the fact that the imposition of patriarchy has transformed Indigenous societies by diminishing Indigenous women's power, status, and material circumstances."[5] Patriarchy, in other words, is inseparable from colonialism.

Indigenous feminism foregrounds Indigenous relationships to place and dominant society, which on a global scale vary from country to country. In the US this is articulated in the language of tribal sovereignty and Native nationhood. This wave of modern rights-based American Indian activism began with SAI, a collection of Western-educated Indian professionals who embraced the Progressive Era values of reform that tended to believe education and government action were key to improving Indian lives. Their work influenced what led to positive change in federal Indian policy in the 1930s with the passage of the Indian Reorganization Act of 1934. It was progressive for its goals to promote self-determination, but also for the way Native women worked side by side with Native men at a time when white women were still barred from many leadership organizations.

The women of SAI are remembered to this day for their bold leadership and fearless voices. There are many noteworthy examples, but a few women stand out as significant players. One of SAI's founding members was Laura Cornelius Kellogg of the Wisconsin Oneida tribe. She was widely traveled and well educated and taught at two Indian boarding schools. As a public intellectual she was known for her visionary ideas to transform the Indian Service (also known as Office of Indian Affairs, predecessor of the Bureau of Indian Affairs), advocacy for preserving traditional Native knowledge, and fighting for land rights of her tribe and others in Southern California. The *Los Angeles Times* in 1904 described Kellogg as "one of the most interesting Indian women in the United States."[6]

Marie Louise Bottineau Baldwin, Turtle Mountain Ojibway, was the first American Indian woman to become an attorney. At a time of extreme pressure for Indian people to assimilate into white society and when women were fighting for the vote, Baldwin—a respected employee of the Indian Service—was publicly outspoken on the equity built into Native cultures and "went even further, claiming the cultural superiority of Native societies, especially in terms of the position of women."[7] Her strong Indigenous feminist stance was highly influential on mainstream suffragists when she participated in a suffrage parade the weekend of President Woodrow Wilson's inauguration.

Gertrude Simmons Bonnin, also known by her Lakota name Zitkála-Šá, is one of the most widely written about women of SAI. Bonnin was a multitalented Native renaissance woman who wrote several books and was an accomplished musician (she wrote the first Native American opera, *The Sundance Opera*), teacher, editor, and political activist. Perhaps her greatest influence during the Progressive Era came through her leadership in the National Council of American Indians.

Formed after the dissolution of SAI in 1923, Bonnin was chosen as president and remained in that post until the end of her life in 1938.

SAI suffered from internal disharmony among its members, even those who had previously been friends, like Gertrude Bonnin and Marie Bottineau. Conflict stemmed from differences in views on the ritual use of peyote in a new religious movement that was sweeping through reservation communities (now known as the Native American Church) and from distrust of the Indian Service, where many of SAI's members worked. American Indians' formal organizing followed a trajectory from SAI to the National Council of American Indians, formed in 1924 under Bonnin's leadership, to the emergence of the National Congress of American Indians (NCAI) in 1944, which was the beginning of the notorious termination era. NCAI was (and still is) a forum for tribal leaders to work together on solving problems in Indian country that stemmed from the violation of tribes' treaty rights. Their approach was to lobby lawmakers and use other "official" channels to assert and strengthen tribal rights. But something else was brewing in the streets of big cities where Indians had been sent on a relocation work program, especially in Minneapolis and San Francisco. In 1968 in Minneapolis, police brutality against Indians inspired a grassroots response, giving birth to the American Indian Movement (AIM) under the male leadership of Dennis Banks, Russell Means, Vernon and Clyde Bellecourt, and others. The following year, college students in the San Francisco Bay Area hatched a plan to reclaim the defunct prison island of Alcatraz and turn it into an American Indian cultural center. The Alcatraz Island occupation lasted a year and a half and became a flashpoint for AIM, beginning a series of other actions that were considered militant by the mainstream press and federal government. It was followed by the Trail of Broken Treaties and the occupation of the BIA building in Washington, DC, in 1972, and the seventy-one-day standoff at Wounded Knee in 1973.

Referred to as the Red Power movement, the activism of the 1960s and '70s was cultivated largely by young urban Indians, and while women were involved, it was visibly dominated by men who had become so acculturated to dominant white society they had limited knowledge of their tribes' matrilineal and matriarchal cultures.[8] This translated into sexist, repressive behavior toward women. One of the most profoundly destabilizing aspects of colonization on Native life has been in the relationships between men and women. This "patriarchal colonialism"[9] is particularly applicable to the 1960s and '70s and led to a new generation of Native women's organizing.[10] By 1974 some of the AIM women came together and formed the Women of All Red Nations (WARN). Lorelei De Cora Means, Phyllis Young, Janet McCloud, Madonna Thunderhawk, and others organized WARN based on earlier concepts of tribal women's traditions. Some of these women are still involved in activist organizing; Phyllis Young was instrumental from the beginning of the Standing Rock resistance as a council member who was present and very outspoken in SRST's meeting with Energy Transfer Partners in September 2014, and Madonna Thunderhawk was at Oceti Sakowin for much if not all of its duration.

WARN formed initially as a response to the extensive arrests of Native men after the Wounded Knee occupation. But the group quickly advanced its objective, focusing on Native women's health issues, especially exposing that the federal government had forcibly sterilized thousands of Indian women without their knowledge. During the occupation of the BIA building in 1972, WARN members seized secret files documenting the sterilizations at Indian Health Service facilities. In a 1974 WARN study stemming from those documents, the group contended that as many as 42 percent of Native women of reproductive age had been unknowingly sterilized in an official government eugenics program that targeted poor and other women of color.[11] The WARN study slightly predated a 1975 study by the General Accounting Office, under the direction of South Dakota senator James Abourezk, that confirmed much of WARN's data and led to several lawsuits and the reform of the Indian Health Service's reproductive health-care practices. Both the WARN study and the GAO report coincided with other research findings, exposing a pattern that between 25 and 35 percent of all Indian children were being removed from Indian homes and placed in foster care, adoption, or other institutions. The studies' findings led to the passage of the Indian Child Welfare Act in 1978.[12] It seems important to note that in the larger context of American history, forced sterilizations and removal of Indian children clearly fit within the pattern of structural genocide identified in chapter 2. As WARN evolved, it incorporated other issues pertinent to American Indian women's health, notably the effects of Black Hills uranium extraction on the Pine Ridge reservation in South Dakota, which was causing miscarriages, birth defects, and various forms of cancer.

Women of All Red Nations became a launching pad for other Native women's organizing and was initially connected to organizing on the tribal level. For example, some of the WARN women were involved in the leadership of the Oglala Sioux Civil Rights Organization (OSCRO) of the early 1970s. On the Pine Ridge reservation, the OSCRO was formed in response to the reactionary tribal government led by chairman Dick Wilson, who was widely perceived to be a puppet of the US government. Under Wilson's direction, the notorious GOON (guardians of the Oglala Nation) squad, carried out a campaign of violent intimidation against AIM activists and other traditionalists working to reform their government. Other women's organizations sprang up, such as the Northwest Indian Women's Circle, founded in 1981 by WARN's Janet McCloud, and the Indigenous Women's Network (IWN) in 1985.[13]

The Indigenous social movements of the 1960s and '70s continued to build upon and overlap with each other, because all the issues facing American Indians were interconnected—the result of their history of colonization and modern forms of colonial exploitation and abuse. A good example is how WARN's exposing of uranium poisoning linked Native women's reproductive health problems to environmental contamination. Environmental contamination, especially related to uranium, was not a new issue in Indian country in the 1970s. As we have seen, in the Southwest on and near the Navajo Nation, uranium mining had been going on since the late 1930s, and by the 1970s its deadly health effects were well known, reaching a catastrophic crescendo with the Rio Puerco spill in 1979. But what was new was the way WARN linked this long-recognized issue to reproductive health.

Native women's activism was always distinctly connected to environmental activism in order to protect communities from toxic development and was part of a larger pattern of organizing that led to the international arena. The International Indian Treaty Council, for example, was not a women's organization, but American Indian women played significant roles throughout its history and IITC became the first Indigenous entity to achieve United Nations nongovernmental organization status in 1977. Andrea Carmen joined the staff of IITC in 1983, and since 1992 she has been the organization's executive director. On the international scene another visible shift began to occur with the rise of the climate justice movement. Indigenous peoples worldwide became more visible as it became apparent that they, along with more vulnerable peoples in the undeveloped, Indigenous, and fourth world, were on the frontlines of climate change, even though they had been excluded from international processes like the Kyoto Protocol. Grassroots movements and organizations emerged from Indigenous communities all over the world, bringing attention to the effects climate change, the fossil fuel industry, and government collusion were having on their communities. And women were conspicuously at the forefront of those movements and organizations. With the rise of the internet, mass organizing became infinitely easier, enabling people to connect across international and cultural lines. For instance, in 2004 a group of thirteen international Indigenous women came together from communities as diverse as the Dakotas, the Alaskan Tundra, Oaxaca, Tibet, and Nepal to form an "alliance of prayer, education and healing for our Mother Earth, all Her inhabitants, all the children, and for the next seven generations to come."[14] Calling themselves the Council of Thirteen Indigenous Grandmothers, the council held gatherings every year for thirteen years in the home territory of each member.

In 2012 Indigenous women's organizing vaulted into mainstream visibility when four mostly First Nations women came together to oppose a suite of proposed Canadian laws that were seen as a threat to the environment and a simultaneous assault on Native rights.[15] Primarily through the vehicle of social media, they vowed to be "idle no more," and a new Indigenous women–led environmental rights movement was born. Spreading like wildfire, the Idle No More movement was international within weeks, especially taking hold in the US. The movement failed to stop the legislation it formed to oppose, but it galvanized the attention of Canadians and Americans, awakening many to the ways the struggles of Indigenous peoples fighting toxic development were everybody's struggles, not just Indigenous peoples'.

In 2013 women were once again out front with the Summer Heat campaign, organized by Winona LaDuke, Naomi Klein, and Bill McKibben. It was a coordinated effort to bring people out into the streets to oppose the fossil fuel industry. San Francisco's Idle No More group mobilized more than two thousand people on the first anniversary of a massive explosion at a Richmond refinery that sent fifteen thousand people to the hospital. It was led by Pennie Opal Plant of mixed Yaqui, Cherokee, and Choctaw

heritage. Idle No More groups continue to work within Canada and beyond to stem the tide of fossil fuel development.

Meanwhile, fueling the climate justice movement was disturbing
new information that the greenhouse gases (GHG) in the atmosphere
were accumulating faster than scientists previously predicted. The
scientific community has long maintained that to prevent global catastrophic scenarios, global warming must remain under two degrees Cel-
sius. But in 2012 the United Nations Environmental Program released
a report claiming that GHG emissions were approximately 14 percent
higher than what would be required by the end of the decade to limit
warming to two degrees.[16] Then in 2013, the concentration of GHGs had
surpassed the critical threshold of four hundred parts per million, representing a 41 percent increase caused by humans.[17] On the heels of Idle
No More, another group of North American Indigenous women (some
of the same organizers of the San Francisco Idle No More group) came
together to create the Indigenous Women of the Americas—Defenders
of Mother Earth Treaty in 2015. The treaty acknowledges natural laws of
Mother Earth and Father Sky, and that the "laws have been violated to
such an extreme degree that the sacred system of life is now threatened
and does not have the capacity for life to continue safely in the way in
which it has existed for millions of years."[18] Reflecting a growing sense
of collective urgency, it calls for all women of the Earth (1) to nonviolently
rise up and work to influence government leaders and those in seats of
power to adapt human-made laws in accordance with natural laws in a
spirit of love, and (2) to conduct prayer ceremonies on each new moon
and every solstice and equinox.

The treaty links the violence done to the Earth with the violence done
to women, naming the crisis of missing, murdered, raped, and enslaved
women in Indigenous communities worldwide. Because of the activism
of First Nations women in Canada and the country's Truth and Recon-
ciliation Commission, the decades-old problem has become more visible
in recent years. In 2012 Canadian statistics indicated that Indigenous
women represented 16 percent of all female homicides between 1980 and
2012 despite being only 4 percent of the population; a 2014 report from
the Royal Canadian Mounted Police counted a total of 1,181 murdered and
missing Indigenous women and girls, 164 missing and 1,107 murdered in
that thirty-two-year span. The government of Canada launched a national

inquiry into the problem of missing and murdered Indigenous women in 2016.[19] The problem is mirrored in the United States with numerous studies confirming that American Indian women experience rates of sexual and domestic violence far higher than all other demographic groups. A 2016 Department of Justice study indicated that more than four in five (84 percent) American Indian and Alaska Native women experienced violence in their lifetimes; 56 percent experienced sexual violence, and 55 percent have experienced physical violence by an intimate partner.[20] According to the DOJ's website, American Indian women are two and a half times more likely to experience sexual assault crimes compared to all other races.[21] Globally, the problem of human sex trafficking in Indigenous communities came to the forefront with the 2014 genocide of Yezidi people in Iraq. At the hands of the Islamic State (ISIS), thousands of Yezidi men were massacred, and more than three thousand women were kidnapped and swept into a system of modern slavery.

CULTURAL CLASHES AT STANDING ROCK

Against the backdrop of the countless seen and unseen actions by Indigenous women working for the protection of their communities and future generations, a critical mass seemed to have been reached, making the #NoDAPL demonstration at Standing Rock possible. Massive global resistance to Big Oil, decades of political organizing by Native people, networking across multiple spheres of interest, and sophisticated use of social media all account for the groundswell that made the Standing Rock convergence possible. It was stunning not only for the sheer scope of support it received but also for the way it brought together a diverse array of people from the farthest reaches of the globe. Aside from the dangerous encounters with a militarized police force and pro-pipeline propaganda, Oceti Sakowin seemed to be a well-oiled machine. Human-interest news stories emphasized harmonious teamwork in feeding the growing crowds and the daily chores of managing a village-size camp out on an isolated prairie. Medics expertly handled injuries inflicted by police weapons, mace, and dogs. Lawyers staffed the legal tent and helped prepare defenses for the hundreds of those arrested. On "Facebook hill," the only spot in the camp with a reasonably good cell signal, a stationary bicycle generated enough electricity to recharge phones as long as someone was pedaling. The hill became the place for press conferences and social media updates that kept the world informed on a daily basis. In general people were well behaved.

But something else was lurking just underneath the surface, a familiar tension that surfaced in a particularly gendered way. It was reminiscent of the roadblocks that have plagued relationships between environmentalists and Native people in the past, only this time it manifested in a particular way among the women. About the time the friction became public, I had been asked to participate in a conference panel on the topic of Indigenous feminist issues. Intrigued by what was playing out on the ground at Standing Rock, I decided that I would make a closer study of the conflict in order to understand the underlying dynamics as the topic for my conference presentation. At the same time, I had also been working as a freelance journalist writing for Indian Country Media Network and writing about Standing Rock from a distance. Like thousands of other people, I felt compelled to go there, but a busy work and travel schedule made it difficult.

For weeks I had been glued to the many live Facebook feeds coming out of Oceti Sakowin. I'd been watching the evening of November 21 when the water cannon attacks in the subfreezing nighttime temperatures unfolded. That was the moment I decided the time had come to go, and I found an opening in my schedule to make the trip. Traveling with a couple of friends—a brilliant young Kul Wicasa doctoral student named Nick Estes, who had become a trusted advisor to his relatives who were the headmen at Oceti Sakowin, and Carolina Ramos, who was going to donate her lawyer skills—we left Southern California on Thanksgiving Day, unavoidably driving east into a snowstorm. After a harrowing drive in near-blizzard conditions and a road closure that forced us to sleep in the car in the parking lot of a truck stop in Rock Springs, Wyoming, we finally made it to Oceti Sakowin after thirty-six hours in the car.

I was at Standing Rock for just a few days. Thanksgiving weekend was when the population swelled to its largest numbers—some estimating thirteen thousand people or more. It's impossible to say when the ratio of Native to non-Native people shifted, but by that weekend it was clear that non-Natives far outweighed the Native population. What I was most struck by was my perception that despite that more non-Native than Native people were in the camp, it was nonetheless a space dominated

by Native people. The rules for engagement were based on Lakota protocol, and everything was conducted in ceremonial fashion. It was peaceful
and focused. Oceti Sakowin was, in other words, Indigenous, culturally
sovereign space. The community at the Standing Rock camps was, however, far from an Indigenous cultural utopia. By all accounts, things were
less complicated when the camps were still populated with a majority
of Native people. When the violence started in September, people began
pouring into the camps from all over the United States and the world,
and the population demographic began shifting. Standing Rock had become a lightning rod and symbol of global resistance against fossil fuel
development.

While there was cooperation and people chipping in with the heavy
work of chopping wood, sorting out donations, cooking, structure building, and other chores of managing a large semipermanent encampment,
in my conversations I also heard dissatisfaction with the way things were
going. There were complaints from the Native folks that the non-Native
people were treating their visit more like it was a music festival than a site
of serious political resistance. There were accounts of drug and alcohol
use, which was strictly prohibited, and other transgressions that signaled
violations of Indigenous protocol in what appeared to me as a cultural
conflict in which dominant European American values were consciously
or unconsciously in competition with Lakota values. I first became interested in how the differences were playing out among the women months
earlier, in September when a controversy arose about how women were
expected to dress in camp. According to Lakota tradition, in a ceremonial
context, women are expected to wear long skirts. This is also true in other
tribal contexts—it is common throughout Indian country—and different tribal people have different ways of expressing what wearing skirts
means, but for all tribal cultures it is, if nothing else, a simple matter of
respect.

There were murmurings of some of the non-Native women objecting
to wearing skirts. After all, from their perspective, wearing skirts in a
camping environment seemed impractical. Not surprising, most seemed
not to have been aware of the protocol and arrived at the camps without
the appropriate attire. It became such an issue that Native women organized sewing brigades to make skirts for the women who were without them. Well-known Native clothing designer Bethany Yellowtail, for

example, came from Los Angeles armed with two hundred yards of cloth and other sewing materials to contribute to the skirt-making effort. The skirt issue is relevant because it is emblematic of the differences in world-view across not just cultural but also gendered lines. In this instance, for non-Native women, wearing skirts might seem not just impractical but also oppressive, perhaps invoking a time when women were socially required to dress in certain ways, a history they fought hard to change. For Native women on the other hand, wearing skirts is a way of honoring tradition and expressing identity and cultural pride.

Indigenous social ethics and Native peoples' authentic connection to land are what historically has drawn white settlers to emulate Native American cultures in myriad problematic and convoluted ways, even while they were trying to exterminate Native people. In local histories they also write Indians out of landscapes as extinct or somehow disap-peared and relate histories of themselves as original to place in "replace-ment narratives."[22] In these ways white people unconsciously and often consciously enact the conditioning that has mythologized their superior-ity, even while they venerate the values that shape Native societies. To explain it, psychologists have applied the framework of critical race psy-chology to account for ways the centering of whiteness in dominant so-ciety manifests in narratives of neoliberal individualism and, borrowing from critical social theory, in "possessive investments in whiteness" to de-scribe how racism is reproduced on individual and institutional levels.[23] Simply stated, possessive investment in whiteness refers to an American social structure whose default reference point is white and middle class, a system that benefits primarily white people.[24]

In social movements, this dynamic can result in troubled relation-ships between affinity activist groups; we have seen how it plays out in the environmental movement in particular, and how relationships be-tween Native and non-Native people go sideways. These are invisible, un-spoken, typically unrecognized, but always-present assumptions about white cultural superiority that structure society at every level. I'm argu-ing it's why the disharmony between Native and non-Native men and women manifested at Standing Rock, even in culturally sovereign Indig-enous space, and by extension, why relationships go wrong in the broader environmental movement.

To further understand these dynamics, I sought to gather stories of individual women and men who were willing to go on record with their experiences. In these interviews (which were conducted predominantly with women) my goal was to understand how their experiences exemplified, or conversely concealed, the cultural differences between Native and non-Native people, and women in particular. The interviews produced stories that not surprisingly reflected a range of experiences and viewpoints. The difference in worldview is especially poignant in the example of two particular interviewees, one whom I'll refer to as Sue and another I'll call Darcy (both pseudonyms). Sue is a Native journalist who traveled back and forth between her home community and Standing Rock numerous times and wrote many stories for Native American media. She is solidly grounded in a Native identity and grew up in a reservation community. Sue recounted several instances where Native and non-Native worldviews collided. She commented that "the topic of the skirts took on rich meaning because it symbolized so many different things," especially relative to prayerful resistance and Native identity. She spoke at length about what she called the "hippie" or "rainbow" people, whom she characterized as "New Agey," and she witnessed several events where "rainbow women" overstepped boundaries of Indigenous protocol in a number of ways.

One example of boundary crossing occurred in October. In August a series of two women's meetings had been held, led by esteemed Lakota elder Faith Spotted Eagle, who delivered teachings about traditional women's knowledge, including perspectives on skirts and the need to understand patriarchy and how it has affected Native communities. A few weeks later, in October, a call was announced from the central fire (Oceti Sakowin's central gathering place) for another women's meeting. Thinking this was another meeting with Spotted Eagle, Sue went to the meeting only to find it being run by a white woman. She described the woman having a "New Agey staff" that was being used as a talking stick (a communication implement Native people often use to regulate meetings), with children's handprints all over it. Not a style of talking stick that can be identified as "traditional," Sue recounted feeling uncomfortable about the staff, not sure if the children's parents had given permission for what she believed was an exploitation of the children. Only about ten women were present, mostly non-Native, but one was a Native woman who appeared to have been brought to the meeting by the white woman and who spoke in disrespectful and vulgar ways. Sue saw the Native woman as a "token Indian," there to "legitimize her [the white woman's] meeting." "It was something like the *Survivor* television show or *Lord of the Flies*. . . . It was just goofy," she recalled. Sue saw the meeting as the white woman inappropriately taking upon herself the authority to call the meeting and then use it as a "soapbox, as though she was teaching something new as a Native woman."

Sue illustrated how for many non-Native people the journey to Standing Rock became a narrative of personal healing, "losing sight of the mission to protect water. For Native people it was 'we' versus 'I'm here to tell my story.'" This was exemplified by the white woman who used the meeting to talk about things like "healing the inner child." As the staff was passed around, women described stories about selling personal belongings to finance their trips, or "the spirit calling" them. As Sue explained, for Native people "personal healing might have been a by-product [of coming to Standing Rock] but not the mission." Sue also spoke about a sense of fatigue in dealing with the "hippies," whom she was accustomed to dealing with. "Over the years I've noticed that what they bring is an extractive tendency to want us to share mystical knowledge for them to take for themselves, so I don't have a positive history of respect from that community. They don't have respect for traditions or boundaries."

This concept of taking was also expressed by Darcy, a young non-Native college student from Colorado who had come to Standing Rock with a group of thirteen non-Native friends, initially as part of an assignment for a Native art history class she was enrolled in. There was potential funding for the trip that would have required her to "bring something back," presumably knowledge or experience. This weighed heavily on her, causing an "internal conflict that I'm still ethically and morally putting together." In our video conversation I could see the pain in her face as she talked. "My friend said she wanted to be part of history," Darcy told me, "but what are we doing that's ever giving?" She also spoke of not being aware of the need for skirts or of prohibitions about women who are on their monthly "moontime." This is a Lakota protocol that restricts women from ceremonies or from certain ceremonial contexts (such as a sacred fire) and from handling food, based on the idea that this is a time of spiritual power for women that needs to be guarded. Darcy said some women in her group were on their cycles, but that because they "didn't feel like it aligned with their own morals, they decided to work in the kitchen anyway." Darcy said, "I had never sat in a place where all of a sudden I had no idea how to fit in, which was an incredible learning experience and has allowed me to be empathetic, and try to understand how everyday life may be for people who are not white. But I was not prepared mentally to step back in my morals."

To Darcy and her friends, it was obvious that they were in the midst of a radically different culture than the mainstream society they were accustomed to, one that constructed its own ideas of what's normal and acceptable. But as well meaning as they were coming in to the culturally sovereign space of Oceti Sakowin, they were unwilling in differing degrees to adjust their behavior to meet these new circumstances. This translates into a willfully disrespectful dismissal of Indigenous cultural values. We might attribute this attitude to youthful recalcitrance, but considered with other stories I heard, it was a phenomenon not limited to age group. The difference in views between the Native and non-Native interviewees revealed ruptures that Native people are far more aware of and conversant in than non-Natives are. In cultural sovereign space, Native values rooted in communal well-being supersede values of individual fulfillment and emphasize the virtues of contributing and giving over extractive taking. It's fair to say that the nearly yearlong tenure of the Standing Rock encampments left no one unchanged, as exemplified by the testimonies of some of the people I spoke with and countless testimonials that can be found in news stories and personal blogs. But as much as solidarity was expressed across cultural lines, it also exposed the insidious ways the systemic nature of racism manifests in even the most liberal and well-meaning activists. This is a lesson non-Native activists will need to absorb if they are to build effective partnerships with Native peoples in the future.

In light of the conflicts at Standing Rock and other events exemplified in chapter 6, there are still many examples of ways Indian and non-Indian environmental activists have successfully worked together, even if it was an afterthought or the result of another initial exclusion. In the next chapter we will look at other examples of how coalition building has worked to achieve the common goal of environmental protection, but in a way that highlights ongoing contradictory orientations to land and concepts of sacredness and justice.

CHAPTER SEVEN

Sacred Sites and Environmental Justice

*The question has been asked, yet we hear no response: "What part of
sacred don't you understand?" Essentially we're saying why isn't it
enough for us to say a site is sacred and should be set aside
and protected and respected because it's integral for our spiritual
practice to be continued.*

—KLEE BENALLY, NAVAJO ACTIVIST[1]

To be born American Indian today is to have survived a holocaust of a
very particular kind, one whose evidence is everywhere, all the time.
After a pattern of simultaneous denial and justification of the five-
centuries-long genocidal rampage on the continent and the settler
population believing they knew what was best for the land and original
inhabitants, Indigenous peoples focus on revitalizing their cultures and
healing from intergenerational trauma. In the new postapocalyptic world,
landscapes that for millennia contained the origin stories of the people
often became unrecognizable. Skyscrapers mushroomed from ancestral village sites, concrete entombed burial grounds, and superhighways
paved over ancient trade routes. Even in all their resilience, the trauma
of surviving an apocalypse of unspeakable proportions is an inescapable
reality for today's Native people. Adding insult to injury, as if the injury
weren't bad enough, they are forced to fight to retain access to what remains of their homelands. Today the sanctity of these places is defined by
their ancient religious significance, or simply by their state designation
as a "traditional cultural property" when only a remnant of an ancestral
place remains. Protecting sacred sites is one of the most difficult and
pressing issues Native people now face. Widely varying histories and legal relationships to federal and state governments result in a complex
tangle of circumstance, which means that approaches to protecting such

sites are far from universal. Negative court decisions still haunt efforts to protect sites, because they construct the legal framework from which other sacred site battles are waged. Some sacred sites involve treaty rights and some do not. Sacred site protection battles are sometimes fought as religious freedom issues, but such cases have met with little success, given that Western conceptions of religion and sacredness that construct legislation and govern court decisions are dramatically different—and unrecognizable—from Indigenous conceptions. As this chapter argues, viewing sacred site protection as an environmental justice issue can be a more effective framework for sacred site protection, adding another layer of legal protection at the very least, in light of the limited capacity for justice the legal and policy landscape currently offers. At the same time, it highlights ways Native peoples are working in successful partnerships to protect land for sometimes different but ultimately mutually beneficial reasons.

TRUST LAND, TREATY RIGHTS, AND STANDING ROCK

Indian reservations are lands reserved in treaties, by executive order, or congressional acts. They are not gifts of the federal government to tribes; they are products of massive land cessions by tribes that created the United States (though not all tribes had treaties). The legal foundation of Indian reservations rests upon the principle of trust. The federal government holds Indian lands as the trustee for tribal nations in what's sometimes called "aboriginal title"; reservation lands are also called "trust lands," and tribes with reservations are considered federally recognized tribes. Trust lands are not subject to the same property laws as fee simple lands (such as property taxes and local zoning laws) because of American Indians' inherent sovereignty as preconstitutional peoples. Tribes can also own land in fee simple, but unless they are placed in trust status, they are no different from other fee simple lands, subject to taxes and other property-based legal regimes. On trust lands tribal governments have jurisdiction within the boundaries of those lands, so protecting sacred sites on reservations is a matter of tribal sovereignty. But original tribal territories invariably extended far beyond current boundaries, and areas beyond those boundaries always contain important cultural sites or resources.

Written into the treaties that ceded tribal lands to the US were rights for Native peoples to access the ceded lands for hunting, fishing, and other cultural resources. Treaty making ended with an act of Congress in 1871, but after that, countless unilateral actions by the settler US government shrank reserved treaty lands. As we have seen, the most notorious of those actions was the Dawes Act, which within half a century reduced treaty-reserved lands by two-thirds in what Indians consider to be blatant treaty violations. In many cases lands were just seized without ratified treaties or other legal instruments, as was the case in California where eighteen treaties were made but never ratified. Oceti Sakowin, the Great Sioux Nation, comprised several separate but related bands of Lakota who were joined together on the Great Sioux Reservation by the Treaty of Fort Laramie in 1851, is a textbook example of lands reserved through treaties but later diminished by acts never agreed to by the Lakota, Nakota, and Dakota people. The result was the fragmentation of the Great Sioux Reservation into smaller reservations known today as Pine Ridge, Rosebud, Lower Brulé, Crow Creek, Yankton, Sisseton Wahpeton, Santee, Cheyenne River, and Standing Rock.

The Dakota Access Pipeline was controversial not only because it was rerouted to avoid Bismarck and threatened Standing Rock's water source but also because its route was directly in the path of sacred lands outside today's reservation boundary lines, and still well within the unceded territory of the original Great Sioux Reservation. More than one desecration occurred. The first occurred in early September 2016 when bulldozers cut a one-hundred-fifty-foot-wide swath of land for a stretch of two miles that contained eighty-two cultural features and twenty-seven burials, the event that immediately preceded the first of the violent attacks on water protectors. SRST chairman Dave Archambault asserted that the tribe had not been properly consulted as required under federal law, despite numerous letters sent to the Army Corps of Engineers requesting consultation.[2] A second desecration occurred on October 17 when Energy Transfer Partners' construction workers unearthed another cultural site and for ten days failed to report it to the North Dakota Public Service Commission permitting agency, which SRST perceived as violating conditions of the permit and the National Historic Preservation Act.[3]

The violation of Standing Rock's sacred sites is an example of how easily it can occur, even when treaty rights, in theory, grant a measure of legal protection to federally recognized tribes. Things are infinitely more complicated for tribes who don't have land bases or who are not federally recognized, or both. This is exemplified by one particular sacred-site battle in Southern California that culminated in 2008 in the homelands of the Acjachemen people.

PANHE: AN INDIGENOUS PLACE AT THE CROSSROADS

The Acjachemen people, also known as the Juaneño Band of Mission Indians, occupied much of today's Orange County, California, overlapping territories with their northerly Tongva neighbors and more southerly Luiseño, or Payómkawichum, neighbors in numerous village groups. The largest of the ancient Acjachemen village sites is known as Panhe (which means "the place at the water"), and its center lies within the San Mateo Creek watershed within San Mateo Creek Campground. Complicating jurisdiction over Panhe is that the campground lies within San Onofre State Beach, a three-thousand-acre coastal canyon area under a fifty-year lease from the Department of the Navy, which owns Camp Pendleton Marine Base adjacent to the San Onofre Nuclear Generating Station—and that the Acjachemen are not a federally recognized tribe. In other words, Panhe is located within a state park, which is within a military base next to a nuclear plant. Acjachemen people today affirm their ancestral knowledge that prior to colonization Panhe referred to the entire valley that now constitutes parts of Camp Pendleton and San Onofre State Beach and much of today's town of San Clemente. What is currently recognized as Panhe is confined to a small area within San Mateo Campground, where there is still a burial and ceremonial site. Panhe is considered the most sacred of all Acjachemen places.

Panhe is confirmed by archeologists to be at least 9,600 years old, making it one of just a few remaining sites of such antiquity in the state that have not been bulldozed and built upon. In 1981 Panhe received an official Determination of Eligibility for the National Register of Historic Places by the National Park Service, and in the same year it was recorded with the State Historic Preservation Office, at which point it became organized as the San Mateo Archeological District. In 1989 the state agency California Native American Heritage Commission added Panhe to its Sacred Lands inventory as a result of extensive documentation by

Acjachemen elders.⁴ In addition to middens (waste heaps often consisting of shells, indicating ancient human habitation), human remains had
been found within the boundaries of San Onofre State Beach, once in
1969 during construction of the nuclear plant, and then again years later,
during a military construction project at Camp Pendleton when twelve
sets of remains were found.⁵ Despite Panhe's enduring cultural significance to the Acjachemen, or Juaneño, people, it is entirely out of their
control. Without federal recognition, the Acjachemen have no access to
what few federal laws there are protecting Native American sacred sites
and religion.

Panhe was threatened by plans to build a toll road through the San
Mateo Creek watershed, which became widely known in 2006. The 241
toll road was proposed by the privately owned Transportation Corridor
Agencies (TCA) to alleviate traffic on California's main artery, Highway 5.
The bulk of the controversy emerged when the public became aware that
the last six-mile segment skirting San Clemente in the south would cross
into Camp Pendleton and the state park, where it would finally connect
to Highway 5, dangerously close to the Trestles surf break, where San
Mateo Creek empties into the ocean. Trestles is one of the most coveted
and famous surf spots in California and even the world. In this section,
the proposed road would run parallel to the creek for approximately two
miles, adjacent to the campground, and a scant twenty feet from Panhe.⁶
Environmental impact studies revealed that the creek bed would likely be
completely torn up as the highway's one-hundred-foot-high pillars would
be anchored into bedrock, totally disrupting the creek's flow by diversion. More alarming was the effect such dramatic disruption would have
downstream at Trestles. A primary determinant of wave quality is the
topography of the ocean bottom. Excessive silt deposits washing downstream from road construction would undoubtedly degrade the near-
perfect wave quality that Trestles is famous for, an effect that would be
unmitigatable once inflicted. When the surf community got wind of the
threat to Trestles in 2006, it was game on; for them Trestles was sacred
ground, and any threat to it was intolerable. That was when the anti-toll
road movement became organized as a campaign, "Save Trestles, Stop
the Toll Road." The mass distribution of bumper stickers and lawn signs
all over San Clemente had awakened the sleeping giant, and suddenly everyone had an opinion, and it wasn't in support of the toll road. The news

that Trestles was in danger spread like wildfire far beyond the California surf community, making the "Save Trestles" campaign an international issue.[7] What followed was a flurry of organizing across multiple stakeholder lines involving surfers, environmentalists, and a group of American Indian people called the United Coalition to Protect Panhe (UCPP).

The UCPP came together as a grassroots group of Acjachemen tribal members in 2007 to bring attention to the American Indian aspect of the toll road issue, since few others were concerned with it, let alone even knew about it. They also saw it as an opportunity to expand their ceremonial use of Panhe while they worked to protect it. Their strategy was to build alliances with environmentalist and surf organizations like the Sierra Club and Surfrider Foundation—those with whom they otherwise had little connection—to enhance public perceptions about why the toll road must not be built. Although the UCPP was a relative latecomer to the campaign, their work took things in a critical direction. The UCPP alerted the California Coastal Commission about the toll road's impact on the sacred site. The Coastal Commission must comply with the Coastal Act and other state laws, including laws related to tribal cultural resources, and it is the agency who grants the final permits to development projects in the coastal zone.[8] What is clear in hindsight is that few people outside the Native community and the Coastal Commission realized the important role Panhe would ultimately play in the fight to stop the toll road.

Numerous legal attempts to stop the toll road were ongoing, including one lawsuit filed by the California Native American Heritage Commission (CNAHC), which was based on the enforcement of state laws protecting Native Americans' right to free exercise of religion. In fact, one of the UCPP's key achievements was its appeal to the CNAHC, eventually triggering the lawsuit. After several years of battles waged by multiple stakeholders, the toll road's death knell came on February 6, 2008, when by a vote of eight to two the Coastal Commission denied the permit certification, arguing that it was inconsistent with the Coastal Act because of policy violations and the road's impact on environmentally sensitive habitat areas, wetlands, public access and recreation, surfing, public views, water quality, *archeological resources*, energy and vehicle miles traveled, and conflict resolution. Illustrating the importance of the "archeological resources" (sacred sites), Commissioner Mary Schallenberger stated,

There is a huge disconnect in understanding between the Native American culture, and the—what would I call it?—the rest of the culture of California. . . . What I learned and came to respect is that for the Native Americans, quite often, their sacred sites are different. They are absolutely tied to, and integral to a specific place on the earth. Churches, synagogues, and I believe mosques can be moved. They can be moved, and they can be reblessed, or whatever that particular religion calls for, and the worship can go on in a different building in a different place. With the Native Americans, that is often not the case.[9]

Besides the Coastal Commission, other government agencies that opposed the project included the State Department of Parks and Recreation, California Native American Heritage Commission, State Historic Preservation Office (SHPO), and the federal Advisory Council on Historic Preservation. All agreed with the Coastal Commission's determination that based on the draft environmental impact report, no reasonable mitigation was possible in all areas of concern. In particular, regarding the archeological resources, the commission's report stated that "the impacts to the Juaneño/Acjachemen people who currently use the ceremonial site are completely unmitigated."[10] Also at issue in the report was that Panhe should have been evaluated as a "traditional cultural property" (TCP) based on the advice of SHPO, which had not been done, and because it hadn't, there was inadequate information to make a determination for consistency.[11] After the Coastal Commission denied the toll road permit, TCA appealed to the US Commerce Department, who denied the appeal later that year. The Save Trestles campaign was a success, at least for the time being, but everybody knew that the fight wasn't over—the forces of development weren't going to give up that easily. In the meantime, a larger alliance had been formed among twelve national and state environmental organizations, called the Save San Onofre Coalition, and in 2016 the coalition reached a settlement agreement with TCA to end the six lawsuits that had been filed against them. In the settlement, TCA agreed to abandon the 241 route through the San Mateo Creek watershed and pursue other alternatives.

ENVIRONMENTAL JUSTICE AND INDIGENOUS DIFFERENCE

In chapter 1 we saw that environmental justice as it is ordinarily conceived of is inadequate for tribal nations in the US, because it fails to acknowledge broader histories of colonization and current frameworks of sovereignty, however limited they are within the modern State system. Indigenous peoples face political circumstances that differ dramatically from other ethnic minorities; their pre-State connections to ancestral homelands and traditional cultures, which they are constantly fighting to protect, mean a different relationship to the State, as they are political relationships based on treaties and inherent sovereignty. Chapter 1 described how the State—in this case, the US government—interferes in the collective continuance of a people, disabling their systems of responsibility, which are built upon place-based knowledge accumulated over vast periods of time. Inherent to these systems of responsibility is the concept of sanctity, that which is held to be sacred within Indigenous worldviews. Differentiating a mainstream EJ framework from an Indigenized EJ framework must also, therefore, proceed from the assumption that Indigenous worldviews reflect a different relationship to land, a relationship that does not separate people or culture from land, nor creates anthropocentric hierarchies within nature. Simply put, from an Indigenous perspective, nonhuman life forms have agency in a way that they do not in dominant Western cultures. Likewise, the religious significance of a place is the spiritual glue that binds peoples to their homelands.

The US legal system has been incapable of recognizing Indigenous peoples' very different relationship to land largely because of its recognition of land as property. In cases where sites are successfully protected, the protection is based on concepts Western law is able to reconcile. In the case of Panhe, a measure of legal protection was available via state law by virtue of Panhe's location on publicly owned lands that had been designated as an "archeological resource" deserving of protection, a framework that recognizes Panhe's relevance to the Acjachemen people (framed as a "cultural resource"). Panhe's eligibility for the National Register of Historic Places and its listing on the CNAHC Sacred Lands Inventory were critical as a protective mechanism, just as an evaluation of it as a traditional cultural property likely would have been, had such an evaluation been made.[12] However, protective frameworks of Panhe that were constructed based on its national historical significance also rather problematically define Panhe in terms of its significance to *all* American people, Acjachemen and non-Acjachemen alike. These kinds of claims amount to a form of settler appropriation of Native culture based on our collective history (all Americans), our State-based heritage, and not exclusively Acjachemen history or heritage. Because Acjachemen history and heritage is *ours*, it is worthy of protecting. Acjachemen identity is effectively submerged into a homogenizing narrative that has the effect of erasing Native concerns, even while it purports to be protecting them. Ironically, Panhe was protectable *because* of its absorption into what eventually became publicly owned or leased lands, subject to laws designed for the homogenized masses that comprise the American public, not necessarily or primarily because of its inherent meaning for Acjachemen people.

The story of Panhe demonstrates how the Acjachemen as constitutionally preexisting sovereign people—even though they are not federally recognized—asserted their political identity as Native people to protect their ancestral lands in response to the threat of the inevitable environmental destruction that would be committed there (constituting further religious desecration and limited access to a religious site) had the toll road been built. Their ancient historical ties to the land were the indisputable vehicle available for them to argue for the protection of the land, while other protective mechanisms used by non-Native people were based on protecting the environment itself, divorced from any aspect of connection between humans and the land (aside from how their recreational use of it would be affected).[13] By and large, this is not a political or ideological avenue that is available to other ethnic minorities in their struggles for environmental justice, highlighting Indigenous difference.

The domination framework of the US settler State means that the State appoints itself as the determiner of identity for Indigenous peoples. Without federal recognition, an Indian group or nation may be Indian by self-definition, amounting to no more than an ethnic classification, but it does not necessarily attach to the rights associated with the political recognition granted through the legal fictions of federal Indian law. Federally recognized tribes, even those without land bases, in theory have the ability to acquire land and have it placed in trust (as difficult as this process is, and as the example of the Federated Indians of the Graton Rancheria illustrates). As Indian trust land, it then becomes subject to the jurisdiction of federal Indian law and a certain level of sovereignty. *If* the Acjachemen (Juaneño) were federally recognized, and *if* they were able to overcome the nearly impossible odds that would result in their acquiring Panhe, and *if* they could achieve the monumental task of having Panhe placed into trust, then by virtue of their federally sanctioned sovereignty they would have had the power to stop the road and protect their sacred site via the mechanisms accorded to them through federal Indian law. The Acjachemen, like many other tribal nations and individual Indians in the United States, inhabit an identity gray zone politically—not non-Indian in the eyes of the state of California, but not necessarily Indian in the eyes of the federal government.[14] As a tribal nation, they are not subject to the laws that would support the limited sovereignty available to federally recognized tribes, but as individual Indians, Acjachemen people are entitled to some of the benefits guaranteed under some legal definitions of "Indian."[15] So to conceptually transcend the limits the US State imposes on Native people through legal definitions of "Indian" or "tribe," EJ frameworks must be able to situate tribal peoples' struggles to protect sacred places with their relationality to land, not with artificial constructions of identity.

THE CONCEPT OF THE SACRED

The very thing that distinguishes Indigenous peoples from settler societies is their unbroken connection to ancestral homelands. Their cultures and identities are linked to their original places in ways that define them, as reflected through language, place names, and cosmology or religion. In Indigenous worldviews, there is no separation between people and land, between people and other life forms, or between people and their ancient ancestors whose bones are infused in the land they inhabit. All things in nature contain spirit (specific types of consciousness), thus the world is seen and experienced in spiritual terms. As many scholars have noted, the Indigenous world is a world of relationships built on reciprocity, respect, and responsibility, not just between humans but also extending to the entire natural world. Indigenous relationships with nature have been stereotyped and appropriated by dominant society in a multitude of ways (such as the ecological Indian), but in reality are rooted in a philosophical paradigm very different from that of dominant Western society.

Native scholars argue that the difference between Indigenous conceptions of the sacred and Western conceptions are their different orientations to time and space. Vine Deloria Jr., in particular, first articulated
these ideas in his pioneering book *God Is Red: A Native View of Religion*
(1973), and later built upon them in his theoretically dense *The Metaphys-
ics of Modern Existence* (1979). In both works Deloria presents fundamental challenges to the Newtonian-Cartesian view of a mechanistic, linear
universe. Identifying Western paradigms and drawing on Deloria, Osage
theologian George Tinker observes that centuries ago Europeans adopted
a perceptual orientation based on temporality. Time, as the primary organizing intellectual principle to which a spatial orientation is secondary,
creates a linear and unidimensional world in which human existence is
perceived as motion through space, which is cast as the past, present, and
future.[16] An orientation that favors time over space in which the world
is perceived in terms of progress based on forward motion naturally results in systems of hierarchy. Hierarchies of knowledge and life forms
(evolution; concepts of superiority and inferiority), for example, make it
possible for a paradigm of domination to become a guiding principle in a
society. The sacred is also perceived in terms of history; places are sacred
because of the events associated with them and contained within time.
For instance, for Christians, Jews, and Muslims, Deloria argues, particular sites in the Holy Land are sacred primarily because of their historical
significance more than a sense of rootedness in them, as is true in Native
American cultures.[17]

For Indigenous peoples, a spatial orientation emphasizes human
linkages with place, and all the elements of that place, spanning time.
These connections are reflected by and infused in all aspects of Native
life, including identity, culture, and ceremonial cycles, as people recognize themselves as having been placed there by spiritual forces to which
they are responsible. But this responsibility is a two-way street, and the
elements of those places are seen to be responsible to the people as well;
this reciprocal relationship forms a sense of kinship with the land itself.[18]
The emotional bonds of people to place reflects an egalitarianism that
does not distinguish hierarchies of importance, and as Tinker observes,
"humans lose their status of 'primacy' and 'dominion.' . . . American Indians are driven by their culture and spirituality to recognize the personhood of all 'things' in creation."[19] Said another way, for Indigenous people

land and all its elements have agency by virtue of their very life energy in a way that they do not in Western cultures. Humans are only part of the natural world, neither central to nor separate from it.

LEGAL INADEQUACIES, COALITION BUILDING, AND AMERICAN INDIAN EJ

The story of Panhe is a study of how, in the absence of federal protection, the laws of a state government (California) were used to protect an American Indian sacred site based on a combination of factors, and not primarily it being a Native sacred site. Yet while the salvation of Trestles was celebrated as the most significant achievement of stopping the toll road, in the big picture, few seemed to realize the importance of protecting Panhe still contributed to that victory. The comments of Commissioner Mary Schallenberger quoted above are telling for how an American Indian religious paradigm was fortunately able to seep into the awareness of a powerful government official and effect a positive outcome.[20] The Indigenous idea that recognizes agency in sacred places helps shift the balance of power that currently favors Eurocentric configurations of justice, which deny Indigenous spiritual realities and the rights of the Earth.

Yet despite existing legal EJ frameworks and laws to protect their religious freedoms, Native peoples continue to fight for the protection of sacred sites within an inadequate and often unjust system. During the period of forced assimilation, the US banned American Indians from practicing their traditional religions through a variety of rules and laws, notably the Indian Religious Crimes Code (also known as the Code of Indian Offenses, 1883), which imposed prison sentences and suspended rations for those caught leading or participating in Indigenous ceremonies.[21] More than half a century after Indians were granted citizenship, they finally received full protection for freedom of religion. In 1978 Congress passed the American Indian Religious Freedom Act (AIRFA) to officially outlaw government bans on American Indian religions. The law guarantees access to sacred sites but does not guarantee environmental integrity or the conditions necessary for religious practices in natural open spaces. US courts routinely deny Native legal appeals to protect lands where there are sacred sites, the precedent having been set in the Supreme Court case *Lyng v. Northwest Indian Cemetery Protective Association* (1988). In *Lyng* the court ruled that building a road through a site of traditional spiritual significance and ceremonial practice of three tribes in Northern California (Karuk, Tolowa, and Yurok) did not constitute a violation of their freedom of religion. The court argued that "the First Amendment bars only outright prohibitions, indirect coercion, and penalties on the free exercise of religion."[22] *Lyng* set a dangerous precedent that continues to haunt Native American battles to protect sacred sites. While AIRFA guarantees access to sacred sites, the *Lyng* decision illustrates why and how the Karuk, Tolowa, and Yurok tribes were unable to find protection for their sites based on the act. It comes down to differences in how religion is conceived in Western and Indigenous worldviews.

The high-profile case to protect the San Francisco Peaks perfectly illustrates how the legal system failed to recognize the significance of Native American spiritual beliefs and the desecration of a sacred site on publicly owned lands at the hands of powerful developers. The San Francisco Peaks in Arizona is sacred to at least thirteen tribal nations in the Four Corners region of the Southwest (upward of hundreds of thousands of individual Indians) for the way it figures into their creation stories and for the centrality of the mountain to the spiritual practices and other cultural activities of those people. In the 1970s the US Forest Service allowed the building of a ski resort, against the protests of the tribes who, based on their beliefs about the sanctity of the place, felt that the mountain should be protected from development. Then in the early 2000s the resulting Snowbowl Ski Resort applied for a permit to expand the resort and add snowmaking equipment that would utilize reclaimed sewage water. The tribes responded with a massive campaign and two lawsuits to oppose the permit, arguing that the use of treated effluent would pose significant health risks to all people, particularly those who still use the mountain to gather plants for medicine and other traditional practices. When the lawsuit came before the Ninth Circuit Court of Appeals in 2009, a narrow interpretation of the American Indian Religious Freedom Act again made the law unavailable to protect the land. The court claimed that the only effect of the proposed upgrades is on "the Plaintiffs' subjective, emotional religious experience. That is, the presence of recycled wastewater on the Peaks is offensive to the plaintiffs' religious sensibilities. . . . The diminishment of spiritual fulfillment—serious though it may be—is not a 'substantial burden' on the free exercise of religion."[23] Twice the Supreme Court declined to review the lower court's decision, and while the Obama administration had the power to intervene, it chose not to. The campaign to stop the development is still active despite its setbacks, but now focuses on technical legal maneuvers supporting claims that the Forest Service was negligent in disseminating appropriate information to the public regarding the potential health threats, effectively eliminating an argument based on religious or spiritual meaning.

The Save the Peaks campaign, like the campaign to protect Panhe, relied upon diverse coalitions of groups with similar objectives to accomplish their goals. In these campaigns, Native people find themselves aligned with groups who have often been their opponents, particularly in the environmentalist community, as we observed in chapter 5. In these cases the need for coalition building between environmentalists and Native peoples is clear, as was true in the Panhe struggle to preserve a particular place, even if for different reasons, facilitated relatively easy alliances. Professor of geography and Native studies Zoltán Grossman did an exhaustive two-decade-long study of unlikely alliances between Native peoples and otherwise unrelated—and sometimes antagonistic—groups across multiple regions of the US to show the effectiveness of this kind of organizing. In one of the most recent and visible examples of successful coalition building that Grossman covers, the ironically named Cowboy Indian Alliance (CIA) was instrumental in the stunning defeat of the Keystone XL Pipeline by the Obama administration in 2015. White ranchers and Native people had begun organizing informally in South Dakota as early as 1987, when they came together initially to oppose a gunnery range where the Honeywell Corporation would test depleted uranium-tipped munitions deep in the Black Hills country—the place of origin for the Lakota and the location of large cattle ranches that were already suffering economically. The Honeywell project was averted, and the alliance would not converge again until 2000 when it successfully blocked a coal-transporting railroad operation. The CIA moniker was revived a third time in 2013 after American Indians, First Nations people in Canada, and non-Native agricultural and environmental allies organized across international boundaries with the signing of a treaty to collectively oppose the southern leg of the Keystone XL Pipeline, which was designed to transport Alberta tar sands oil to American ports in the Gulf of Mexico. The pipeline would not only threaten the underground Ogallala Aquifer everybody depended on but also subject ranchers and farmers to land seizure through imminent domain laws. Recognizing the irony of the gathering, Chief Phil Lane poignantly remarked,

Those ranchers came in and spoke to that council, and they shared their heart. . . . So finally we came back after the treaty signing . . . we had about ten or fifteen ranchers there, they all got up to speak . . . and one after another they got up and said they're infuriated. They said . . . "How could this happen? How can people take our land? How can they do this to us?" And of course . . . we didn't see a smile but everybody knew what we was thinking about from our side. . . . So finally, this last sister got up to speak, and she just said, "I just am so infuriated, they're coming and taking our land . . . they just can't do it without our consent. . . . This is our land that our families have lived in since . . . you know, how long they have been there." And said, "They're treating us just like . . . just like . . . ," and then one of the relatives said, "Just like the Indians." And all of the [sic] sudden there was this beautiful pause and everybody's like, "Yes!" And one of my relatives walked over to her and says, "Welcome to the tribe, *welcome* to the tribe."[24]

Returning to Southern California, several years after the Panhe victory, a similar battle played out in Orange County in the wealthy coastal city of Newport Beach in October 2016—during the Standing Rock occupation. One of the last remaining beachfront open spaces in Southern California was slated for a massive development that included hundreds of upscale homes, a hotel, and shopping mall, but the proposed project was defeated due to the broad coalition building of multiple stakeholders, including environmentalists and tribal people. Referred to as Newport Banning Ranch, the land is an ancient dwelling place of Tongva and Acjachemen people, who know the site as Genga. In that case the Coastal Commission denied permits based on the protection of sensitive habitats and the preponderance of Native sacred sites. In its decision, three of the commissioners stressed the need for Native nations to be properly consulted (which hadn't been adequately done), and one noted that Standing Rock was a good example of why.[25]

As Native peoples have stressed decolonization as the appropriate path to social justice, coalition building continues to gather steam as one of the most effective decolonizing strategies for protecting sacred sites. Worldwide, Indigenous peoples are joining forces with each other and with non-Native peoples, fighting not only to stop endless expropriation of their lands by multinational forces driven by market fundamentalism but also to produce a paradigm shift that acknowledges their worldviews as a legitimate and necessary basis for understanding the world we all live in. Whether it's fighting the neoliberal structural adjustment programs of the International Monetary Fund, which aim to develop Indigenous lands with toxic industries in so-called developing nations; preventing the dumping of nuclear waste within a sacred mountain (Yucca Mountain); or simply guaranteeing access to a ceremonial ground, all together these battles constitute what Native activists regularly refer to as "environmental justice." Organizations like the Indigenous Environmental Network, Honor the Earth, Cultural Conservancy, Sustainable Nations Development Project, National Environmental Coalition of Native Americans, Seventh Generation Fund, and innumerable others, both within and beyond the United States, focus their efforts to build a web of ideas at the intersection of the concepts of sacred, environment, and justice.

Beth Rose Middleton, whose work examines Native Americans' use of land trusts and private conservation as a means to protect access to sacred sites, challenges the conventional understanding of environmental justice. She acknowledges the history of the land conservation movement in the US that has contributed to Native land dispossession, and that the "cultural foundations of the notion of conservation and public benefit must be interrogated,"[26] particularly since private conservation is hardly private, because it is subject to public statutes, funding, and incentives. She further argues that

> environmental justice is analytically important to private conservation, yet it remains under-discussed and under-utilized in the conservation field. As Mary Christina Wood and Zachary Welcker note, "by integrating humans into conserved landscapes, the tribal trust movement will draw attention to the role of land in the pursuit of social justice and human rights. This dimension has been much ignored by the conservation movement." An environmental justice analysis is essential for expanding conservation tools that have heretofore been used for relatively narrow conservation purposes.[27]

In other words, unless and until legal tools that restore Native peoples' access to ancestral places incorporate Indigenous conceptions of relationality to land in environmental justice projects, those policies will ultimately reproduce relationships of domination that continually hamstring tribal efforts to regain access to these sacred sites. These legal tools include whatever protocols tribes may utilize in the short term, be they conservation and land trusts and easements, environmental law, religious freedom protection, sacred lands inventories, archeological resource protection, and in the long term, whatever new forms we may in the future imagine for sacred site protection.

Environmental justice for Native peoples encompasses a broad spectrum of concerns, from protecting sensitive environmental habitats and communities from the ravages of toxic industries, to the assurance that lands deemed holy by them are still available for their uninterrupted ceremonial, spiritual, and cultural practices. Centering Native peoples in EJ frameworks holds the potential for legal protection that is meaningful and responsive to their specific histories, treaties, and spiritually based cultures. Had there been such a mechanism to which the Army Corps of Engineers and Energy Transfer Partners were accountable, it's not hard to imagine that there might have been a different outcome for the Standing Rock Sioux people. If such a mechanism existed in California law, the added layer of legal protection might have prevented the Transportation Corridor Agencies from designing a road alignment that threatened Panhe in the first place. As the cases examined in this chapter illustrate, despite their often-troubled histories with each other, and even though their relationships with each other are still far from conflict-free, Native and non-Native people nonetheless share connections to land that they each consider sacred, in albeit different ways. In the face of threats by corporate development and toxic infrastructure projects, the need to join forces has never been greater. What's obvious is that Indigenous resistance is increasingly a shared struggle, and that negotiating the tricky terrain of environmental justice frameworks that work for Native peoples' is challenging and demands coordinated responses in ever more creative and innovative ways.

CHAPTER EIGHT

Ways Forward for Environmental Justice in Indian Country

It may be true as Martin Luther King Jr. once said, that the arc of the moral universe is long but it bends towards justice. What is equally true, however, is that most of the time we have to forcibly bend it with our very own hands.

—THOMAS LINZEY, EXECUTIVE DIRECTOR, COMMUNITY ENVIRONMENTAL LEGAL DEFENSE FUND[1]

Throughout this book I have argued that for environmental justice to be responsive to the needs of Native peoples it must be indigenized—tailored to account for their very different histories, relationships to the land, and political relationships to the State. This indigenization must occur across all aspects of the EJ realm, from the halls of academia to policy framework building at the government level and to environmental activist organizing. I have argued, furthermore, that for this process to be effective it must confront both the foundation of white supremacy that inflects the social and legal landscape of the US and the ways white supremacy continues to obstruct those relationships. I have also pointed to ways various groups are navigating these rough waters to form workable, mutually beneficial partnerships. Expanding on this conversation, I close with a chapter highlighting positive trends, with examples of how indications of progressive change can nonetheless be seen, despite renewed threats to the environment and Indian country on the national front. We turn back to California for a view of how some of these changes are taking place.

The defeat of the 241 toll road in San Clemente was a significant victory for many reasons and people, but particularly for Southern California's Indian communities. In a place where the landscape has been dramatically altered in so short a period of time, land protection victories are few and far between. California's hyperdevelopment since the Gold Rush came at the greatest cost to California Indians. The state's prolific growth was built upon a tradition of ethnic cleansing that has been largely hidden from the public.

Perhaps nowhere is the pattern of Indigenous erasure more pronounced than in California's beach lifestyle and surf culture. Several years after the initial toll-road victory, the environmentalist organization Surfrider Foundation produced a short video recounting the successful Save Trestles campaign in an effort to block a renewed threat from developers. As the video showed, their campaign had focused entirely on saving the cobbled rocks responsible for Trestles' perfect waves and the extraordinary water quality of San Mateo Creek. The video makes no mention of the sacred site of Panhe or the critical role Native communities played in the Coastal Commission's denial of the permit.[2] In a few short years, the contributions and perspectives of the Indigenous activists whose efforts were essential to blocking the toll road were forgotten.

Considering the extent of Indigenous erasure in California, the Coastal Commission's decision to oppose a major infrastructure project on the grounds that it would have "unmitigatable" effects on sacred Native lands is all the more noteworthy. To some, it signaled a shifting tide in California's approach to working with tribal nations. More generally, it animated the possibility of a new beginning for the environmental community's relationship to Indigenous peoples and their specific needs within the movement.

The Coastal Commission's landmark decision fit within a growing trend of pro-Indian decision making in the state. In 2014 the California legislature passed Assembly Bill 52, which expands the California Environmental Quality Act review process to include a "traditional cultural resource" assessment for lead agencies that prepare certain environmental documents, in effect augmenting Senate Bill 18 of 2004, which provides limited protections for nonreservation lands and nonfederally recognized tribes through tribal consultation. Further, in 2012 the California Natural Resources Agency adopted a Tribal Consultation Policy in response to an executive order by Governor Jerry Brown, which explicitly signaled the government's intention to "encourage communication and consultation with California Indian Tribes."[3]

Native and non-Native groups fought and won a battle similar to the Save Trestles campaign against big corporate development in 2014, also in Orange County. Eight years after the successful protection of Panhe, the Coastal Commission denied a permit for the Newport Banning Ranch development at the traditional site of Genga in Newport Beach, in the shared ancestral territory of Tongva and Acjachemen people. The development would have crammed yet another upscale mall, a hotel and resort, and hundreds of homes for the wealthy on four hundred acres of the only remaining beachfront open space in the region. The efforts of the activist coalitions organizing against the developers were characterized by an increased level of attention and deeper respect for Native nation perspectives and paradigms. They heeded the wisdom of the Panhe fight and understood that stronger protection for traditional cultural resources was most effective in protecting land where numerous sacred sites were documented and worked favorably to restore a landscape that had also been damaged from decades of oil drilling.[4] Greater recognition of Native history and rights at the governmental level and more respectful, functional relationships between activist groups and American Indians at the community level is indicative of this larger productive trend in environmental protection efforts.[5] In the face of an intensifying climate change crisis, relentless land development, and ongoing consolidation of power in the fossil fuel industry, it may well be that organizing around Native land rights holds the key to successfully transitioning from a fossil-fuel energy infrastructure to one based on sustainable energy. This paradigm shift would bring environmental justice closer to Indigenous peoples and other vulnerable communities in the United States.

However, as we have seen, the imperialist roots of federal Indian law present daunting obstacles to justice for American Indians. If American Indians are to experience real environmental justice—which means not only ending the poisoning of their environments but also regaining access to and protection of their sacred sites and ancient territories—it means confronting a "state built on the pillars of capitalism, colonialism, and white supremacy."[6] The confrontation must occur at all levels, from the individual to the institutional, and ultimately dismantle the legal, social, and policy frameworks that uphold an ongoing system of domination. Indigenizing environmental justice in these ways goes beyond a distributive model of justice.

Dismantling the mechanisms of domination—or decolonization—as the path to environmental justice for Indian country is admittedly a gargantuan and idealistic task. It's probably even unthinkable to many in positions of power. The barriers are formidable, given the depth and breadth of American prejudice against Indigenous peoples. Tribal sovereignty theoretically means that tribal nations are the third sovereign power in the US, alongside federal and state. And although federal law acknowledges the inherent sovereignty of Native nations through centuries of treaty relationships and often works in partnership with them through shared power, it is nonetheless a restricted form of sovereignty animated by imperialist legal foundations: the doctrine of discovery, domestic dependent nationhood, and the plenary power doctrine. These doctrines control Native peoples' lives and resources via intense regulation by the United States Bureau of Indian Affairs, meaning that Native people are more legally managed than all other people in the country, and arguably unconstitutionally contrary to the original treaty-based relationships. These are all constituent parts of what constructs the US domination-based legal paradigm.

The domination paradigm is continually supported by people invested in maintaining power across a broad spectrum of American political interests that keep tribal governments disempowered. At the state level, vociferous grassroots antitribal sovereignty movements still work endlessly to extinguish what limited sovereignty the US legal system recognizes. For example, in Washington State the group Citizens Equal Rights Alliance (CERA)—also known as the "Ku Klux Klan of Indian country"—has led a decades-long campaign to end tribal treaty rights. The group Stand Up California actively opposes tribal gaming and led the unsuccessful fight against the Federated Indians of the Graton Rancheria's casino. In recent years conservative religious groups, including the Goldwater Institute in Arizona, work to undermine the Indian Child Welfare Act, a law passed in 1978 to stop the systematic and widespread removal of Indian children from their homes and tribal cultures.

At the federal level the strength of tribal sovereignty is subject to the ideological leanings of whoever happens to be in power. When all three branches of government—executive, legislative, and judicial—are stacked with conservatives, we see significant threats not only to tribes but also to issues tribes and environmentalists alike care about.[7] In the

Trump administration and Republican-ruled Congress, the antienvironmental sentiment is rampant. In fewer than two years they granted the final permit for the Dakota Access Pipeline, approved the Keystone XL Pipeline, eviscerated the EPA and overturned dozens of environmental protection laws, shrank Bears Ears National Monument by 90 percent, and scrubbed mention of climate change from all government websites, including the US Federal Emergency Management Agency's (FEMA) strategic plan and the list of national security threats. In January 2018 the administration's Department of the Interior drafted the largest-ever proposal for offshore oil and gas lease auctions. And this is just the beginning. In early 2018 the *New York Times* identified no fewer than sixty-seven environmental rules the administration rolled back in deference to the fossil fuel industry.[8]

In a neoliberal, market-fundamentalist world, a federal government controlled by conservatives has historically meant deregulation and the prioritization of industry over the protection of the environment. For Native communities, conservative governments also represent a particular threat of new forms of termination or other tactics to gut tribal sovereignty while dressed up in the language of liberation and improvement as it was in the 1950s.[9] As we have seen, in times of extreme political hostility, tribal governments must remain vigilant and assert what political power they do have.

RESILIENCY IN ACTION

We have seen how constructive alliance building is crucial in activist movements to protect against cannibalistic and predatory development. Sometimes coalitions are ephemeral, forming as the need arises and disbanding as campaigns for environmental justice are won and lost. Others involve increasingly radical partnership with local communities to form private land trusts and conservation easements. When tribal governments can, they purchase back ancestral lands, and if they are federally recognized, they usually have the lands transferred from fee simple to trust status, incorporating them into existing reservations.

In other cases, alternative land arrangements maintain or facilitate regaining access to dispossessed ancestral lands. As Beth Rose Middleton's study of land trusts notes, private land trusts are growing at a rate far faster than parks, preserves, wilderness areas, and other methods of public conservation.[10] Organized as nonprofits, land trusts are used not only to conserve "wilderness" areas but also to ensure open spaces for human use. The Trust for Public Lands is one such organization that specializes in creating parks close to urban areas. It also has a Tribal and Native Lands Program that has worked with more than seventy tribes to protect more than two hundred thousand acres of ancestral land in cases where tribes are unable to acquire land in trust.[11] Land trusts are often led by tribal groups—some federally recognized tribes, some not—and perhaps not surprising, are frequently found in California.

One well-known example, the Native American Land Conservancy (NALC), was initially formed in 1997 by Chemehuevi and Cahuilla tribal members to protect the Old Woman Mountains, a site considered sacred by Colorado River tribes in the Mojave Desert two hundred twenty miles east of Los Angeles.

As is the case with NALC, some conservancies and land partnerships focus on employing traditional ecological knowledge to restore damaged ecosystems. Some, like the Maidu Summit Consortium, work within formal agreements with state and federal agencies. Though the Mountain Maidu groups are not federally recognized, tribal members organized the consortium, partnering with various institutions like the US Forest Service, California Department of Fish and Wildlife, and numerous other environmental groups, land trusts, and grassroots organizations to protect and rehabilitate 2,325 acres of the Humbug Valley in the Sierra Nevada through traditional management practices.[12]

Tribes work with governments in other ways to preserve access to ancestral lands out of tribal control. Since the 1990s tribes have partnered with governments at all levels in collaborative land and watershed management arrangements in projects to assure access to and revitalization of cultural resources like salmon and other fisheries, caribou, and other wild game and resources. Increasingly these collaborations incorporate traditional methods of ecological management and knowledge with conventional sustainability sciences to maintain or restore ecological integrity, but also to retain sites based on their religious significance.[13] The recent controversy over the Bears Ears National Monument in Utah is an ideal example of a site where tribes came together with the

environmental movement and federal government in a productive, collaborative arrangement.

Bears Ears is a region of profound sanctity to numerous tribes in the
Southwest's Colorado Plateau, which, as we have seen, has a history of
being exploited for intense mineral and fossil fuel extraction. In 2016,
tribes worked with the federal government during the last days of the
Obama administration to place more than a million acres of spiritually,
archeologically, and environmentally sensitive lands in monument status under the 1906 Antiquities Act. The monument designation would
provide strong protections for places where uranium and oil rich areas
are likely to come under siege by extractive industries. The Bears Ears
Intertribal Coalition consisted of the Navajo, Hopi, Zuni, Ute Mountain,
and Ute Indian Tribe, with the support of at least twenty-five other tribal
nations and conservation organizations. Together they worked with the
administration to create an advisory commission to ensure that tribes
with ancient ties to the land would have a voice in how the land is used.
Other notable examples of tribes working cooperatively with the federal government to establish national monuments include Canyon de
Chelly and Navajo National Monument, which are within Navajo Nation
boundaries in Arizona, but Bears Ears was significant for the intertribal
coalition and advisory arrangement in addition to the sheer size of the
monument.

However, the conservative Utah opposition argued that the land
should remain in state control, wrongfully claiming that previously allowed public use of the land would be restricted under the new federal
designation. When Republicans secured control of both the executive
and legislative branches of government in 2017, the stage was set for the
monument shrinking by at least 85 percent under secretary of the interior Ryan Zinke, who was acting on a Trump campaign promise. Not
long after the decision was made to roll back protections for Bears Ears,
the *Washington Post* broke a story that Energy Fuels Resources (USA),
a uranium processing company, had lobbied the administration for the
monument shrinkage from January until September of 2017, despite numerous public claims by the administration that the plan was unrelated
to energy or mining.[14] Lawsuits were immediately filed against various
agencies of the Trump administration (including Trump himself; Ryan

Zinke, secretary of the Department of the Interior; and others), challenging the legality of the move to eviscerate the monument, and as of this writing the complaints are still in litigation. The continuing Bears Ears saga stands as an example not only of how ideological differences between conservatives and liberals play out in environmental policy but also of the fragility of laws and other policy frameworks that determine what happens to ancestral Indian lands due to the fickleness of the US political system.

RIGHTS OF NATURE AND COMMUNITY RIGHTS

After decades of fighting losing battles against pollutive and damaging resource extraction projects, communities have needed to pursue alternative routes to environmental protection. Following successes abroad, the movement to recognize the rights of nature, and a related undertaking known as the Community Rights movement, is proliferating. Both movements acknowledge the need to transform legal approaches that inevitably favor the neoliberal global economy at the expense of ecosystems.

Since 2008, the rights of nature (RON) approach has helped activists in Ecuador, Bolivia, India, and New Zealand imbue nature with legal rights in much the same way American courts have given rights to corporations. These laws have been instrumental in protecting ecosystems inherent in natural landscapes like mountains and rivers. Ecuador in 2008 and Bolivia in 2009 went so far as to rewrite their national constitutions to include RON in their legal frameworks. This new language is based on Indigenous worldviews rooted in right relationship with nature and *buen vivir*, the good life. New Zealand (known as Aotearoa to the Maori, who are the Indigenous people of New Zealand) did not amend their constitution but instituted other legal mechanisms to grant personhood to the Whanganui River and Te Urewera National Parks in 2013. Following the Aotearoa example, in 2017 India granted personhood to the Ganges and Yamuna rivers.

Legal personhood means that these natural entities have the same rights as humans under national law and that humans can represent nature in the courts. As a result, tribal nations in the United States are beginning to institute rights of nature laws in their communities. In 2016 the Ho Chunk nation in Wisconsin began amending their constitution with the mission of "giving legal standing to nature" and denying the legal personhood of any corporation or business entity that violates the law.[15] The following year the Ponca Nation of Oklahoma, nicknamed "Earthquake Capital of the world" as a result of pervasive fracking, incorporated RON as a statute in their tribal legal code.[16]

Creating RON statutes and constitutional amendments is a way for tribal governments to codify customary law into Western-style governance mechanisms in accordance with federal Indian law. The Ponca statute, for example, acknowledges this when it claims:

> We believe that Ponca Law has always recognized Right [sic] of Nature, and therefore we resolve that the following shall be immediately recorded as the customary law of the Ponca Tribe, existing since time immemorium until the end of all days.[17]

The statute then lays out a list of articles clarifying what those rights are and the penalties for violating those rights, and further characterizing those violations as misdemeanors or felonies. Even outside the RON framework, the incorporation of customary law into formal governing mechanisms transforms traditional cultural protocols into enforceable law, enabling the protection of biodiversity and important cultural resources like plant and animal-based medicines.[18]

While tribal sovereignty can, to an extent, enable tribal communities to protect themselves from unwanted corporate encroachments that compromise the environment within their boundaries, the demonstrations at Standing Rock showed that those boundaries are sometimes contested. Furthermore, beyond currently recognized boundaries there is little tribal sovereignty can do to stop projects that will affect both Indigenous and non-Indigenous communities alike. RON laws are still so new in the United States that they haven't been thoroughly tested in the courts. Questions remain about whether they can be applied extrajudicially; that is, outside jurisdictions that enact them, such as Indian reservations.[19] Relative to nontribal RON, a test-case lawsuit in the state of Colorado seeking personhood for the Colorado River was rendered incomplete in December 2017 when the attorney representing the case was threatened with sanctions and subsequently withdrew.[20]

In the US more than three dozen municipalities have since 2006 enacted RON laws. But often, local communities who attempt to resist fracking, GMO farming, pipelines, and other environmentally offensive and health-threatening practices or attempt to institute RON laws find themselves preempted by state laws, private property laws, regulatory regimes, and corporate privilege. Both elected and appointed government officials fail to protect communities—small municipalities are sued by megacorporations for passing bans against polluting industries, and environmental lawyers are increasingly sanctioned by judges and attorneys general. Despite these challenges, the movement to strengthen community rights is building, led by organizations like Community Environmental Legal Defense Fund (CELDF), National Community Rights Network, and Movement Rights, which specializes in Indigenous issues. Through the creation of formal community rights networks (CRNs), these organizations help communities to exercise self-governance by passing community bills of rights and working toward state and federal constitutional amendments that empower local self-governance. CRNs in Colorado, Hawaii, New Hampshire, Ohio, Oregon, Pennsylvania, and Washington are taking a long-term approach to changing the status quo through various amendments to their state constitutions that would end state preemption and challenge the primacy of corporate "rights." So far, no state has successfully passed one of these amendments, but in early 2018 New Hampshire became the first state to consider a community rights amendment. Bill CACR19, the New Hampshire Community Rights Amendment, was debated in the House with fully one-third support of legislators, which is seen by CELDF as "signifying the growing support for Community Rights that is building across the U.S."[21] Given this is CACR19's first pass through the New Hampshire legislature, its eventual success is not difficult to imagine. Strengthening community self-determination then opens a wider path to enforceable rights of nature laws, since community rights include environmental rights, such as the right to clean air and water. Greater self-determination and the freedom from preemption mean greater latitude to pass regulations that protect communities from toxic industries. As a bottom-up phenomenon, community rights start at the local level and move to the state and national levels. Until states begin enacting community rights amendments, municipalities and other local jurisdictions will continue to pass community rights ordinances and rights of nature laws to assert community self-determination and self-governance in defiance of the legal status quo.

The community rights movement holds promise for all kinds of populations facing exposure to toxic or otherwise undesirable development projects without their consent—especially for those communities that have traditionally sought environmental justice: people of color and low-income communities. For reservation populations RON legislation is integral to self-determination and collective rights and provides the opportunity to codify customary law and Indigenous worldviews of relationality to the natural world into more formal westernized governance mechanisms. Smaller reservations and rancherias will benefit from the community rights organizing done in nearby areas beyond their control, so long as non-Native activists are conscientious in reaching out to their Indigenous neighbors by acknowledging their histories and doing the work of respectful coalition building.

OTHER PATHWAYS TO INDIGENOUS ENVIRONMENTAL JUSTICE

Achieving true environmental justice in Indian country must ultimately engage a wide variety of strategies, from creative organizing and functional partnerships at the community level to formal organizing initiatives and evolving environmental justice policies at the local, state, federal, and international levels that respond to American Indians' specific histories, legal statuses, and assertions of sovereignty. As the framework of settler colonialism gains traction and becomes more widely understood and accepted in activist movements and governmental institutions there will be more opportunities for honest community dialogue and decolonizing action.

These conversations are gradually taking place. In one especially interesting example, members of a non-Native community in the original homelands of the Karuk, Yurok, Shasta, and Konomihu peoples in Northern California began a movement to consciously decolonize the region. They started a public conversation about how to change their relationship with the Native community by changing their relationship with the land. Created in 2014, the Unsettling Klamath River (UKR) project began with a small group of white activists led by Laura Hurwitz, who was working on a master's thesis that interrogated the area's history of settler colonialism and issues of white settler responsibility. The study focused on "back-to-the-landers"—the counterculture settlers who migrated to the area and built a cannabis industry that has led to skyrocketing land values and profound ecological impacts that further alienated Indigenous peoples from their homelands in the last half century. Hurwitz, herself a white settler, posed the question "Back to whose land?" The study was inspired by Unsettling Minnesota, a project begun in 2009 by Dakota and non-Dakota activists with a ten-week class titled "Dakota Decolonization: Solidarity Education for Allies," and Unsettling America, a decentralized network of autonomous groups and individuals committed to "mental and territorial decolonization throughout Turtle Island and the 'Americas.'"[22]

UKR identified several different portals, or openings, through which white settlers continued flooding into the area, among them nonprofit internships, AmeriCorps programs, the cannabis economy, and Black Bear Ranch, which is a commune established as a land trust in 1968 under the moniker "Free land for free people."

UKR's organizers raised tough questions about closing the portals and tearing down fences that blocked access to Indigenous sacred sites and other cultural resources, and it conducted public meetings to educate the community about decolonization. One of their most essential tasks was to brainstorm ways to repatriate land, including bringing Native people into the land trust, creating housing for some Indigenous families, and creating a support network. Reactions to talk of decolonizing ranged from curiosity and openness to hostility and rage. Some claimed to have "saved" the area due to their land stewardship and environmental activism, asserting that their presence prevented logging, pesticide spraying, and other environmental ills, playing into what Hurwitz identified as a white savior narrative. Relationships were strained and broken, especially at Black Bear Ranch. Hurwitz analyzed these responses as settler fragility and described debates about whether the unsettling movement should try to avoid making people "uncomfortable." Hurwitz's own opinion was that while it wasn't the goal to hurt loved ones, discomfort with the topic of decolonization is unavoidable and should be directly confronted.[23]

While the Unsettling Klamath River project is a work in progress and has yet to accomplish any measurable decolonizing action, it did start a powerful conversation—one that could potentially be replicated in other contexts. In this regard, it succeeded in metaphorically unsettling the settler population by blowing the lid off myriad unspoken assumptions about what it means to "go back" to a land that was stolen to begin with, and it exposed the ways in which even the most progressive and antiestablishment of countercultures are rooted in white supremacy and settler privilege. By attempting to dismantle the structures of settler society, the conversation started by UKR revealed that it is not a matter of liberal versus conservative ideology but about challenging the foundation of a country built on genocide, slavery, and private property.

At the state and local level, new strategies are being implemented to accomplish protection of sacred sites, and as the examples of Panhe and Genga illustrate, California is a leader in these approaches. In the East San Francisco Bay Area in 2011, a type of burial site known as a shellmound was threatened by the proposed building of a waterfront park on public land. It was ultimately protected through the efforts of the Yocha Dehe and Cortina Bands of Wintun Indians, who entered into a conservation and cultural easement agreement with the city of Vallejo to protect the site, known today by its traditional name Sogorea Te (also known as Glen Cove), setting a precedent and providing a blueprint for future arrangements of this kind, under California SB 18. For the first time, a tribe's case for protecting a sacred site was bolstered by invoking the United Nations Declaration on the Rights of Indigenous Peoples (UNDRIP).[24]

In another promising development, in 2016 the California legislature passed AB 2616, charging the Coastal Commission with the responsibility to incorporate an environmental justice policy framework into its mandate to protect the coast and coastal access. At the time of this writing, the commission is consulting with California tribal people about what environmental justice means specifically for them. At the same time, the commission is also developing a Tribal Consultation Policy to more clearly articulate and improve communications between tribes and the commission in "its mission to protect, maintain, and where feasible, enhance and restore the resources of California's coast and ocean for present and future generations," acknowledging Indigenous traditional knowledge as essential to sustainable coastline management.[25] After circulating the Draft Tribal Consultation Policy, the commission solicited comments from tribes and individuals up and down the state, asking for their insights and contributions. In March 2018 the commission issued Form W6d, a twenty-four-page compilation of comments it had received to that point, annotated with the commission staff's initial responses to the comments. Comments ran the gamut from suggesting relatively small changes in language to advocating for the commission to endorse broad Indigenous rights concepts, including UNDRIP, which the staff agreed with. The commission's addition of two full paragraphs recognizing California's colonial and genocidal history was a direct result of that feedback. Assuming the final tribal consultation and environmental justice policies include these principles and language, it will represent a considerable step forward in governmental accountability to Indigenous peoples, going much farther than the EPA's *Plan EJ 2014* reforms and helping to reverse the pattern of California Indian erasure at the governmental level.

Yet, significant hurdles remain. Still to be resolved is the tension between consultation and consent at all levels of government. What does meaningful consultation look like? And what powers of recourse do tribal nations possess when insurmountable obstacles present themselves in the consultation process, especially for nonfederally recognized tribes? The highest standard for relationships between Indigenous peoples and State governments enshrined in UNDRIP is the right to free, prior, and informed consent, not just consultation. So, if local, state, and federal governments legislate the minimal principles of tribal consultation and simultaneously endorse UNDRIP with its superior principles of free, prior, and informed consent, which values take precedence? These are questions that have not been adequately addressed in the US. As the example of Standing Rock made plain, too often the domination paradigm is the default response. Tribal rights, even those circumscribed by domestic law, are often dismissed or ignored. This leads to an even greater question: What can tribal nations realistically do in the face of a legal game that is rigged against them?

Karla General, an attorney formerly at the Indian Law Resource Center, has recommended strategies to help bring federal law into compliance with UNDRIP. First, tribes and non-Native advocates can call on presidents to strengthen Executive Order 13175, Consultation and Coordination with Indian Tribal Governments, to provide for free, prior, and informed consent as the highest standard of consultation, which is the established guideline in the UN declaration and other human rights law obligations, such as International Labor Organization (ILO) 169.[26] This measure would also require that the US support United Nations efforts to pass protocols to implement and monitor states' compliance with UN-DRIP, as none currently exist.[27] Additionally, the US should be pressured by both internal and external parties to comply with international agreements specific to environmental issues, including Indigenous protection clauses like those contained in the *Convention on Biological Diversity* and the *Rome Declaration* (2009).

Second, relative to protecting sacred sites, tribal governments should call on Congress to amend the American Indian Religious Freedom Act to explicitly provide for the protection of sacred places, not just access to them.[28]

Another potent strategy within the power of tribal governments is to continue building intergovernmental relationships at all levels. In addition to the plethora of examples of intergovernmental cooperation we have explored, tribal governments regularly institute agreements with local governing entities, such as cross-deputation of law enforcement officers across jurisdictions. In cases when tribes have incorporated customary law and protocols based on tribal values of relatedness to the natural world into formal legal mechanisms, enforceable environmental protections expand to include non-Native people when intergovernmental arrangements are made with neighboring jurisdictions.[29]

Finally, Executive Order 12898 and the EPA's official definition of environmental justice should be amended to include language that acknowledges the historic, political, and cultural differences of Native peoples, acknowledges Indigenous worldviews, protects sacred sites, and admits the US's history of colonization and genocide, as the California Coastal Commission's Tribal Consultation and EJ policies did. Indigenizing EJ definitions in these ways would go a long way toward meaningful accountability and decolonizing the relationship between Native people and the United States.

As its history with American Indians has shown, the US complies with laws it makes or agrees to only haphazardly at best, and often not at all. Indians have always had to fight to defend their lives, lands, and treaties. Resistance became a way of life a long time ago; only the tactics change. The federal government has never relinquished power over Native people without a fight, and the degree to which it has is directly attributable to work initiated by Native people themselves. In other words, more than any "granting" of rights by the United States, it is their bold assertions of self-determination, aided at times by powerful allies, that accounts for progress Native people have made in their relationships with the United States over the last century. Indigenous peoples have learned that no one is coming to save them, just as environmentalists have learned that their American legal system is a rigged game against the environment and their own communities. This is a pattern engrained by the forces of white settler colonialism and domination paradigms, but the growing sophistication in using education, law, and politics to advance tribal self-determination will continue to build a wall of defense against environmentally destructive corporate and government encroachments. There is no denying that the fossil fuel industry as we once knew it is dying. Even as its government puppets desperately grasp to hold on to power as the final drops of oil and gas are sucked from the Earth, the last chunks of coal are wrenched from the ground, and the nuclear industry continues to perpetuate the lie of its comparable cleanness, effective partnerships with allies in the environmental movement will provide the best defense for the collective well-being of the environment and future generations of all Americans, Native and non-Native alike. In the long run, environmental justice for American Indians is environmental justice for everyone . . . and for the Earth herself.

Acknowledgments

In the journey of life there are often many roads to one destination, especially when it comes to learning and knowledge production. This is true of my experience as a scholar and writer. This book is borne from my circuitous route through higher education and the world of community-engaged Indigenous research and activism as I have struggled to link what I have often experienced as seemingly disparate worlds. When life has thrown curveballs, I have learned to adapt and use changing circumstances to my advantage, and it has taken me to unexpected places.

I was approached by my editors at Beacon Press, Gayatri Patnaik and Will Myers, with the idea to write this book soon after the publication of my first book, coauthored with Roxanne Dunbar-Ortiz, *"All the Real Indians Died Off" and 20 Other Myths About Native Americans*. Roxanne and I were in the middle of a national book tour, and the book was enjoying great reviews and sales. At that time, November 2016, the standoff at Standing Rock was in full swing, and I had spent Thanksgiving weekend traveling there with an assignment from Indian Country Today Media Network (ICTMN). We had also just experienced the national tragedy of the election of Donald Trump, which portended an ominous future in the fight to stop the Dakota Access Pipeline and for the entire planet, given the pro-fossil-fuel and climate-change-denying ideologies of Trump and his ilk. Gayatri and Will decided the time was ripe for Beacon to produce a book on Indigenous environmental justice, especially considering a relative scarcity of books on the topic.

It was a perfect project for me, because I had spent the last several years writing about it, all through graduate school and after receiving my master's degree, and as I pursued a career as a researcher and a journalist in Native media. I had intended to pursue a PhD but changed my mind for a variety of reasons (those pesky curveballs), including a move back to coastal Southern California, the place of my birth. After graduating in 2011, I was recruited by the Center for World Indigenous Studies, where for several years I worked on many different projects related to advancing Indigenous self-determination, both domestically and internationally, and have written news stories and a column for ICTMN.

My master's thesis was based on a case study of Panhe and its role in the 241 toll road and "saving Trestles" controversy. In the thesis, I argued that the field of environmental justice as it existed in the United States was inadequate for Indigenous peoples, and it needed to be "Indigenized" to fit their unique circumstances. The day I orally defended the thesis, after a short deliberation, my committee advisors returned to the room and informed me that it passed (with distinction), but only under one condition: that I promise to continue doing this work. This book is thus the fulfillment of that promise. While I decided against pursuing a doctorate, I have nevertheless continued my research and writing on the topic of Indigenous environmental justice and branched out into other areas to pioneer related topics, such as understanding the relationship of surf culture to settler colonialism, which I hope will be the subject of a future book.

This book stems from and builds on my master's thesis research project. I like to think that it is one possible version of what a PhD dissertation might have looked like, had I gone down that road. In that sense then, the book you hold in your hands represents an alternative road that led to one of the inevitable destinations on my life's journey: a contribution to the literature on Indigenous environmental justice. I would like to thank my committee advisors at the University of New Mexico, Alyosha Goldstein, Lloyd Lee, and David Correia, who oversaw my initial work on this project. Thanks to the entire faculty of Native American Studies at UNM, especially Tiffany Lee, who encouraged me as a writer, and Gregory Cajete, who helped mentor me and whose brilliant work I teach at California State University at San Marcos; and thanks to Joely Proudfit, whose faith in my work brought me there. Thanks to Lydia Heberling and Christina Juhasz-Wood for reading and critiquing early chapter drafts. Gratitude to my old friend Pennie Opal Plant for her tireless work on Indigenous environmental justice issues and to her husband, also an old friend, Michael Horse for generously giving of his artistic talent for the cover of this book. Thank you, Roxanne Dunbar-Ortiz and Gayatri Patnaik, for bringing me into the Beacon Press family, and Will Myers for your editorial excellence, and to Joanna Green for stepping into Will's place. I would like to acknowledge Rebecca Robles and Angela Mooney D'Arcy of the United Coalition to Protect Panhe for your undying devotion to Panhe and for your support. *Muchas gracias* to Rudy Ryser and Leslie Korn at the Center for World Indigenous Studies for always believing in me and for your inspiration. And finally, thank you, TW, for your ongoing support and love, without which this would have been much more difficult.

Notes

INTRODUCTION: THE STANDING ROCK SAGA

1. "Official Red Warrior Camp Communique," December 15, 2016, https://redpowermedia.wordpress.com/tag/red-warrior-camp.

2. "Where Are Liquids Pipelines Located?," Pipeline 101, source of information given as American Energy Mapping, 2013, http://www.pipeline101.com/where-are-pipelines-located.

3. "Pipelines Explained: How Safe Are America's 2.5 Million Miles of Pipelines?" ProPublica, November 15, 2012 (updated December 6, 2016), https://www.propublica.org/article/pipelines-explained-how-safe-are-americas-2.5-million-miles-of-pipelines.

4. Philip Wight, "Down the Line: Exploring the Environmental History of Pipelines," January 23, 2017. Excerpted from his PhD dissertation in process, "Arctic Artery: An Environmental History of the Trans-Alaska Pipeline System, 1945–2012," Brandeis University, http://niche-canada.org/2017/01/23/down-the-line-exploring-the-environmental-history-of-pipelines.

5. The #NoDAPL movement is only one part of the story of the Dakota Access Pipeline and exists within the context of the Standing Rock Sioux Tribe's legal battle to prevent its construction on tribal treaty territory. It's an extremely complex story that does not need to be told in its entirety here. For this reason, only aspects of it that are relevant to Indigenous resistance more broadly will be recounted in this book.

6. Amy Dalrymple, "Audio: Tribe Objected to Pipeline Nearly 2 Years Before Lawsuit," *Bismarck Tribune*, November 30, 2016, http://bismarcktribune.com/news/state-and-regional/audio-tribe-objected-to-pipeline-nearly-years-before-lawsuit/article_51f94b8b-1284-5da9-92ec-7638347fe066.html.

7. Amy Dalrymple, "Pipeline Route Plan First Called for Crossing North of Bismarck," *Bismarck Tribune*, August 18, 2016, http://bismarcktribune.com/news/state-and-regional/pipeline-route-plan-first-called-for-crossing-north-of-bismarck/article_64d053e4-8a1a-5198-a1dd-498d386c933c.html.

8. Standing Rock Sioux Tribe v. US Army Corps of Engineers, Complaint for Declaratory and Injunctive Relief, filed July 27, 2016, at Earthjustice.org, http://earthjustice.org/sites/default/files/files/3154%201%20Complaint.pdf.

9. Sarah Sunshine Manning, "And Then the Dogs Came," *This Week from Indian Country Today*, Fall 2016, 14. https://ictmn.lughstudio.com/wp-content /uploads/2016/10/DAPL-Magazine-2016_PREVIEW_r1.pdf.

10. NYC Stands with Standing Rock, Standing Rock Syllabus, "Timeline of United States Settler Colonialism," 2016, https://nycstandswithstandingrock .wordpress.com/standingrocksyllabus.

11. Estes, "Fighting for Our Lives."

12. The permitting process to acquire the necessary easements through which the pipeline could cross was incremental and known as a "nationwide permit." By the time construction had reached the edge of Lake Oahe, the final easement hadn't yet been granted. The incremental strategy meant that the company could get away with less environmental regulation. The easements required environmental assessments, not a full environmental impact statement (EIS), per the National Environmental Protection Act. SRST believed that a full EIS should have been performed within treaty territorial boundaries, which would have meant compliance with more stringent laws regarding sacred site protection and tribal consultation.

13. To the naked eye, the region where the pipeline was designed to go appears as a desolate, deserted landscape, but in reality it was a significant place of ceremony and prayer. A Lakota archeologist on August 29 revealed it to be an ancient burial site, which was completely missed by the North Dakota State Historic Preservation Office, which was involved with the initial environmental assessment. Upon the discovery, and seeing the construction path headed directly toward the site, but still miles away, SRST on September 2 filed an immediate injunction to halt construction. The following day— the day of the dog attacks—the company's construction equipment showed up and bulldozed the site in what appeared to be a "willful act of treason to North Dakota preservation laws" and deliberate desecration of a burial site. Dave Archambault Sr., "Sacred Grounds Destroyed," *This Week from Indian Country Today* (Fall 2016): 16, https://ictmn.lughstudio.com/wp-content /uploads/2016/10/DAPL-Magazine-2016_PREVIEW_r1.pdf.

14. On September 9, 2016, only moments after a federal judge denied granting a temporary injunction to halt construction, the Departments of the Army, Interior, and Justice issued a joint statement that the Army Corps would not authorize construction pending a review of current laws, statutes, and practices for infrastructure projects like DAPL, and they requested the company voluntarily stop construction.

15. ICTMN staff, "Breaking: Dakota Access Lake Oahe Work Stopped Pending Standing Rock Sioux Appeal," Indian Country Media Network, September 17, 2016, https://indiancountrymedianetwork.com/news/politics/breaking -dakota-access-lake-oahe-work-stopped-pending-standing-rock-sioux-appeal.

16. "Timeline of Events," Earthjustice, latest update August 31, 2018, http:// earthjustice.org/features/faq-standing-rock-litigation.

17. In July of 2018 Lakota People's Law Project announced that the North Dakota attorney general's office determined that the Dakota Access Pipeline never legally acquired title to the ranchland that water protectors were camped on, effectively nullifying the many trespassing charges that had been brought against the water protectors.

18. Indigenous Environmental Network, "Citing 1851 Treaty, Water Protectors Establish Road Blockade and Expand Frontline #NoDAPL Camp," Indian Country Media Network, October 24, 2016, https://indiancountry medianetwork.com/news/native-news/citing-1851-treaty-water-protectors -establish-road-blockade-and-expand-frontline-nodapl-camp.

19. Theresa Braine, "Conflicting Accounts Emerge After Treaty Camp Police Action," Indian Country Media Network, October 28, 2016, https:// indiancountrymedianetwork.com/news/native-news/conflicting-accounts -emerge-after-treaty-camp-police-action.

20. "Police and Military Attack Oceti Sakowin Treaty Camp," *Unicorn Riot*, October 27, 2016, http://www.unicornriot.ninja/?p=10476.

21. Steve Russell, "Patriots Acquitted in Malheur as DAPK Water Protectors Get Maced," Indian Country Media Network, October 28, 2016, https://indiancountrymedianetwork.com/news/native-news/patriots -acquitted-in-malheur-as-dapl-water-protectors-get-maced.

22. "Standing Rock: 100+ Injured After Police Attack with Water Cannons, Rubber Bullets and Mace," *Democracy Now*, November 21, 2016, https://www.democracynow.org/2016/11/21/headlines/standing_rock _100_injured_after_police_attack_with_water_cannons_rubber_bullets _mace.

23. Christine Hauser, "Obama Says Alternate Routes Are Being Reviewed for Dakota Pipeline," *New York Times*, November 2, 2016, https://www.nytimes.com/2016/11/03/us/president-obama-says-engineers -considering-alternate-route-for-dakota-pipeline.html.

24. Harper Neidig, "Clinton Campaign Urges Both Sides in Dakota Protests to Work Out Solution," *The Hill* (blog), October 27 2016, https:// thehill.com/blogs/blog-briefing-room/news/303211-clinton-campaign-urges -both-sides-in-dakota-protests-to-work.

25. Lauren McCauley, "'What a Crock': Clinton Breaks DAPL Silence with Statement That Says 'Literally Nothing,'" *Common Dreams*, October 28, 2016, http://www.commondreams.org/news/2016/10/28/what-crock-clinton-breaks -dapl-silence-statement-says-literally-nothing.

26. "CEO Confident Dakota Access Pipeline Will Be Completed Under Trump Presidency," CBS News, November 11, 2016, http://www.cbsnews .com/news/dakota-access-pipeline-energy-transfer-partners-ceo-kelcy-warren -breaks-silence.

27. Caroline Kenny, Gregory Krieg, Sara Sidner, and Max Blau, "Dakota Access Pipeline to Be Rerouted," CNN, December 5, 2016, http://www.cbsnews

.com/news/dakota-access-pipeline-energy-transfer-partners-ceo-kelcy-warren
-breaks-silence.

28. Athena Jones, Jeremy Diamond and Gregory Krieg, "Trump Advances
Controversial Oil Pipelines with Executive Action," CNN, January 24, 2017,
https://www.cnn.com/2017/01/24/politics/trump-keystone-xl-dakota-access
-pipelines-executive-actions/index.html.

29. ICMN Staff, " 'Absolutely False': No Contact from Trump Administration, Archambault Says," Indian Country Media Network, February 24, 2017,
https://indiancountrymedianetwork.com/news/politics/archambault-false
-no-contact-trump/?mqsc=ED3873590.

30. About the relationship of water to the Lakota people, Edward Valandra
wrote, "The mainstream public sees ours as an environmental action: when
an oil pipeline fails, the spill contaminates the water, rendering it unsafe to
drink. 'Mni Wiconi—Water Is Life!' also calls to the fact that all life would
die without clean water. Protecting water from contamination falls within the
environmental paradigm, and therefore becomes a universal aspiration.
However, Phil Wambli Numpa, the Sicangu Lakota Treaty Council's executive
director, pushed beyond Western environmental, racial, and development
paradigms. He explains that 'water is alive: we call it mni wiconi, water is
life.' That water is alive—and therefore possesses personality or personhood
—defines our cultural response to the DAPL. Our definition challenges the
West's anthropocentrism, which accords person/peoplehood only to humans.
Hence, the Western way of life would both deny and defy water as having
personhood. Yet the United States can arbitrarily recognize fictional entities
like corporations as legal persons, while denying personhood to humans who
become subject to the Thirteenth Amendment's slavery exception." Edward
Valandra, "We Are Blood Relatives: No to the DAPL," *Hot Spots, Cultural
Anthropology* website, December 22, 2016, https://culanth.org/fieldsights/1023
-we-are-blood-relatives-no-to-the-dapl.

CHAPTER ONE: ENVIRONMENTAL JUSTICE THEORY AND ITS LIMITATIONS FOR INDIGENOUS PEOPLES

1. "Environmental Justice History," Energy.gov, https://energy.gov/lm
/services/environmental-justice/environmental-justice-history, accessed March
9, 2017.

2. US General Accounting Office, *Siting of Hazardous Waste Landfills and
Their Correlation with Racial and Economic Status of Surrounding Communities*
(Washington, DC: GAO, 1983).

3. The term "uncontrolled toxic waste sites" was defined as "closed and
abandoned sites on the EPA's list of sites which pose a present and potential
threat to human health and the environment." While statistics were gathered
for Native Americans in communities with uncontrolled toxic waste sites, it

appears that the study did not count abandoned uranium mines in the Southwest or on reservations in other regions—which number in the thousands—or uranium enrichment facilities, such as the Hanford site in Washington State, which has been known for decades to be leaking radioactive waste in the surrounding area and into the Columbia River. If these had been factored in, it is reasonable to assume the numbers would have been higher for the American Indian demographic.

4. Pulido, *Environmentalism and Economic Justice.*

5. *Principles of Environmental Justice,* adopted at the First National People of Color Environmental Leadership Summit, Washington, DC, October 24–27, 1991, http://www.ejnet.org/ej/principles.html.

6. "Environmental Justice: Timeline," A Voice: African American Voices in Congress, http://www.avoiceonline.org/environmental/timeline.html, accessed October 1, 2018.

7. Mike Ewall, "Legal Tools for Environmental Equity vs. Environmental Justice," *Sustainable Development Law and Policy* 13, no. 1 (2012–13), http://www.ejnet.org/ej/SDLP_Ewall_Article.pdf.

8. "Learn About Environmental Justice," Environmental Justice, Environmental Protection Agency website, https://www.epa.gov/environmentaljustice/learn-about-environmental-justice, accessed October 23, 2018.

9. Cutter, "Race, Class, and Environmental Justice."

10. "Learn About Environmental Justice," EPA.

11. US Commission on Civil Rights, *Not in My Backyard: Executive Order 12898 and Title VI as Tools for Achieving Environmental Justice,* chap. 1, http://www.usccr.gov/pubs/envjust/ch1.htm, accessed March 10, 2017.

12. US Commission on Civil Rights, *Environmental Justice.*

13. Devon J. Peña, "Toward an Environmental Justice Act," March 2, 2011, http://www.newclearvision.com/2011/03/02/toward-an-environmental-justice-act.

14. Clifford Rechtschaffen, Eileen Gauna, and Catherine A. O'Neill, "Introduction: History of the Movement," in Rechtschaffen, Gauna, and O'Neill, *Environmental Justice: Law, Policy & Regulation* (Durham, NC: Carolina Academic Press, 2009).

15. Gross and Stretesky, "Environmental Justice in the Courts," 205–32.

16. Ewall, "Legal Tools for Environmental Equity vs. Environmental Justice."

17. Cutter, "Race, Class, and Environmental Justice."

18. Ibid.

19. Pulido, *Environmentalism and Economic Justice.*

20. See Kosek, *Understories.* For more on land grant issues, see, for example, María E. Montoya, *Translating Property: The Maxwell Land Grant and the Conflict over Land in the American West, 1840–1900* (Berkeley: University of California Press, 2002).

21. Eric Cheyfitz convincingly argues, however, that the material promises of liberal democracy have collapsed in a rhetoric of disinformation, because economic equality has deliberately been left out of the constitutional and legal framework of the United States. See Cheyfitz, *The Disinformation Age.*

22. Schlosberg, "Reconceiving Environmental Justice," 518.

23. Standing Rock Sioux tribal chairman Dave Archambault appealed to the UN Human Rights Council in Geneva in September 2016, and UN officials later visited the protest camps. Several high-ranking officials denounced the human rights abuses, referring to them as "inhuman and degrading conditions." Max Bearak, "U.N. Officials Denounce 'Inhuman' Treatment of Native American Pipeline Protestors," *Washington Post*, November 15, 2016, https://www.washingtonpost.com/news/worldviews/wp/2016/11/15/u-n-officials -denounce-inhuman-treatment-of-north-dakota-pipeline-protesters/?utm_term =.8f6a14f1b906. It was unclear why SRST focused their efforts on human rights abuses without interrogating the United States' violation of the free, prior, and informed consent clause of UNDRIP.

24. Schlosberg, "Reconceiving Environmental Justice."

25. Karl Marx, "Genesis of the Industrial Capitalist," chap. 31 in *Capital, Volume One: A Critique of Political Economy*, 1867.

26. Wolfe, "Settler Colonialism and the Elimination of the Native."

27. Several Native scholars have pointed out the hegemonic nature of State recognition of tribal nations. See, for example, Glen Coulthard, *Red Skin, White Masks: Rejecting the Colonial Politics of Recognition* (Minneapolis: University of Minnesota Press, 2014), and Audra Simpson, *Mohawk Interruptus: Political Life Across Borders of Settler States* (Durham, NC: Duke University Press, 2014).

28. For in-depth critical analysis of Indigenous sovereignty, see especially Taiaiake Alfred, *Peace, Power, Righteousness: An Indigenous Manifesto* (Ontario: Oxford University Press, 1999); Joanne Barker, ed., *Sovereignty Matters: Locations of Contestation and Possibility in Indigenous Struggles for Self-Determination* (Lincoln: University of Nebraska Press, 2005); and Scott Richard Lyons, *X-marks: Native Signatures of Assent* (Minneapolis: University of Minnesota Press, 2010). For more on the paradigm of domination, see Newcomb, *Pagans in the Promised Land.*

29. Anne Bonds and Joshua Inwood, "Beyond White Privilege: Geographies of White Supremacy and Settler Colonialism," *Progress in Human Geography* 40, no. 6 (November 2015): 715.

30. Norman K. Denzin and Yvonna S. Lincoln, preface to Denzin, Lincoln, and Smith, *Handbook of Critical and Indigenous Methodologies*, x.

31. Franke Wilmer, *The Indigenous Voice in World Politics* (Thousand Oaks, CA: Sage Publications, 1993), quoted in Smith, *Decolonizing Methodologies*, 111. In mainstream economics, economic surplus is the net gain between the cost of production and the selling price of goods. Similarly, but in Marxist terms,

"surplus value" is the core value or goal of capitalism and cannot be separated from private property and worker exploitation.

32. See Andrea Smith, "Heteropatriarchy and the Three Pillars of White Supremacy: Rethinking Women of Color Organizing," in *Women in Culture: An Intersectional Anthology for Gender and Women's Studies*, ed. Bonnie Kime Scott, Susan E. Cayleff, Anne Donadey, and Irene Lara (Chichester, UK: Wiley-Blackwell, 2016), 404.

33. Wanda McCaslin and Denise C. Breton, "Justice as Healing: Going Outside the Colonizers Cage," in Denzin, Lincoln, and Smith, *Handbook of Critical and Indigenous Methodologies*, 512.

34. Ibid.

35. Kyle Powys Whyte, "Indigenous Experience, Environmental Justice, and Settler Colonialism" (April 25, 2016), SSRN: https://ssrn.com/abstract =2770058 or http://dx.doi.org/10.2139/ssrn.2770058.

36. Some scholars have referred to Indigenous cultural difference as the "cultural dilemma." See Ranco et al., "Environmental Justice, American Indians and the Cultural Dilemma."

37. Federal Indian policy is grounded in several principles that form the core of federal Indian law, with the trust responsibility as one of the bedrock legal principles. The often-controversial trust doctrine holds that the federal government serves as the trustee for Indian reservation lands and assets, to whom the government is legally and morally accountable. For an excellent discussion on the trust doctrine, see David E. Wilkins and K. Tsianina Lomawaima, *Uneven Ground: American Indian Sovereignty and Federal Indian Law* (Norman: University of Oklahoma Press, 2001).

38. Indigenous Peoples Work Group, *Recommendations for Fostering Environmental Justice for Tribes and Indigenous Peoples*, 1, 12, https://www.epa.gov /environmentaljustice/recommendations-fostering-environmental-justice -tribes-and-indigenous-peoples, accessed April 11, 2017.

39. See *Policy on Environmental Justice for Working with Federally Recognized Tribes and Indigenous Peoples*, https://www.epa.gov/sites/production/files /2015–02/documents/ej-indigenous-policy.pdf, accessed April 13, 2017.

40. Ibid., 6.

41. See *Announcement of U.S. Support for the United Nations Declaration on the Rights of Indigenous Peoples Initiatives to Promote the Government-to-Government Relationship and Improve the Lives of Indigenous Peoples*, https://2009 -2017.state.gov/documents/organization/154782.pdf, accessed October 8, 2018.

42. Ibid., 3. There is a growing body of literature on the meaning of self-determination in UNDRIP, and contrary to the Obama administration's definitive claim that the declaration created a new definition for the concept, there is much disagreement about this. It stands to reason that if this were the case, and a new definition of self-determination was reserved for Indigenous peoples living under conditions of State domination, then the US (and Canada, New

Zealand, and Australia) would not have been so reluctant to endorse the declaration to begin with. The administration's position is thus a revisionist version that doesn't accurately reflect the declaration's intent.

43. The term "benevolent supremacy," describing US foreign policy in the Middle East, was coined by Melani McAlister in her book *Epic Encounters: Culture, Media, and U.S. Interests in the Middle East Since 1945*, updated ed. (Berkeley: University of California Press, 2005).

CHAPTER TWO: GENOCIDE BY ANY OTHER NAME

1. Andrew Jackson: "Fifth Annual Message," December 3, 1833, *The American Presidency Project*, https://www.presidency.ucsb.edu/node/200846, accessed October 23, 2018.

2. Quoted in Peter Nabokov, *Native American Testimony: A Chronicle of Indian-White Relations from Prophecy to the Present, 1492–1992* (New York: Penguin, 1992), 151–52.

3. The concept of deracination—literally, to pull up by the roots—has been applied by Indigenous scholars as an apt metaphor for describing the process of land dispossession.

4. Vickery and Hunter, "Native Americans: Where in Environmental Justice Research?"

5. Lord and Shutkin, "Environmental Justice and the Use of History."

6. Vickery and Hunter, "Native Americans: Where in Environmental Justice Research?"

7. US Supreme Court justice Clarence Thomas in particular has critiqued the complexity of federal Indian law several times. But as at least one commentator noted, when court justices critique the "complexity" of federal Indian law, it seems to precede a restriction on tribal authority. Matthew L. M. Fletcher, "Commentary on 'Confusion' and 'Complexity' in Indian Law (Updated with Blake Watson Materials)," *Turtle Talk* (blog), Indigenous Law and Policy Center, Michigan State University College of Law, May 2, 2011, https://turtletalk.wordpress.com/2011/05/02/commentary-on-confusion-and-complexity-in-indian-law.

8. For more on the racist underpinnings of the Supreme Court's Indian law decisions, see Robert A. Williams, *Like a Loaded Weapon: The Rehnquist Court, Indian Rights, and the Legal History of Racism in America* (Minneapolis: University of Minnesota Press, 2005).

9. Whyte, "Indigenous Experience, Environmental Justice and Settler Colonialism."

10. At least one scholar (who specializes in environmental jurisprudence and Indigenous peoples) has used the phrase in this way. In her book *Environmental Justice and the Rights of Indigenous Peoples: International and Domestic Legal Perspectives*, Laura Westra articulates the idea of environmental deprivation, connecting it to genocide (174).

11. The inherent contradiction of a landscape populated by "wild" Indians versus a virgin wilderness can be seen as a reflection of the historical ambivalence of European settlers' relationship to Indigenous peoples. Referencing the work of early American writers like D. H. Lawrence (and others), Dakota scholar Philip Deloria wrote of this American ambivalence in his 1998 book *Playing Indian*. He explained that Americans were torn between their desire to be like Indians, who represented perfect freedom and an authentic connection to the continent on one hand and the need to extirpate them on the other (3). Virgin wilderness narratives are a way to discursively eliminate Indigenous peoples from the land as a form of erasure or extirpation.

12. Dunbar-Ortiz, *An Indigenous Peoples' History of the United States*, 41.

13. Ibid., 61–62.

14. James F. Brooks, *Captives and Cousins: Slavery, Kinship, and Community in the Southwest Borderlands* (Chapel Hill: University of North Carolina Press, 2002).

15. See Brett Rushforth, *Bonds of Alliance: Indigenous and Atlantic Slaveries in New France* (Chapel Hill: University of North Carolina, 2012).

16. Other important Indian slavery studies include Allan Gallay, *The Indian Slave Trade: The Rise of the English Empire in the American South, 1670–1717* (New Haven, CT: Yale University Press, 2012), and Margaret Ellen Newell, *Brethren by Nature: New England Indians, Colonists, and the Origins of American Slavery* (Ithaca, NY: Cornell University Press, 2015).

17. Reséndez, *The Other Slavery*, 266.

18. See, for example, Lindsay, *Murder State*; Benjamin Madley, *An American Genocide: The United States and the California Indian Catastrophe* (New Haven, CT: Yale University Press, 2016); and George Harwood Phillips, "Indians in Los Angeles, 1781–1875: Economic Integration, Social Disintegration," *Pacific Historical Review* 49, no. 3 (August 1980): 427–51.

19. Lindsay, *Murder State*, 27.

20. See Kimberley Johnson-Dodds, "Early California Laws and Policies Related to California Indians," California Research Bureau, 2002, https://www.library.ca.gov/crb/02/14/02–014.pdf.

21. Lindsay, *Murder State*, 154.

22. Ibid., 157.

23. Reséndez, *The Other Slavery*, 284.

24. Ibid., 294.

25. The Treaty of New Echota, which traded all Cherokee land east of the Mississippi River in exchange for money and an equal amount of land in the Oklahoma Territory, was controversial because it had been negotiated by a group under the leadership of John Ridge, who wrongly claimed to represent the Cherokee Nation. In retaliation, other Cherokees assassinated Ridge and two other treaty negotiators in 1839, the year after the final march of the Cherokees.

26. Clara Sue Kidwell, *The Effects of Removal on American Indian Tribes*, http://nationalhumanitiescenter.org/tserve/nattrans/ntecoindian/essays /indianremoval.htm, accessed October 8, 2018.

27. The reservation system itself can be seen as a tactic of genocide. They were much smaller than what was needed to support those who depended on subsistence lifestyles. Off-reservation hunting was necessary due to constant shortages of government food rations and was severely punished. The passage of the Dawes Act in 1887 placed even greater strains on Indians with the legalized theft of two-thirds of treaty-reserved lands, which contributed to conditions of starvation and malnutrition.

28. For more on the history of Round Valley, see for example, Lynwood Carranco and Estle Beard, *Genocide and Vendetta: The Round Valley Wars in Northern California* (Norman: University of Oklahoma Press, 1981); William J. Bauer, *We Were All Like Migrant Workers Here: Work, Community, and Memory on California's Round Valley Reservation* (Chapel Hill: University of North Carolina Press, 2009); Frank H. Baumgardner, *Killing for Land in Early California: Indian Blood at Round Valley* (New York: Algora, 2006).

29. Whyte, "Indigenous Experience, Environmental Justice and Settler Colonialism."

30. The Medicine Lodge Treaty was contested by leaders and members of the various bands, having not been ratified by three-quarters of the male population as required, rendering it invalid. The tribes were moved anyway, and a lawsuit was filed and decided in the Supreme Court in 1903. The notorious decision in *Lone Wolf v. Hitchcock* ruled in favor of the federal government. While the court admitted the tribes never appropriately ceded their lands, it also said that Congress always held the political power to act unilaterally. This was the precedent that articulated the plenary power doctrine, in which Congress is deemed to hold ultimate authority over Indian nations and is one of the bedrock principles in federal Indian law today.

31. Much of the Malheur reservation later became the Malheur National Wildlife Refuge and was the site of the Bundy standoff against federal marshals in 2016. The Bundys were acquitted by a federal jury on October 27, 2016, the same day of the first militarized attacks on the 1851 Treaty Camp at Standing Rock.

32. Donald Fixico, *Termination and Relocation: Federal Indian Policy, 1945–1960* (Albuquerque: University of New Mexico Press, 1986).

33. Lawrence William Gross, "The Comic Vision of Anishinaabe Culture and Religion," *American Indian Quarterly* 26, no. 3 (2002): 436– 59. Native studies professor Cutcha Risling Baldy even teaches courses using zombie apocalypse movies to illustrate to non-Natives what it feels like to be a Native living in a postapocalyptic world. See her blog *Why I Teach the Walking Dead in My Native Studies Classes*, April 24, 2014, https://

thenerdsofcolor.org/2014/04/24/why-i-teach-the-walking-dead-in-my-native
-studies-classes.

34. Scholars have debated the original indigenous population for decades.
Here I rely on Henry F. Dobyns's figures. See "Estimating Aboriginal American
Population: An Appraisal of Techniques with a New Hemispheric Estimate,"
Current Anthropology 7 (1966): 295–416, and "Reply," 440–44. See also Dobyns,
Native American Historical Demography: A Critical Bibliography (Bloomington:
University of Indiana Press, 1976), 1; and *Their Number Become Thinned: Native
American Population Dynamics in Eastern North America* (Knoxville: University
of Tennessee Press/Newberry Library, 1983), 2.

35. Yuchi Muscogee scholar Daniel Wildcat contends that many Native
people were and are subject to four distinct removals. The first removal was
physical removal from homelands, the second occurred with the removal of
children from their homes during the boarding-school era, the third removal
was the psychocultural removal of Indian identities in the boarding schools
(the embodiment of cultural genocide, he says), and some will experience a
fourth removal as their homes become uninhabitable due to sea-level rise and
other environmental disruptions due to climate change. See Wildcat, *Red Alert*.

36. See, for example, Kathleen Brown-Rice, "Examining the Theory
of Historical Trauma Among Native Americans," *Professional Counselor* 3,
no. 3 (2013); M. Brave Heart, J. Chase, J. Elkins, and D. B. Altschul, "Historical
Trauma Among Indigenous Peoples of the Americas: Concepts, Research,
and Clinical Considerations," *Journal of Psychoactive Drugs* 43, no. 4 (2011);
M. Y. H. Brave Heart and L. M. DeBruyn, "The American Indian Holocaust:
Healing Historical Unresolved Grief," *American Indian and Alaska Native
Mental Health Research* (1998); Eduardo Duran, *Healing the Soul Wound:
Counseling with American Indians and Other Native Peoples* (New York: Teachers
College Press, 2006).

37. See Public Law 103–150 (1993), a joint resolution apologizing for the
overthrow of the Hawaiian Kingdom government, and an apology resolution
toward Native Americans buried deep within the 2010 Defense Appropriations
Act, H.R. 3326, Public Law No. 111–118.

38. Wolfe, "Settler Colonialism and the Elimination of the Native," 403.

39. See full text at "Rome Statute of the International Criminal Court," July
17, 1998, http://legal.un.org/icc/statute/99_corr/cstatute.htm, accessed October 23, 2018.

40. Office of the UN Special Adviser on the Prevention of Genocide,
"Analysis Framework," 3, http://www.un.org/ar/preventgenocide/adviser/pdf
/osapg_analysis_framework.pdf.

41. McDonnell and Moses, "Raphael Lemkin as Historian of Genocide in
the Americas," 514.

42. Card, "Genocide and Social Death."

CHAPTER THREE: THE COMPLICATED LEGACY OF WESTERN EXPANSION AND THE INDUSTRIAL REVOLUTION

1. Nabokov, *Native American Testimony*.

2. "About My Gas Mask Paintings . . . via the Official Blog of Bunky Echo Hawk," March 14, 2014, archived at https://lucian.uchicago.edu/blogs /atomicage/2015/09/03/about-my-gas-mask-paintings-via-the-official-blog -of-bunky-echo-hawk/, accessed October 25, 2018.

3. Clint Carroll, *Roots of Our Renewal: Ethnobotany and Cherokee Environmental Governance* (Minneapolis: University of Minnesota Press, 2015).

4. Quoted in Newcomb, *Pagans in the Promised Land*, 76. Scholars generally agree that the intent of the Johnson case was to establish clarity in American land acquisition law by addressing what turned out to be a manufactured and collusive dispute between two white men to defraud the court, not primarily to establish a basis for federal Indian law. As legal scholar Lindsay Robertson asserted, what should have been a much simpler, concise decision turned into a complex affair involving peripheral questions about Indians, with ultimately tragic consequences for them. For a case study on the legal fraud of the decision, see Robertson's *Conquest by Law: How the Discovery of America Dispossessed Indigenous Peoples of Their Lands* (New York: Oxford University Press, 2005).

5. The origin of the term "Manifest Destiny" is typically attributed to an 1845 editorial in the *United States Magazine and Democratic Review*—an organ of the Democratic Party—by the publication's editor, John O'Sullivan. Discussing the US and Great Britain's dispute over the Oregon Territory, O'Sullivan wrote that "the right of our manifest destiny [is] to overspread and to possess the whole of the continent which Providence has given us for the development of the great experiment of liberty and federated self-government entrusted to us."

6. Papal bulls are edicts or public decrees delivered by the pope.

7. For a more in-depth discussion of Story's opinion, see Newcomb, *Pagans in the Promised Land*, 81–85.

8. Ibid., 23–36.

9. Modern Native scholars have identified numerous popular culture representations that arose in the latter nineteenth century, perpetuating the myth of the vanishing Indian. It laments the inevitable demise of the "dying race" of American Indians and the purity of their cultures. See Roxanne Dunbar-Ortiz and Dina Gilio-Whitaker, *"All the Real Indians Died Off" and 20 Other Myths About Native Americans* (Boston: Beacon Press, 2016).

10. Elliott West, "American Indians and the Transcontinental Railroad," Gilder Lehrman Institute of American History, https://ap.gilderlehrman .org/history-by-era/development-west/essays/american-indians-and-trans continental-railroad, accessed October 8, 2018.

11. The growing harshness of the treaties is reflected in treaty language,

as analyzed by a Princeton University study. Treaties were made with tribes until 1871 when Congress removed the president's ability to negotiate treaties with the Nations. Negotiations continued, however, in the form of ratified "agreements"; while they differed little in effect, they nonetheless "ushered in an aggressive new regime of conquest and ruin for native peoples." Arthur Spirling, "US Treaty-Making with American Indians: Institutional Change and Relative Power, 1784–1911," January 11, 2011, 6, https://www.princeton .edu/~pcglobal/conferences/methods/papers/Spirling.pdf.

12. Report of Gen. William Tecumseh Sherman, in *Report of the Secretary of War*, 1883, 48th Cong., 1st sess., House Executive Document 1, Pt. 2, Serial 2182, quoted in West, "American Indians and the Transcontinental Railroad."

13. William G. Thomas III, "How the Railroads Took Native American Lands in Kansas," December 11, 2010, http://railroads.unl.edu/blog/?p=125.

14. "Extermination of Buffalo," Enclopedia.com, http://www.encyclopedia .com/history/encyclopedias-almanacs-transcripts-and-maps/buffalo -extermination, accessed October 8, 2018.

15. Theodore Steinberg, quoted in David P. Billington, Donald C. Jackson, and Martin V. Melosi, "The History of Large Federal Dams: Planning, Design, and Construction in the Era of Big Dams," US Department of the Interior Bureau of Reclamation, 2005, 2, https://www.usbr.gov/history/HistoryofLarge Dams/LargeFederalDams.pdf.

16. Jerilyn Church, Chinyere O. Ekechi, Aila Hoss, and Anika Jade Larson, "Tribal Water Rights: Exploring Dam Construction in Indian Country," *Journal of Law, Medicine, and Ethics* 43 no. 1 (Spring 2015): 60–63, https://www.ncbi .nlm.nih.gov/pmc/articles/PMC4699571.

17. "Environmental Impacts of Dams," International Rivers, https://www .internationalrivers.org/environmental-impacts-of-dams, accessed October 8, 2018.

18. Celia McMichael, Jon Barnett, and Anthony McMichael, "An Ill Wind? Climate Change, Migration, and Health," *Environmental Health Perspectives* 120, no. 5 (May 2012): 646–54, https://www.ncbi.nlm.nih.gov/pmc/articles /PMC3346786.

19. Pierini, "How Did the Hetch Hetchy Project Impact Native Americans?"

20. "Columbia River Treaty Fishing Access Sites Oregon and Washington Fact-Finding Review on Tribal Housing Final Report," Cooper Zietz Engineers, Inc., for Portland District US Army Corps of Engineers, November 19, 2013, https://www.eenews.net/assets/2015/12/21/document_daily_01.pdf.

21. White, *The Organic Machine*.

22. Ken Kesey's classic 1962 book *One Flew Over the Cuckoo's Nest* is a testament to this trauma in the character of Chief Broom Bromden, the protagonist through whose perspective the story is told. As an Indigenous person of the Columbia River, Broom's mental illness is directly connected to the drowning

of Celilo Falls and the interruption of the ancient fishing cultures of the Yakama, Umatilla, Walla Walla, and other related Columbia River peoples. For an analysis of this perspective, see Leise, "Ken Kesey's *One Flew Over the Cuckoo's Nest*," 62–79. For more on the cultural impacts of Columbia River damming, also see Barber, *Death of Celilo Falls*.

23. In 1992, Congress approved the restoration of the Elwha River through the Elwha River Ecosystem and Fisheries Restoration Act. By 2014 both the Elwha and Glines Canyon Dams were removed. A similar initiative is taking place on the Klamath River, with the scheduled removal of four dams.

24. "Revisiting the Reign of Terror," CBS News, April 30, 2017, http://www.cbsnews.com/news/killers-of-the-flower-moon-revisiting-the-reign-of-terror-on-the-osage-nation.

25. Voyles, *Wastelanding*.

26. Grinde and Johansen, *Ecocide of Native America*, 208.

27. Ibid., 214.

28. "Justice Department Surpasses $2 Billion in Awards Under the Radiation Exposure Compensation Act," *Kayenta Today*, March 2, 2015, http://www.kayentatownship-nsn.gov/blog/?p=5624.

29. Voyles, *Wastelanding*.

30. LaDuke, "Indigenous Environmental Perspectives."

31. Terri Hansen, "Northern Cheyenne Sue to Block Coal Mining on Public Lands," *Indian Country Today*, April 14, 2017, https://newsmaven.io/indiancountrytoday/archive/northern-cheyenne-sue-to-block-coal-mining-on-public-lands-hPtxUVh1_0GncLXXPSQ9MA.

32. Michelle Tolson, "Yakama Nation Fights for Nuclear Waste Cleanup at Hanford Site," *Earth Island Journal*, May 21, 2014, http://www.earthisland.org/journal/index.php/elist/eListRead/yakama_nation_fights_for_nuclear_waste_cleanup_at_hanford_site.

33. La Duke, "Indigenous Environmental Perspectives."

34. Moore-Nall, "The Legacy of Uranium Development on or near Indian Reservations and Health Implications Rekindling Public Awareness." This is an excellent synopsis of all the uranium mine sites in Indian country.

35. Terri Hansen, "Kill the Land, Kill the People: There Are 532 Superfund Sites in Indian Country!," *Indian Country Today*, June 17, 2014, https://newsmaven.io/indiancountrytoday/archive/kill-the-land-kill-the-people-there-are-532-superfund-sites-in-indian-country-LpCDfEqzlkGEnzyFxHYnJA.

36. See Grinde and Johansen, *Ecocide of Native America*.

37. Short, *Redefining Genocide*. In a collection of case studies, Short highlights the example of the Alberta tar sands development as a clear case of the connection between ecocide, genocide, and bottom of the barrel energy development.

38. Sherry L. Smith and Brian Frehner, introduction to Smith and Frehner, *Indians and Energy*, 8.

39. Ibid.

40. Melissa K. Nelson, "Introduction: Lighting the Sun of Our Future—How These Teachings Can Provide Illumination," in Nelson, *Original Instructions*, 3.

41. Clayton Thomas-Muller, "Front Line of Resistance: Indigenous Peoples and Energy Development," in Nelson, *Original Instructions*, 239–46.

42. Rebecca Tsosie, "Cultural Sovereignty and Tribal Energy Development: Creating a Land Ethic for the Twenty-First Century," in Smith and Frehner, *Indians & Energy*, 263–79.

43. After years of intense protests by Navajo activists, the ill-fated Desert Rock plant was never built. The Navajo Nation does, however, own the Navajo Generating Station, a 2,200-megawatt coal-fired power plant in conjunction with the Bureau of Land Management and is supplied by Peabody Energy's Kayenta Mine. The aging power plant narrowly averted a shutdown by the EPA in 2017 for its inability to meet regulations limiting nitrogen oxide emissions, but its lease was extended until 2019. As of this writing the plant's future is uncertain.

44. Title 4, chapter 9 of the *Navajo Nation Code Is the Environmental Policy Act*. The cornerstone of the policy implies the Fundamental Law without directly naming it as such, whereby "the protection, restoration and preservation of the environment is a central component of the philosophy of the Navajo Nation . . . and that it is the policy of the Navajo Nation to use all practicable means to create and maintain conditions under which humankind and nature can exist in productive harmony." See http://www.navajonationepa.org/Pdf%20files/NN%20EnvPolicy.pdf.

45. Even after the EPA granted permits, the ill-fated power plant for years fought an uphill battle due to opposition from the state of New Mexico because of the environmental impact of yet another coal plant in the region, opposition from the neighboring Mountain Ute tribe, and legal challenges to the permit by the Sierra Club and its allies. Among its allies was the group Diné Citizens Against Ruining Our Environment (CARE).

46. Tsosie, "Cultural Sovereignty and Tribal Energy Development," 278.

CHAPTER FOUR: FOOD IS MEDICINE, WATER IS LIFE

1. Here I defer to the spelling used by the famous Colville novelist and activist Christine Quintasket, also known as Mourning Dove, in *Mourning Dove: A Salishan Autobiography* (Lincoln: University of Nebraska Press: 1990).

2. Vanessa Ho, "Native American Death Rates Soar as Most People Are Living Longer," *Seattle Post Intelligencer*, March 11, 2009, http://www.seattlepi.com/local/article/Native-American-death-rates-soar-as-most-people-1302192.php.

3. Although an analysis of the federal Indian Health Service is beyond the scope of this chapter, it's important to point out that federal neglect most commonly takes the form of chronic underfunding of IHS. Health care for

American Indians has been affirmed time and again, beginning in the early twentieth century, as a trust responsibility that descends from the hundreds of treaties the US made with tribal nations in exchange for land. But the agency has never been adequately funded to meet the needs of Indian country, as was starkly revealed in a 2003 study commissioned by the US Commission on Civil Rights, "A Quiet Crisis: Federal Funding and Unmet Needs in Indian Country."

4. "Disparities," Indian Health Service Fact Sheet, https://www.ihs.gov /newsroom/factsheets/disparities/, accessed October 8, 2018.

5. "Disparities," Indian Health Service Fact Sheet, https://www.ihs.gov /newsroom/factsheets/disparities/, accessed October 8, 2018.

6. "Changing the Course of Diabetes: Turning Hope into Reality," Indian Health Service, Special Diabetes Program for Indians, 2014 Report to Congress, https://www.ihs.gov//newsroom/includes/themes/responsive2017 /display_objects/documents/RepCong_2016/SDPI_2014_Report_to_Congress .pdf.

7. "Diné Food Sovereignty: A Report on the Navajo Nation Food System and the Case to Rebuild a Self-Sufficient Food System for the Diné People," Diné Policy Institute, April 2014, 52, http://www.dinecollege.edu/institutes/DPI /Docs/dpi-food-sovereignty-report.pdf.

8. Clint R. Carroll, Carolyn Noonan, Eva M. Garroutte, Ana Navas-Acien, Steven P. Verney, and Dedra Buchwald, "Low-Level Inorganic Arsenic Exposure and Neuropsychological Functioning in American Indian Elders," *Environmental Research* 156 (July 2017), http://www.sciencedirect.com/science/article/pii /S0013935116305321.

9. Cay Leytham-Powell, "Trace Arsenic Linked with Deteriorating Health Among American Indian Elders," *Colorado Arts and Sciences Magazine*, August 25, 2017, https://www.colorado.edu/asmagazine/2017/08/25/trace -arsenic-linked-deteriorating-health-among-american-indian-elders.

10. In addition to health disparities, Native Americans consistently rank at the top of all social ills, including poverty, violence against women, police murder rates, youth suicide, and education levels.

11. Whyte, "Indigenous Food Systems, Environmental Justice, and Settler-Industrial States."

12. Depopulation due to disease is not thought to be a result of poor health. On the contrary, it was the absence of certain diseases on the continent that led to death from previously unencountered contagions. Having not been exposed to microbes that caused influenza, measles, small pox, and a host of other diseases, Indian bodies did not possess the antibodies to fight what were common illnesses among Europeans. Some studies in American Indian health disparities, however, note the presence of diseases like pneumonia and tuberculosis in pre-Columbian America and have claimed that American Indian health has always exhibited disparities compared to Europeans, even before their arrival, and problematically posit genetic determinism as a possibility.

13. Gregory Cajete, "Indigenous Foods, Indigenous Health: A Pueblo Perspective," in Cajete, *A People's Ecology.*

14. Ibid., 87–89.

15. Ibid., 95.

16. When Pueblo people talk about corn, they are talking about "Indian" corn—what's often called maize—not the nutritionally deficient, genetically modified corn seen in modern supermarkets.

17. Cajete, "Indigenous Foods, Indigenous Health: A Pueblo Perspective," in Cajete, *A People's Ecology,* 91.

18. Heidi Bruce, "Muckleshoot Foods and Culture: Pre-20th Century Stkamish, Skopamish, Smulkamish, and Allied Longhouses," *Fourth World Journal* 16, no. 1 (Summer 2017). Landscape cultivation to increase food availability was also widely practiced throughout Indigenous California.

19. Melissa K. Nelson, "Re-Indigenizing Our Bodies and Minds Through Native Foods," in Nelson, *Original Instructions,* 189.

20. LaDuke, *Recovering the Sacred,* 168.

21. In 1988, the Ojibwe filed a lawsuit against Busch Agricultural Resources for false and misleading advertising, because the company had marketed their product as "authentic" Minnesota lake rice, with an image of two Indians in a canoe harvesting wild rice, when in fact the rice was commercially grown in California. The lawsuit, settled out of court, was considered a small victory when state laws were changed to add the term "paddy rice" to "wild rice" on packaging.

22. Amanda Raster and Christina Gish Hill, "The Dispute over Wild Rice: An Investigation of Treaty Agreements and Ojibwe Food Sovereignty," *Agriculture and Human Values* 34, no. 2 (May 2016): 267–81.

23. Biopiracy happens when corporations patent plants originating in Indigenous cultures for profit, without compensation or recognition of those people, an appropriation of Indigenous knowledge. One criticism is that when patents are privately held Indigenous communities are deprived of the right to commercially develop those resources. As this case points out, however, the commercial ownership of knowledge itself is considered anathema to many Indigenous peoples.

24. Ibid.

25. LaDuke, *Recovering the Sacred.*

26. For more on the history of the trouble and subsequent agreements, see the film *A River Between Us.*

27. Jamie Bissonnette Lewey, "For the Penobscot Nation, the Water in the River Is the Blood in Their Veins," *Bangor Daily News,* January 5, 2016.

28. Anderson, *Tending the Wild.*

29. The Colville reservation is composed of twelve bands who historically lived in separate territories and groups with distinct histories, customs, and governing systems. They have been forced to operate as one tribe since the reservation was formed in 1872.

30. Michelle Chino, Darlene R. Haff, and Carolee Dodge Francis, "Patterns of Commodity Food Use among American Indians," *Pimatisiwin: A Journal of Aboriginal and Indigenous Community Health* 7, no. 2 (2009): 279–89.

31. "Frequently Asked Questions," Indian Affairs, US Department of the Interior website, https://www.bia.gov/frequently-asked-questions, accessed October 8, 2018.

32. Numerous legal actions were enacted to outlaw the practice of American Indian religious traditions, such as the *Indian Religious Crimes Code* (1883), which imposed prison terms on those caught engaging in ceremonies; the BIA's *Rules of Indian Courts*, which directed Indian agents to put an end to traditional religious practices and gatherings; and the Dawes Act, which institutionalized Christianity within the boarding school system to prevent the perpetuation of Native religions.

33. Because of the secretive nature of Native plant medicine knowledge, aside from early anthropological texts there is a dearth of modern literature on the use of traditional American Indian medicinal plants, especially about their contemporary use. However, with threats due to climate change and other environmental changes, there is a recognition of the need for relevant research relative to the protection of these important cultural resources. For more on the revitalization of Native plant medicines, see Clint Carroll's study, *Roots of Our Renewal: Ethnobotany and Cherokee Environmental Governance* (Minneapolis: University of Minnesota Press, 2015).

34. Checkerboarding happened within reservation boundaries when original allottees sold or otherwise lost their allotments to private, non-Indian landowners. The result was a land mass that became a "checkerboard" of trust and fee simple lands.

35. Besides causing the initial destruction of communities, dam construction is connected to some of the ongoing health problems in Indian country through the loss of traditional foods and habitats that support them. See Jerilyn Church, Chinyere O. Ekechi, Aila Hoss, and Anika Jade Larson, "Tribal Water Rights: Exploring Dam Construction in Indian Country," *Journal of Law, Medicine, and Ethics*, Supplement S1, 43, no. 1 (Spring 2015): 60–63.

36. Ogallala Aquifer Initiative 2011 Report, United States Department of Agriculture, https://www.nrcs.usda.gov/Internet/FSE_DOCUMENTS /stelprdb1048827.pdf.

37. Cynthia Brougher, "Indian Reserved Water Rights Under the Winters Doctrine: An Overview," June 8, 2011, http://nationalaglawcenter.org /wp-content/uploads/assets/crs/RL32198.pdf.

38. Robert Anderson, "Water Rights, Water Quality, and Regulatory Jurisdiction in Indian Country," *Stanford Environmental Law Journal* (September 2015).

39. See, for example, McCool, *Native Waters*.

40. K. Cozzetto et al., "Climate Change Impacts on the Water Resources of

American Indians and Alaska Natives in the U.S.," *Climatic Change* 120 (2013): 569–84.

41. Anderson, "Water Rights, Water Quality, and Regulatory Jurisdiction in Indian Country."

42. Ed Williams, "Small Tribe, Big River: Isleta Eyes Pollution in the Rio Grande," Public Health New Mexico, February 19, 2015, http://publichealthnm .org/2015/02/18/small-tribe-big-river-isleta-eyes-pollution-in-the-rio-grande.

43. "EPA Says It Won't Repay Claims for Spill That Caused Yellow Rivers," CBS News Online, January 13, 2017, https://www.cbsnews.com/news/gold -king-mine-spill-colorado-rivers-epa-claims.

44. Noel Lyn Smith, "Group to Present Update on Mine Spill Study," *Farmington Daily Times*, May 23, 2017, http://www.daily-times.com/story /news/local/navajo-nation/2017/05/23/group-present-update-mine-spill-study /102020678.

45. Cozzetto et al., "Climate Change Impacts on the Water Resources of American Indians and Alaska Natives in the U.S."

46. Ibid., 575–76.

47. Ibid.

48. *Food Sovereignty: Valerie Segrest at TedxRainier*, YouTube video, https:// www.youtube.com/watch?v=RGkWI7c7400.

49. The *Feeding Ourselves Report* can be found at http://indigenousfood andag.com/wp-content/uploads/2017/01/FeedingOuselves2015.pdf.

50. In 2016, I attended one of the conferences, held in Cherokee territory in Tulsa, Oklahoma, as a member of the Center for World Indigenous Studies research team, which was at the time partnered with the Muckleshoots in the most recent phase of the MFSP. Over two and a half days, conference presentations ranged from heirloom seed preservation in the Cherokee Nation to debates on organic food certification in the Choctaw Nation—which grows much of its own food for its casino restaurant business—and even a geothermal greenhouse project on the Pine Ridge Reservation in South Dakota.

51. Valerie Segrest, Rudolph C. Ryser, Heidi G. Bruce, Dina Gilio-Whitaker, and Leslie E. Korn, *Muckleshoot Food Sovereignty Assessment: Conclusions of Nine-Month Study (October 2016–2017)*, June 22, 2017.

52. The concept of Indian survivance was captured by Ojibwe scholar Gerald Vizenor and describes a process of active survival whereby Native peoples adapt their cultures to modern circumstances.

CHAPTER FIVE: (NOT SO) STRANGE BEDFELLOWS

1. Quoted in Anderson, *Tending the Wild*, 156–57.

2. Michael Popejoy, "The Beginnings of American Naturalism in Our Own Backyard," Emerson and the Environment series, April 1, 2014, Harvard University Sustainability webpage, https://green.harvard.edu/news/beginnings -american-naturalism-our-own-backyard.

3. The terms "preservation" and "conservation" are often used interchange-ably, but there are distinctions. According to the National Park Service, "Con-servation is generally associated with the protection of natural resources, while preservation is associated with the protection of buildings, objects, and land-scapes. Put simply conservation seeks the proper use of nature, while preserva-tion seeks protection of nature from use." "Conservation vs. Preservation and the National Park Service," lesson plan, National Park Service website, https://www.nps.gov/klgo/learn/education/classrooms/conservation-vs-preservation.htm, accessed October 8, 2018.

4. Spence, *Dispossessing the Wilderness*, 5.

5. See, for example, the online version of *Selections from the "Indian Note-books" (1847–1861) of Henry D. Thoreau*, a collection of notes Thoreau kept, which appear to have been intended for an eventual book. Richard Fleck, ed., Thoreau Institute at Walden Woods, 2007, https://www.walden.org/wp-content/uploads/2016/03/IndianNotebooks-1.pdf.

6. The literature on Thoreau and Muir is vast and entire volumes could still be written. It would be especially useful to see Indigenous perspectives. A couple of notable examples are the works of Robert F. Sayre and Richard F. Fleck. Sayre is admittedly more realistic in his critique of Thoreau's adherence to the "savagist" paradigm, although he believes Thoreau was able to overcome his savagism to some degree later in life. I see Fleck, on the other hand, as more an apologist for Thoreau's savagism. See Sayre, *Thoreau and the American Indians*, and Fleck, *Henry Thoreau and John Muir Among the Native Americans*.

7. Henry David Thoreau, Journal 10, chap. 6, "January, 1858," 251–52, Walden Woods Project Online, February 2016, https://www.walden.org/wp-content/uploads/2016/02/Journal-10-Chapter-6.pdf.

8. See Fleck's *Selections from the "Indian Notebooks"* for Thoreau's refer-ences to Morton. Morton advanced the theory of craniology in early race studies, in which skull size was believed to determine intelligence and culture and to distinguish certain innate differences between people of different "races." His work, along with that of other scientists of the time who set out to prove the inferiority of non-white people, laid the groundwork for the field of anthropol-ogy and is now referred to as "scientific racism."

9. In his 1983 treatise *Changes in the Land: Indians, Colonists, and the Ecology of New England*, William Cronon addresses Thoreau's lamenting of the woods of Walden as "maimed" and "imperfect," raising the question, "What are we to make of the wholeness and perfection which he thought preceded it? It is tempting to believe that when the Europeans arrived in the New World they confronted Virgin Land, the Forest Primeval, a wilderness which has existed for eons uninfluenced by human hands. Nothing could be further from the truth. . . . Indians had lived on the continent for thousands of years, and had to a significant extent modified its environment to their purposes" (12).

10. For more on the history of national parks and tribal relations, see

Robert H. Keller and Michael F. Turek, *American Indians and National Parks* (Tucson: University of Arizona Press, 1998); and Phillip Burnham, *Indian Country, God's Country: Native Americans and the National Parks* (Washington, DC: Island Press, 2012).

11. Keller and Turek, *American Indians and National Parks*, 52. The authors also offer a rare critique of George Bird Grinnell, an early anthropologist and naturalist who was instrumental in the creation of Glacier National Park and later founder of the Audubon Society. Grinnell is known for his close relationship with the Blackfeet, but his extensive writing on Indian cultures reflects his belief in their inferiority, and his work ultimately contributed to the violation of Blackfeet treaty rights and their expulsion from the park. See note 10, page 56, for an analysis of Grinnell's Indian views.

12. Galen Clark, who came to the valley for the first time in 1855, had extensive knowledge of Indian land cultivation in Yosemite Valley, which he described as necessary not only for food propagation but also to protect from enemy incursions. Galen Clark, letter to the Board of Commissioners of the Yosemite Valley and Mariposa Big Tree Grove, August 30, 1894, quoted in Anderson, *Tending the Wild*, 157.

13. Another early California pioneer, Lafayette Bunnell, understood the parklike landscape he observed as a product of human intervention. Quoted in Anderson, *Tending the Wild*, 158.

14. Anderson, *Tending the Wild*. Original text by Belgian gold miner Jean-Nicholas Perlot, in *Gold Seeker: Adventures of a Belgian Argonaut During the Gold Rush Years*, trans. H. H. Brentnor (New Haven, CT: Yale University Press, 1985).

15. Anderson, *Tending the Wild*.

16. The Ahwaneechee Miwok of Yosemite had intermarried extensively with other Sierra Miwok, Mono Paiute, Yokuts, and other ex-mission Indians and are often referred to as the Yosemite Indians.

17. Spence asserts that the creation of Yellowstone rested on the idea of the landscape as a "national 'Wonderland' and against the background of renewed military campaigns to curtail movements of several western tribes." *Dispossessing the Wilderness*, 56.

18. Ibid., 157n30.

19. Ibid., 116.

20. Anderson notes that from a California Indian perspective, the term "management" doesn't apply, as it is a Western concept. Rather, it's a "caring for" of the plants and animals in a "deeply experiential relationship of reciprocity with them." *Tending the Wild*, 153.

21. Muir was the son of a strict Scottish Calvinist, and although he rejected the Calvinism of his childhood, he maintained a strong Christian worldview and saw himself in a role we would today call white savior. In a 1978 essay by Richard Fleck, in which he makes the case for Muir's evolution based on his journals and other written work, Muir actively proselytizes to the Natives and

imagines himself as something of a cultural hero to them. Fleck even makes the dubious claim that "it wasn't long until the Indians with Muir began to take delight in things they never before enjoyed like seeing glaciers and hearing the roar of icebergs breaking off into the bay." See "John Muir's Evolving Attitudes toward Native American Cultures," *American Indian Quarterly* 4, no. 1 (February 1978): 19–31.

22. Merchant, "Shades of Darkness."

23. Michael P. Cohen, "History: Origins and Early Outings," *The History of the Sierra Club: 1892–1970* (San Francisco: Sierra Club Books, 1988), https:// vault.sierraclub.org/history/origins.

24. Shepard Krech III, *The Ecological Indian: Myth and History* (New York: W. W. Norton, 2000).

25. See the film *Reel Injun* for an in-depth look at de Corti's life and the degree to which he adopted an off-screen Indian persona.

26. Castaneda, often referred to as a father of the New Age movement, was an anthropology student at UCLA who passed his work off as serious scholarship, earning a doctorate based on it and megafame and wealth. He was later found to have lied about nearly everything, from the existence of Don Juan to where he was born, and he even had his doctorate rescinded. One commentator called the episode "the largest literary and academic fraud in history." Wallace Sampson, "An Original: Richard de Mille, Carlos Castaneda, and Literary Quackery," Science-Based Medicine website, June 25, 2009, https:// sciencebasedmedicine.org/an-original-richard-de-mille-carlos-castaneda -literary-quackery.

27. Other examples of counterculture and New Age fakery include Jamake Highwater, Ruth Beebe Hill, Lynn Andrews, Mary Summer Rain, Hyemeyost Storm, and James Arthur Ray, just to name a few.

28. Smith, *Hippies, Indians, and the Fight for Red Power*, 8.

29. Paul C. Rosier, "'Modern America Desperately Needs to Listen': The Emerging Indian in an Age of Environmental Crisis," *Journal of American History* (December 2013): 711–35.

30. LaDuke, *All Our Relations*.

31. Ibid.

32. Robert Miller notes, however, that the major environmental groups— particularly Greenpeace—did not oppose the hunt, probably because gray whales had rebounded to record high numbers. "Tribal Cultural Self-Determination and the Makah Whaling Culture," in *Sovereignty Matters: Locations of Contestation and Possibility in Indigenous Struggles for Self-Determination*, ed. Joanne Barker (Lincoln: University of Nebraska Press, 2005), 123–52.

33. Chris Clarke, "When Green Groups Fought Native Rights: The Timbisha Shoshone in Death Valley," *KCET Link*, January 2, 2017, https:// www.kcet.org/shows/tending-the-wild/when-green-groups-fought-native-rights -the-timbisha-shoshone-in-death-valley.

34. Brett Wilkinson, "Smaller Salamander Protection Zone Unveiled for Sonoma County," Center for Biological Diversity, republished from the *Press Democrat*, August 30, 2011, https://www.pressdemocrat.com/news/2291244-181 /smaller-salamander-protection-zone-unveiled.

35. Smith, *Hippies, Indians, and the Fight for Red Power*, 142.

36. According to the *Wall Street Journal*, in 2011 the top five Western oil producers posted record profits, exceeding $140 billion ("Oil Giants Profits Soar, but Investors Aren't Sold," *Wall Street Journal*, October 27, 2017, https://www.wsj.com/articles/profits-jump-at-exxon-chevron-bp-total-shell -1509109079). Even after the oil market crashed in 2014, Reuters reported that the production of shale oil (which relies on fracking technology) made the US the world's top net exporter of oil—2.5 million barrels a day in 2016 ("Why Record U.S. Oil Exports Are Poised for Even More Growth," Reuters, July 26, 2017, https://www.reuters.com/article/us-usa-oil-exports/why -record-u-s-oil-exports-are-poised-for-even-more-growth-idUSKBN1AC0ER).

CHAPTER SIX: HEARTS NOT ON THE GROUND

1. "Why the Founder of Standing Rock Sioux Camp Can't Forget the Whitestone Massacre," *Yes Magazine*, September 3, 2016, http://www .yesmagazine.org/people-power/why-the-founder-of-standing-rock-sioux-camp -cant-forget-the-whitestone-massacre-20160903.

2. See Sally Roesch Wagner, *Sisters in Spirit: Haudenosaunee (Iroquois) Influence on Early American Feminists* (Summertown, TN: Native Voices Book Publishing, 2001).

3. K. Tsianina Lomawaima, "The Mutuality of Citizenship and Sovereignty: The Society of American Indians and the Battle to Inherit America," *American Indian Quarterly* 37, no. 2 (Summer 2013): 334.

4. See Wagner discussing her work in the video *Sisters in Spirit: The Iroquois Influence on Early American Feminists*, August 5, 2013, YouTube video, https://www.youtube.com/watch?v=3HoLpdHpQQQ.

5. Shari M. Huhndorf and Cheryl Suzack, "Indigenous Feminism: Theorizing the Issues," in *Indigenous Feminism: Politics, Activism, Culture*, ed. Shari M. Huhndorf, Cheryl Suzack, Jeanne Perrault, and Jean Berman (Vancouver: UBC Press, 2010), 3.

6. Cristina Stanciu, "An Indian Woman of Many Hats: Laura Cornelius Kellogg's Embattled Search for an Indigenous Voice," *American Indian Quarterly* 6, no. 3 (Summer 2013): 87–115.

7. Cathleen Cahill, "Marie Louise Bottineau Baldwin: Indigenizing the Federal Indian Service," *American Indian Quarterly* 6, no. 3 (Summer 2013): 63–86.

8. Bruce E. Johansen, "Women of All Red Nations (WARN)," in Johansen, *Encyclopedia of the American Indian Movement* (Santa Barbara, CA: Greenwood, 2013), e-book, https://publisher.abc-clio.com/9781440803185/312.

9. M. A. Jaimes Guerrero, " 'Patriarchal Colonialism' and Indigenism: Implications for Native Feminist Spirituality and Native Womanism," *Hypatia: A Journal of Feminist Philosophy* 8, no. 2 (Spring 2003): 58–69.

10. The most notorious example of Native men's oppression of women is the story of the murder of Anna Mae Aquash in 1975. It's a sordid tale of lies, cover-ups, and collusion to protect some of AIM's most high-profile members (both men and women), spanning decades. It also involves undercover FBI informants planted to destabilize the movement under the COINTEL program. The case went unsolved until two male AIM members were finally convicted in 2004 and 2010, but according to an investigative piece in the *New York Times*, prosecutors were never convinced that they acted alone. See Eric Konigsberg, "Who Killed Anna Mae?," *New York Times Magazine*, April 25, 2014, https://www.nytimes.com/2014/04/27/magazine/who-killed-anna-mae.html.

11. Johansen, "Women of All Red Nations." For an excellent accounting of the history of forced sterilization in Indian country, see Sally J. Torpy, "Native American Women and Coerced Sterilization: On the Trail of Tears in the 1970s," *American Indian Culture and Research Journal* 24, no. 2 (2000).

12. Two studies conducted by the Association on American Indian Affairs, one in 1969 and one in 1974, led to the ICWA legislation.

13. Some of these very women also initiated American Indians' work in the international arena in the 1980s. Both WARN and the IWN sent delegations to the United Nations and other international conferences and forums, including the historic Women's International Conference in Beijing in 1985, to advocate for Indigenous rights. Their work contributed to what eventually resulted in the creation of the United Nations Declaration on the Rights of Indigenous Peoples in 2007.

14. "Alliance Statement," International Council of Thirteen Indigenous Grandmothers, October 13, 2004, http://www.grandmotherscouncil.org/alliance-statement.

15. The women who started the Idle No More movement are Nina Wilson, Sheelah McLean, Sylvia McAdam, and Jessica Gordon. All but McLean are First Nations women.

16. Nancy Tuana and Chris J. Cuomo, "Climate Change: Editors' Introduction," *Hypatia, Special Issue on Climate Change* (Summer 2014).

17. Ibid.

18. See the National Institute of Justice Research Report, André B. Rosay, *Violence Against American Indian and Alaska Native Women and Men: 2010 Findings from the National Intimate Partner and Sexual Violence Survey* (Washington, DC: US Department of Justice, May 2016), https://www.ncjrs.gov/pdffiles1/nij/249736.pdf.

19. Background on the Inquiry, Government of Canada, date modified April 22, 2016, https://www.rcaanc-cirnac.gc.ca/eng/1449240606362/1534528865114.

20. Rosay, *Violence Against American Indian and Alaska Native Women and Men.*

21. Tribal Affairs, Office of Violence Against Women, https://www.justice .gov/ovw/tribal-affairs, accessed October 9, 2018.

22. On the topic of authentic connection to land, see, for example, Deloria, *Playing Indian*; Shari Huhndorf, *Going Native: Indians in the American Cultural Imagination* (Ithaca, NY: Cornell University Press, 2001); and Jean M. O'Brien, *Firsting and Lasting: Writing Indians Out of Existence in New England* (Minneapolis: University of Minnesota Press, 2010). These and other scholars argue in essence that the history of displacing Indigenous peoples through violent settlement exposes deeply unsettled feelings about belonging in a land without the ancient ancestral connections that Native people have.

23. Salter and Adams, "Toward a Critical Race Psychology."

24. Lipsitz first wrote about possessive investment in whiteness in a widely read 1999 journal article that later turned into a book. See *The Possessive Investment in Whiteness: How White People Benefit from Identity Politics* (Philadelphia: Temple University Press, 2006).

CHAPTER SEVEN: SACRED SITES AND ENVIRONMENTAL JUSTICE

1. In Jacqueline Keeler, ed., *Edge of Morning: Native Voices Speak for the Bears Ears* (Salt Lake City: Torrey House Press, 2017).

2. Dave Archambault II, "Desecration of Sacred Sites by Oil Company," *Hill*, September 6, 2016, http://thehill.com/blogs/pundits-blog/energy -environment/294680-standing-rock-sioux-chairman-on-desecration-of-sacred.

3. Chelsey Lugar, "DAPL Desecrated Sacred Sites, Took 10 Days to Report to State, as Human Rights Abuses Continue," *Indian Country Today*, November 4, 2016, https://indiancountrymedianetwork.com/history/sacred-places /dapl-desecrated-sacred-sites-took-10-days-to-tell-state-as-human-rights-abuses -continue.

4. Dave Singleton, program analyst at CNAHC, email message to author, August 24, 2011.

5. California Coastal Commission, *W 8b Revised Staff Report and Recommendation on Consistency Certification*, file date March 26, 2007, 190–91.

6. On February 6, 2008, the California Coastal Commission conducted a public hearing to hear testimony from all sectors of the community weighing in on the toll road, drawing some 3,500 people. Milford Wayne Donaldson, state historic preservation officer, when discussing the impacts of the proposed road, testified that "all we know is the impact from that freeway is sitting right on top of the site." Reporter's Transcript of Proceedings, Agenda Item No. 8b, Hearing on Consistency Certification No. 018–07 before the California Coastal Commission, February 8, 2008.

7. Surfing is a multibillion-dollar international industry. The World Surf League (then organized as the Association of Professional Surfers) holds the

world's most prestigious high-stakes surf contests in international locations such as Australia, Brazil, France, Portugal, South Africa, and Tahiti, and at the time of the 241 toll road controversy held four of its contests in the US. Until 2018, Trestles had been one of the stops on the WSL tour, when it was replaced by a high-tech wave pool newly built by former surfing world champion Kelly Slater. Ironically, it was located in California's Central Valley agricultural community of Lemoore, 258 miles from the ocean.

8. The California Coastal Commission was established under the 1976 California Coastal Act. Widely perceived as one of the most powerful land use bodies in the United States, the law and the commission's mandate is to protect the environment of the coastal zone and the public's access to it.

9. *Reporter's Transcript of Proceedings*, February 6, 2008. Quoted in a letter from the City Project/United Coalition to Protect Panhe to Thomas Street at the National Oceanic and Atmospheric Administration (NOAA) and Carlos Gutierrez, US secretary of commerce, May 28, 2008.

10. California Coastal Commission, *W 8b Second Addendum to Commission Packet for Energy, Ocean Resources, and Federal Consistency Division (Update for the Staff Recommendation)*, 4.

11. Ibid.

12. A "traditional cultural property" is an official designation, as defined by National Register Bulletin 38, under the National Park Service, US Department of the Interior.

13. The City Project—an environmental justice law firm—did, however, raise the idea that the toll road was an issue of transportation justice, because building a private road through a public park would disproportionately affect low-income people also by limiting access to affordable recreation and their inability to afford the toll.

14. In 1979 the Acjachemen (Juaneño) filed an application with the Bureau of Indian Affairs for federal recognition. After a grueling thirty-two-year process, they were denied for a second time in March 2011 on grounds that they did not meet four out of the seven necessary standards set forth by the US government.

15. According to Eva Marie Garoutte's research, "a 1978 congressional survey found no less than *thirty-three* separate definitions of Indians in use in different pieces of federal legislation." *Real Indians: Identity and the Survival of Native America* (Berkeley: University of California Press, 2003), 16.

16. George Tinker, "An American Indian Theological Response to Ecojustice," in Weaver, *Defending Mother Earth*, 163.

17. Deloria, *God Is Red*; Grossman, *Unlikely Alliances*, 66.

18. Tinker, "An American Indian Theological Response to Ecojustice," 163.

19. Ibid., 165.

20. Commissioner Schallenberger had worked for many years for the president pro-tem of the state senate and in that position had worked on bills to

protect Native American sacred sites, thus he had a good base of knowledge of Native American worldviews that constitute sanctity.

21. Suzanne J. Crawford, *Native American Religious Traditions* (New York: Routledge, 2007).

22. David H. Getches, Charles F. Wilkinson, and Robert A. Williams Jr., *Cases and Materials on Federal Indian Law,* 5th ed. (St. Paul, MN: Thompson West, 2005), 747. It should be noted, however, that the dissenting opinion of Justice Brennan (who joined Justices Marshall and Blackmun) was uncompromising when he stated, "The land-use decision challenged here will restrain respondents from practicing their religion as surely and as completely as any of the governmental actions we have struck down in the past and the Court's efforts simply to define away respondents injury as nonconstitutional are both unjustified and ultimately unpersuasive." Ibid.

23. "Save the Peaks Coalition News Release: Supreme Court Affirms Tribes Have No Religious Rights," Indigenous Action Media, June 9, 2009, http://www.indigenousaction.org/save-the-peaks-coalition-news-release-supreme-court-affirms-tribes-have-no-religious-rights.

24. Quoted in Grossman, *Unlikely Alliances,* 180–81.

25. See Dina Gilio-Whitaker, "Landslide Vote Quashes 400-Acre Development Project in Southern California," Indian Country Media Network, October 5, 2016, https://indiancountrymedianetwork.com/history/sacred-places/landslide-vote-quashes-400-acre-development-project-in-southern-ca-saves-sacred-sites, accessed May 26, 2018.

26. Middleton, *Trust in the Land,* 3.

27. Ibid.

CHAPTER EIGHT: WAYS FORWARD FOR ENVIRONMENTAL JUSTICE IN INDIAN COUNTRY

1. Thomas Linzey and Mari Margil, keynote speech, Bioneers Conference, 2016, YouTube video, https://www.youtube.com/watch?v=QiXjzgRiAEw.

2. See "Save Trestles Campaign, San Onofre State Beach at Risk of Destruction Again," Surfrider Foundation, 2015, video, https://yhoo.it/1FMQtoi.

3. Exec. Order, B-10–11, https://www.gov.ca.gov/2011/09/19/news17223.

4. As a journalist, I covered the Banning Ranch story for Indian Country Media Network and personally communicated with a Sierra Club spokesperson, Terry Welsh, president of the Banning Ranch Conservancy board of directors. He was not only very interested in the tribal cultural resources aspect of the land, but understood the significance of laws protecting Native American cultural sites to broader environmental interests.

5. See examples from Naomi Klein, who wrote about the "blockadia" phenomenon in *This Changes Everything: Capitalism vs. the Climate* (New York: Simon & Schuster, 2014), and Clayton Thomas-Muller's essay "The Rise of the Native Rights-Based Strategic Framework: Our Last Best Hope to Save Our

Water, Air, and Earth," in the volume *The Winter We Danced*, ed. Kino-nda-niimi Collective (Winnipeg: ARP Books, 2014).

6. Andrea Smith, *Native Americans and the Christian Right: The Gendered Politics of Unlikely Alliances* (Durham, NC: Duke University Press, 2008), 256.

7. This is not to say that Democrats are always better than Republicans on Indian issues. Hillary Clinton's stance on the Dakota Access Pipeline is a clear example of her abandonment of support for Indian country, as is the example of North Dakota senator Heidi Heitkamp during the Oceti Sakowin encampments. While Heitkamp has championed numerous pro-Indian bills and legislation, as an elected official heavily backed by industry money, she consistently supported the pipeline project and failed to act to stop the human rights violations committed by the militarized police and private security firms or address the egregious history of Indian land theft.

8. Nadja Popovich, Livia Albeck-Ripka, and Kendra Pierre-Louis, "67 Environmental Rules on the Way Out Under Trump," *New York Times*, January 31, 2018, https://www.nytimes.com/interactive/2017/10/05/climate/trump -environment-rules-reversed.html.

9. In May 2018 the Trump administration announced a new federal health policy that would classify American Indians as a "racial group" subject to the same Medicaid work rules as all other people, a blatant undermining of tribal sovereignty that troubled even Oklahoma Republican senator Tom Cole. Justin Wingerter, "Oklahoma Tribes and Tom Cole Say 'Troubling' Medicaid Policy Weakens Tribal Sovereignty by Labeling Them a Race," *Oklahoman*, May 7, 2018, https://newsok.com/article/5593676/oklahoma-tribes-and-tosm-cole-say -troubling-medicaid-policy-weakens-tribal-sovereignty-by-labeling-them-a-race.

10. Middleton, *Trust in the Land*, 7–8.

11. "Tribal & Native Lands Program," Trust for Public Lands website, https://www.tpl.org/tribal-native-lands-program#sm.001udhwvgl95dvo10ed2k1 jzwj9vb, accessed October 9, 2018.

12. "Projects," Mountain Maidu Summit website, www.maidusummit.org, accessed October 9, 2018.

13. See Jay T. Johnson, Renee Pualani Louis, and Andrew Kliskey, "Weaving Indigenous and Sustainability Sciences: Diversifying Our Methods (WIS2DOM) Workshop," report from the National Science Foundation workshop, February 13–16, 2013.

14. Juliet Eilperin, "Uranium Firm Urged Trump Officials to Shrink Bears Ears National Monument," *Washington Post*, December 8, 2017, https://www .washingtonpost.com/national/health-science/uranium-firm-urged-trump -officials-to-shrink-bears-ears-national-monument/2017/12/08/2eea39b6-dc31– 11e7-b1a8–62589434a581_story.html?utm_term=.a54feee5604c.

15. The Ho Chunks' technique of amending their constitution is far more complex than passing a statute, as the Ponca did, and as of this writing is still

incomplete. See the Ho Chunk tribal newspaper *Hocak Worak* 32, no. 1 (January 12, 2018), for language and analysis of the amendment, http://www .hocakworak.com/archives/Issue1.pdf.

16. Much controversy exists regarding whether fracking is the cause of earthquakes. The US Geological Survey has consistently denied the connection between earthquakes and fracking, but other studies, such as one conducted in Canada, confirm not just correlation but also causation between fracking and earthquakes. See Xuewei Bao and David W. Eaton, "Fault Activation by Hydraulic Fracturing in Western Canada," *Science,* December 16, 2016, http://science .sciencemag.org/content/354/6318/140.

17. Ponca Tribe of Oklahoma, Resolution 01–01092018, a Resolution Recognizing the Immutable Ponca Tribal Rights of Nature.

18. The Center for World Indigenous Studies conducted an extensive study on how tribal governments protect or regulate plant- and animal-based medicines on reserved lands and found that very few integrated traditional protocols with tribal legal frameworks. See Rudolph Rÿser and Dina Gilio-Whitaker, "Regulating Access to Customary Fourth World Foods and Medicines: Culture, Health, and Governance," *Fourth World Journal* 17, no. 1 (Summer 2018).

19. Mari Margil, attorney with Community Environmental Legal Defense Fund, personal communication with author, June 8, 2018.

20. The lawyer in the case, Jason Flores-Williams, was threatened by the judge with fines and possible disbarment for bringing a frivolous and illegal lawsuit. See Chris Walker, "Attorney to Withdraw Colorado River Lawsuit Under Threat of Sanctions," *Westworld,* December 4, 2017, http://www .westword.com/news/colorado-river-lawsuit-to-be-withdrawn-due-to-potential -sanctions-9746311.

21. "Historic Vote on Community Rights State Constitutional Amendment in NH Legislature," press release, Community Environmental Legal Defense Fund website, March 16, 2018, https://celdf.org/2018/03/press-release -historic-vote-on-community-rights-state-constitutional-amendment-in-nh -legislature.

22. "About," Unsettling American: Decolonization in Theory and Practice website, https://unsettlingamerica.wordpress.com/about, accessed October 9, 2018.

23. See Laura Hurwitz, "Settler Colonialism and White Settler Responsibility in the Karuk, Konomihu, Shasta and New River Shasta Homelands: A White Unsettling Manifesto," master's thesis, Humboldt State University, 2017, https://digitalcommons.humboldt.edu/etd/106. See also Laura Hurwitz and Shawn D. Bourque, "Killing the Settler to Save the Human: The Untidy Work of Unsettling Klamath River Thus Far," *Fourth World Journal* 17, no. 2 (Summer 2018).

24. Karla General, "Securing Rights to Sacred Places with the UN Declaration," Indian Law Resource Center, n.d., http://indianlaw.org/content/securing -indigenous-rights-sacred-places-un-declaration, accessed October 9, 2018.

25. California Coastal Commission, *Draft Tribal Consultation Policy*, August 18, 2017.

26. General, "Securing Rights to Sacred Places with the UN Declaration."

27. The UN General Assembly has been discussing implementation and monitoring protocols at least since the World Conference on Indigenous Peoples in 2014 but has made little progress.

28. General, "Securing Rights to Sacred Places with the UN Declaration."

29. Rÿser and Gilio-Whitaker, "Regulating Access to Customary Fourth World Foods and Medicines."

Selected Bibliography

Anderson, M. Kat. *Tending the Wild: Native American Knowledge and the Management of California's Natural Resources*. Berkeley: University of California Press, 2005.

Barber, Katrine. *Death of Celilo Falls*. Seattle: University of Washington Press, 2005.

Berkes, Fikret. *Sacred Ecology*. 3rd ed. New York: Routledge, 2012.

Cajete, Gregory, ed. *A People's Ecology: Explorations in Sustainable Living*. Santa Fe, NM: Clear Light, 1999.

Card, Claudia. "Genocide and Social Death." *Hypatia: A Journal of Feminist Philosophy* 18, no. 1 (Winter 2003): 63–79.

Carroll, Clint. *Roots of Our Renewal: Ethnobotany and Cherokee Environmental Governance*. Minneapolis: University of Minnesota Press, 2015.

Cheyfitz, Eric. *The Disinformation Age: The Collapse of Liberal Democracy in the United States*. London: Routledge, 2017.

Cronon, William. *Changes in the Land: Indians, Colonists, and the Ecology of New England*. New York: Hill and Wang, 2003.

Cutter, Susan L. "Race, Class, and Environmental Justice." *Progress in Human Geography* 19, no. 1 (1995): 111–22.

Deloria, Philip J. *Playing Indian*. New Haven, CT: Yale University Press, 1998.

Deloria, Vine, Jr. *God Is Red: A Native View of Religion*. 3rd ed. Golden, CO: Fulcrum, 2003.

Denzin, Norman K., Yvonna S. Lincoln, and Linda Tuhiwai Smith, eds. *Handbook of Critical and Indigenous Methodologies*. Los Angeles: Sage Publications, 2008.

Dhillon, Jaskiron, and Nick Estes. "Standing Rock, #NoDAPL, and Mni Wiconi." *Cultural Anthropology* (December 22, 2016). https://culanth.org/fieldsights /1010-standing-rock-nodapl-and-mni-wiconi.

Dunbar-Ortiz, Roxanne. *An Indigenous Peoples' History of the United States*. Boston: Beacon Press, 2014.

Estes, Nick. "Fighting for Our Lives: #NoDAPL in Historical Context." *Red Nation*. September 18, 2016. https://therednation.org/2016/09/18/fighting -for-our-lives-nodapl-in-context.

Fleck, Richard F. *Henry Thoreau and John Muir Among the Native Americans*. Hamden, CT: Shoestring Press, 1985.

Grinde, Donald A., and Bruce E. Johansen. *Ecocide of Native America: Environmental Destruction of Indian Lands and Peoples*. Santa Fe, NM: Clear Light Books, 1995.

Gross, Elizabeth, and Paul Stretesky. "Environmental Justice in the Courts." In *Failed Promises: Evaluating the Federal Government's Response to Environmental Justice*, edited by David Konisky. Cambridge, MA: MIT Press, 2015.

Grossman, Zoltan. *Unlikely Alliances: Native Nations and White Communities Join to Defend Rural Lands*. Seattle: University of Washington Press, 2017.

Huhndorf, Shari M., and Cheryl Susack, eds. *Indigenous Feminism: Politics, Activism, Culture*. Vancouver: University of British Columbia Press, 2010.

Keller, Robert H., and Michael F. Turek. *American Indians and National Parks*. Tucson: University of Arizona Press, 1998.

Kosek, Jake. *Understories: The Political Life of Trees*. Durham, NC: Duke University Press, 2006.

LaDuke, Winona. *All Our Relations: Native Struggles for Land*. Chicago: Haymarket Books, 1999.

———. "Indigenous Environmental Perspectives: A North American Primer." In *Native American Voices: A Reader*, ed. Susan Lobo and Steve Talbot, 353–68. Upper Saddle River, NJ: Prentice Hall, 2001.

———. *Recovering the Sacred: The Power of Naming and Claiming*. Cambridge, MA: South End Press, 2005.

Leise, Christopher. "Ken Kesey's *One Flew Over the Cuckoo's Nest*: Damming the Columbia River and Traumatic Loss." *Interdisciplinary Studies in Literature and Environment* 25, no. 1 (Winter 2018): 62–79.

Lindsay, Brendan C. *Murder State: California's Native American Genocide, 1846–1873*. Lincoln: University of Nebraska Press, 2012.

Lord, Charles P., and William A. Shutkin. "Environmental Justice and the Use of History." *Boston College Environmental Affairs Law Review* 22, no. 1 (1994): 1–26.

McCool, Dan. *Native Waters: Contemporary Indian Water Settlements and the Second Treaty Era*. Tucson: University of Arizona Press, 2006.

McDonnell, Michael A., and Dirk A. Moses. "Raphael Lemkin as Historian of Genocide in the Americas." *Journal of Genocide Research* 7, no. 4 (2005): 501–29.

Merchant, Carolyn. "Shades of Darkness: Race and Environmental History." *Environmental History* 8, no. 3 (2003): 380–94.

Middleton, Beth Rose. *Trust in the Land: New Directions in Tribal Conservation*. Tucson: University of Arizona Press, 2011.

Moore-Nall, Anita. "The Legacy of Uranium Development on or near Indian Reservations and Health Implications Rekindling Public Awareness." *Geosciences* 5 (2015): 15–29.

Nelson, Melissa K., ed. *Original Instructions: Indigenous Teachings for a Sustainable Future*. Rochester, VT: Bear and Company, 2008.

Newcomb, Steve. *Pagans in the Promised Land: Decoding the Doctrine of Discovery*. Golden: Fulcrum, 2008.

Peña, Devon G. "Toward an Environmental Justice Act." *New Clear Vision*. March 2, 2011. http://www.newclearvision.com/2011/03/02/toward-an-environmental-justice-act.

Pierini, Bruce. "How Did the Hetch Hetchy Project Impact Native Americans?" *Snowy Range Reflections: Journal of Sierra Nevada History and Biography* 6, no. 1 (2015). https://www.sierracollege.edu/ejournals/jsnhb/v6n1/pierini.html.

Pulido, Laura. *Environmentalism and Economic Justice: Two Chicano Struggles in the Southwest*. Tucson: University of Arizona Press, 1996.

Ranco, Darren J., Catherine O'Neill, Jamie Donatuto, and Barbara L. Harper. "Environmental Justice, American Indians and the Cultural Dilemma: Developing Environmental Management for Tribal Health and Well-Being." *Environmental Justice* 4, no. 4 (2011): 221–30.

Rechtschaffen, Clifford, Eileen Gauna, and Catherine O'Neill. *Environmental Justice: Law, Policy and Regulation*. 2nd ed. Durham, NC: Carolina Academic Press, 2009.

Reséndez, Andrés. *The Other Slavery: The Uncovered Story of Indian Enslavement in America*. Boston: Houghton Mifflin Harcourt, 2016.

Salter, Phia, and Glen Adams. "Toward a Critical Race Psychology." *Social and Personality Psychology Compass* 7, no. 11 (2013): 781–93.

Sayre, Robert F. *Thoreau and the American Indians*. Princeton, NJ: Princeton University Press, 1977.

Schlosberg, David. "Reconceiving Environmental Justice: Global Movements and Political Theories." *Environmental Politics* 13, no. 3 (Autumn 2004): 517–40.

Short, Damien. *Redefining Genocide: Settler Colonialism, Ecocide, and Social Death.* London: Zed Books, 2016.

Smith, Linda Tuhiwai. *Decolonizing Methodologies: Research and Indigenous Peoples.* London: Zed Books, 1999.

Smith, Sherry L. *Hippies, Indians, and the Fight for Red Power.* Oxford, UK: Oxford University Press, 2012.

Smith, Sherry L., and Brian Frehner, eds. *Indians and Energy: Exploitation and Opportunity in the American Southwest.* Santa Fe, NM: School for Advanced Research, 2010.

Spence, Mark David. *Dispossessing the Wilderness: Indian Removal and the Making of the National Parks.* Oxford, UK: Oxford University Press, 1999.

US Commission on Civil Rights. *Environmental Justice: Examining the Environmental Protection Agency's Compliance and Enforcement of Title VI and Executive Order 12898.* Washington, DC: US Commission on Civil Rights, 2016. http://www.usccr.gov/pubs/Statutory_Enforcement_Report2016.pdf.

Vickery, Jamie, and Lori M. Hunter. "Native Americans: Where in Environmental Justice Research?" *Society and Natural Resources* 29, no. 1 (2016): 36–52.

Voyles, Traci Brynne. *Wastelanding: Legacies of Uranium Mining in Navajo Country.* Minneapolis: University of Minnesota Press, 2015.

Weaver, Jace, ed. *Defending Mother Earth: Native American Perspectives on Environmental Justice.* New York: Orbis Books, 1996.

Westra, Laura. *Environmental Justice and the Rights of Indigenous Peoples: International and Domestic Legal Perspectives.* New York: Taylor and Francis, 2008.

White, Richard. *The Organic Machine: The Remaking of the Columbia River.* New York: Hill and Wang, 1995.

Whyte, Kyle Powys. "Indigenous Experience, Environmental Justice, and Settler Colonialism." April 25, 2016, SSRN: https://ssrn.com/abstract=2770058.

———. "Indigenous Food Systems, Environmental Justice, and Settler Industrial States." In *Global Food, Global Justice: Essays on Eating under Globalization*, ed. M. Rawlinson and C. Ward, 143–56. Newcastle upon Tyne, UK: Cambridge Scholars, 2015.

Wildcat, Daniel. *Red Alert: Saving the Planet with Indigenous Knowledge.* Golden, CO: Fulcrum, 2009.

Wolfe, Patrick. "Settler Colonialism and the Elimination of the Native." *Journal of Genocide Research* (2006): 387–409.

Index

Reséndez, Andrés, 42, 44
reservation system, 81, 82, 93, 130–31, 176n27, 184n34. *See also* forced relocation and displacement; trust responsibility
resistance movements, overview, 10–13
resource use vs. relationship with land, 54–55, 82, 138–40
rice, 78–79, 183n21
Ridge, John, 175n25
rights of nature (RON) approach, 154–55
Rio de Janeiro Earth Summit, 108–9
Rio Puerco River contamination, 65, 118
Rio Tinto Copper Mine, 68
rivers. *See* dam construction and Native displacement; *specific river names*
River That Makes the Sacred Stones. *See* Missouri River
Robertson, Lindsay, 178n4
Robert Wood Johnson Foundation, 88
Rome Declaration (2009), 161
Rome Statute (2002), 51, 68
Rosebud Reservation, 131
Rosier, Paul, 105
rugged individualism, 104, 124

sacred, as concept, 138–40
sacred sites: access to, 137; Bears Ears, 151, 152–54; Black Hills, 143–44; DAPL within, 131–32, 168n13; ETP's destruction of, 4; Genga, 143, 149; Old Woman Mountains, 152; overview of protection of, 129–30; Panhe, 13, 132–38, 140, 191n6; San Francisco Peaks, Ariz., 141–42; Sogorea Te, 159; "traditional cultural property," as official designation, 129, 135, 136, 192n12. *See also* religious practices and traditions
Sacred Stone Camp, 3, 4, 83, 110, 111. *See also* #NoDAPL movement
Safe Drinking Water Act (1974), 19
Saint Regis Mohawk Reservation, 68
salmon: extinction of, 60, 62; fishing practices and relationship with, 62, 73–74, 77, 79–80, 86, 152
Salt Chuck Mine, 68
salvage ethnography, 59
San Francisco Peaks, 141–42
San Juan River, 85
San Mateo Archeological District, 132–33
San Onofre Nuclear Generating Station, 132

San Onofre State Beach, 132–35
Santee Reservation, 131
savage trope, 56, 59, 95, 97, 186n6
Save San Onofre Coalition, 135
Save the Peaks campaign, 142
SB 18 (California), 159
Schallenberger, Mary, 134–35, 192n20
Schlosberg, David, 23
school lunch program, 81
Sea Shepherd Conservation Society, 106
second-wave feminism, 114
segregation, 114
Segrest, Valerie, 87–88
self-determination, as concept, 88–89, 115. *See also* sovereignty
Seminole, 45, 56
Seneca, 61, 113
settler colonialism: decolonizing land project against, 157–59; and environmental justice, 25–26, 39, 107–8; as genocide, 50; historical narrative in, 39–41; loss of food systems from, 75–76; Manifest Destiny, 48, 56, 92, 178n5; overview of, 5; and slavery, 24, 41–44; US government's lack of acknowledgment of, 32–33; westward expansion, 55–62; Whyte on, 38. *See also* genocide; white supremacy
"Settler Colonialism and the Elimination of the Native" (Wolfe), 50
settler industrialism, 75–76
Seven Councils Fire, 5, 10
Seventh Generation Fund, 144
Shasta tribe, 62, 157
Shawnee, 46–47
Sherman, William Tecumseh, 58–59
Sherwood uranium mine, 67
Short, Damien, 69
Shoshone, 67, 68, 93, 106
Shundahai Network, 109
Sierra Club, 99, 101, 105–6, 134, 193n4
Sierra Miwok, 187n16
Silent Spring (Carson), 91
Sinixt, 73
Sisseton Wahpeton Reservation, 131
skirt-wearing issue, 123–24, 125
slavery, 24, 41–44, 46, 55, 121
smallpox, 53
Smith, Linda Tuhiwai, 26
Smith, Sherry L., 105
Snowbowl Ski Resort, 141–42